BLACKSTONE'S GUIDE T

The Civil Justice Refor

BLACKSTONE'S GUIDE TO

THE CIVIL JUSTICE REFORMS 2013

Professor Stuart Sime and Derek French

OXFORD

UNIVERSITY PRESS

OXFORD
UNIVERSITY PRESS

Great Clarendon Street, Oxford, OX2 6DP,
United Kingdom

Oxford University Press is a department of the University of Oxford.
It furthers the University's objective of excellence in research, scholarship,
and education by publishing worldwide. Oxford is a registered trade mark of
Oxford University Press in the UK and in certain other countries

© Stuart Sime and Derek French, 2013

The moral rights of the authors have been asserted

First Edition published in 2013

Impression: 1

Crown copyright material is reproduced under Class Licence
Number C01P0000148 with the permission of OPSI
and the Queen's Printer for Scotland

British Library Cataloguing in Publication Data
Data available

ISBN 978–0–19–968515–8

Printed and bound in Great Britain by
CPI Group (UK) Ltd, Croydon, CR0 4YY

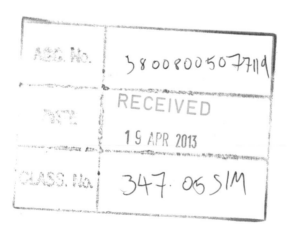

Foreword

Sir Rupert Jackson was faced with a daunting task when the then Master of the Rolls, Sir Anthony Clarke, asked him to carry out a review of the costs of civil litigation. With his customary diligence and perseverance, Sir Rupert produced his preliminary report in May 2009 and his final report in December 2009. The Government published a response in March 2011 and this led, in due course, to the passing of the Legal Aid, Sentencing and Punishment of Offenders Act 2012 which, together with the necessary secondary legislation and changes to the Civil Procedure Rules, will come into force on 1 April 2013. As Lord Neuberger said in the fifteenth implementation lecture, the fact that Sir Rupert carried out such a review from a standing start in November 2008 to legislative implementation in April 2013 is a testament to his unstinting hard work and dedication.

The main provisions in the Act are the changes to funding mechanisms and, in particular, the abolition of the recovery of success fees on conditional fee agreements and after-the-event insurance premiums. Referral fees are also abolished. In their place are a number of new mechanisms. The Act makes it possible to enter into damages-based agreements. General damages are being increased, as the Court of Appeal stated in *Simmons v Castle*, recognizing that claimants will now have to pay costs from damages. Personal injury claims will be subject to qualified one-way cost shifting so that claimants will generally have no costs liability to defendants if they lose. Claimants will also benefit from an additional 10 per cent recovery if they make a successful Part 36 offer.

Secondly, there are changes to the litigation process to reduce cost. Standard disclosure will no longer be ordered by default. Parties will have to put in a disclosure report and what type of disclosure is ordered will take into account knowledge of the cost of standard disclosure. Witness evidence may be limited by the court. Permission to call expert evidence will depend on cost and the issues to be dealt with. The overriding objective is being strengthened to emphasize the need for rules, practice directions and orders to be complied with. ADR will be encouraged and a new ADR Handbook will be used to inform judges, practitioners and others of the possible methods.

The third area of changes relates to costs. Proportionate costs are now defined. They will be a central aim of the litigation process and the overriding objective is also being amended to include this requirement. To make sure that proportionate cost is achieved, a new system of costs management based on costs budgets is being introduced in multi-track cases. Costs and case management will run in parallel to achieve litigation at proportionate cost.

These changes are complex. As Sir Rupert stated, they form a coherent package of interlocking reforms. They need understanding in the context of the overall changes. This Guide by Stuart Sime and Derek French provides an excellent commentary which amply fulfils that purpose. It has been produced by authors experienced in the practice and procedure of civil litigation. This Guide is exactly what the profession requires. The authors have analysed the changes in the Act, the secondary legislation and the Civil Procedure Rules in a clear and systematic way, making it easy to understand the changes and their impact. Such a proper understanding of the changes is also essential to ensure the smooth implementation of the Jackson reforms and further Sir Rupert's aim of promoting access to justice at proportionate cost.

Vivian Ramsey
Royal Courts of Justice
February 2013

Preface

The Civil Justice Reforms of 2013 are intended to implement the main recommendations of Sir Rupert Jackson's *Final Report on Civil Litigation Costs*. Their ultimate purpose, which reflects the terms of reference of Sir Rupert Jackson's Review, is to promote access to justice at proportionate cost.

Ensuring there are methods of funding available to allow potential litigants who might otherwise be unable to afford the costs of legal representation to participate in court proceedings is a major challenge. Without adequate funding arrangements, there is no real access to justice for many people. In the absence of a general right to legal aid, the solution adopted has been to expand the available funding methods that may be used by clients and their legal representatives.

One of the fundamental points made in the *Final Report* was that funding and costs are intimately related. Perhaps the most prominent failing of the post-Woolf civil justice system was the rule permitting the recoverability of success fees under normal party and party costs orders in cases funded under conditional fee agreements. The adverse effect of recoverability on keeping costs under control was graphically described in the *Final Report*, and in many ways the abolition of the recoverability rule is the centrepiece of the 2013 Reforms. Simple abolition of the rule would have altered the balance between the interests of claimants and defendants too much, so it has been allied with a range of measures aimed at ensuring claimants retain genuine access to the courts.

The other side of the equation is that litigation has to be pursued at proportionate cost. Achieving meaningful reductions in legal bills was always going to be a complex and difficult task. The approach has been to introduce a wide range of measures, none of which will make much difference on its own, but which in cumulative effect are intended to bring costs down to reasonable and proportionate levels. Measures being introduced include a more proactive approach to encouraging ADR, through to docketing, more stringent case management, the introduction of costs management, and new arrangements in areas such as disclosure and the use of expert evidence. Perhaps the most significant change is the intended change in culture, with courts and parties each having a role in ensuring litigation is conducted in ways that enable the court to deal with cases justly and at proportionate cost.

Introducing these reforms has required a raft of primary and secondary legislation. This book seeks to provide a practical guide through the maze of new materials, and to assist court users in adjusting to the new landscape and funding methods. Like other books in this series, the first half of the book is a commentary on the full range of innovations being introduced on 1 April 2013. The Appendices include the primary legislation, the provisions of the Courts and Legal Services Act 1990 as amended by the Legal Aid, Sentencing and Punishment of Offenders Act 2012, the new provisions amending the CPR 1998, and other relevant secondary legislation supporting the Reforms. We have been able to take account of all developments up to 25 February 2013. It has been announced that further amendments to the CPR, coming into force on 1 April 2013, will be made after this Guide goes to press. It is thought that, for the purposes of this Guide, the most significant of these further changes will be an amended r 3.12(1), of which there is a note at the end of appendix 3. This will affect what is said at 6.14 to 6.17.

The need for this book was identified by the editors of *Blackstone's Civil Practice* in 2012, and we are very grateful to Sir Maurice Kay for his encouragement in the early stages of this project. We should also like to record our thanks to Victoria Pittman, who has been tireless in providing assistance throughout in steering the book through to publication, and to Andy Redman, who was instrumental in enabling the book to be published at the same time as the implementation of the 2013 Reforms.

Professor Stuart Sime
Derek French

Complimentary eBook version
Oxford University Press are providing all customers of this title with a free electronic version of the book for quick and portable access to the material. In order to claim your eBook, please navigate to http://www.oup.com/uk/booksites/content/9780199685158/ and use the login details as follows: username Jackson, password Reforms010413.

Contents

Contents

List of abbreviations

ADR	alternative dispute resolution
ATE	after-the-event (insurance)
BTE	before-the-event (insurance)
CFA	conditional fee agreement
CLAF	contingent legal aid fund
CLSA 1990	Courts and Legal Services Act 1990
CMC	case management conference
CPD	continuing professional development
CPR	Civil Procedure Rules 1998
DBA	damages-based agreement
ECHR	European Convention on Human Rights
EU	European Union
Final Report	Sir Rupert Jackson's *Review of Civil Litigation Costs: Final Report* (London: TSO, 2010)
Government Response	*Reforming Civil Litigation Funding and Costs in England and Wales—Implementation of Lord Justice Jackson's Recommendations: The Government Response* (Cm 8041, March 2011)
LASPO 2012	Legal Aid, Sentencing and Punishment of Offenders Act 2012
LEI	legal expenses insurance (another name for BTE insurance)
LFA	litigation funding agreement (used in relation to third-party funding)
PD	Practice Direction
Preliminary Report	Sir Rupert Jackson's *Review of Civil Litigation Costs: Preliminary Report* (Ministry of Justice, May 2009)
PSLA	pain, suffering, and loss of amenity
PTR	pre-trial review
QOCS	qualified one-way costs shifting
r	rule
Review, the	Sir Rupert Jackson's Review of Civil Litigation Costs
RSC 1965	Rules of the Supreme Court 1965
s	section
SLAS	supplementary legal aid scheme
SRA	Solicitors Regulation Authority
TCC	Technology and Construction Court
Woolf Report	Lord Woolf, *Access to Justice. Final Report* (London: HMSO, 1996)

1st Implementation Lecture

Cambridge Law Faculty, 'Legal Aid and the Costs Review Reforms (Legal Aid etc Lecture 5)', A Talk by Lord Justice Jackson to the Cambridge Law Faculty on 5 September 2011. <http://www.law.cam.ac.uk/press/news/2011/09/lord-justice-jackson-legal-aid-and-the-costs-review-reforms--recording/1588>.

3rd Implementation Lecture

Lord Justice Jackson's Paper for the Civil Justice Council Workshop on Technical Aspects of Implementation, Third Lecture in the Implementation Programme, 31 October 2011. <http://www.judiciary.gov.uk/Resources/JCO/Documents/Speeches/lj-jackson-third-lecture-implementation-programme-31102011.pdf>.

4th Implementation Lecture

Lord Justice Jackson, 'Focusing Expert Evidence and Controlling Costs'. Fourth Lecture in the Implementation Programme. The Bond Solon Annual Expert Witness Conference, 11 November 2011. <http://www.judiciary.gov.uk/Resources/JCO/Documents/Speeches/lj-jackson-lecture-focusing-expert-evidence-controlling-costs.pdf>.

5th Implementation Lecture

UCL Judicial Institute, Special Lecture by Lord Justice Jackson, 'Achieving a Culture Change in Case Management', 22 November 2011. <http://www.ucl.ac.uk/laws/judicial-institute/docs/Jackson_LJ_Lecture_22Nov2011.pdf>.

6th Implementation Lecture

Lord Justice Jackson, 'Third Party Funding or Litigation Funding'. Sixth Lecture in the Civil Litigation Costs Review Implementation Programme. The Royal Courts of Justice, 23 November 2011. <http://www.judiciary.gov.uk/Resources/JCO/Documents/Speeches/lj-jackson-speech-third-party-funding-or-litigation-funding-23112011.pdf>.

7th Implementation Lecture

Lord Justice Jackson, 'Controlling the Costs of Disclosure'. Seventh Lecture in the Implementation Programme. The Lexisnexis Conference on Avoiding and Resolving Construction Disputes, 24 November 2011. <http://www.judiciary.gov.uk/Resources/JCO/Documents/Speeches/controlling-costs-disclosure.pdf>.

9th Implementation Lecture

Lord Neuberger of Abbotsbury MR, 'Docketing: Completing Case Management's Unfinished Revolution'. Ninth Lecture in Implementation

Programme. Solicitors' Costs Conference 2012, London, 9 February 2012. <http://www.judiciary.gov.uk/Resources/JCO/Documents/Speeches/mor -speech-solicitors-cost-conference-lecture-feb2012.pdf>.

10th Implementation Lecture

Lord Justice Jackson, 'Why Ten Per Cent?'. Tenth Lecture in the Implementation Programme. IBC Conference, London, 29 February 2012. <http:// www.judiciary.gov.uk/JCO%2FDocuments%2FSpeeches%2Flj-jackson -speech-why-ten-percent-29022012a.pdf>.

11th Implementation Lecture

Lord Justice Jackson, 'The Role of Alternative Dispute Resolution in Furthering the Aims of the Civil Litigation Costs Review'. Eleventh Lecture in the Implementation Programme. RICS Expert Witness Conference, 8 March 2012. <http://www.judiciary.gov.uk/Resources/JCO/Documents/ Speeches/lj-jackson-speech-eleventh-lecture-implementation-programme .pdf>.

16th Implementation Lecture

Mr Justice Ramsey, 'Costs Management: A Necessary Part of the Management of Litigation'. Sixteenth Lecture in the Implementation Programme. Law Society Conference. 29 May 2012. <http://www.judiciary. gov.uk/Resources/JCO/Documents/Speeches/costs-management-sixteenth-implementation-lecture-300512.pdf>.

Glossary

additional liability   percentage increase (also known as the success fee) that a legal representative may charge for their work in a case, any premium charged, and / or any amount in respect of provision made by a membership organization.

conditional fee agreement   an agreement between a legal representative and a client under which the legal representative's fee is payable only in specified circumstances. Often called a 'no win no fee' agreement.

contingent legal aid fund   a self-funding scheme, with funds being generated from successful cases.

costs capping   court order limiting the amount of future costs which a party may recover under a costs shifting order.

costs management   management by the court of the steps to be taken and the costs to be incurred by the parties in litigation.

costs management order   court order under CPR, r 3.15, recording the extent to which costs budgets are agreed and the court's approval of costs budgets after appropriate revisions.

costs protection   statutory protection of a party against having to pay costs to the other side in litigation. Applies in favour of litigants in receipt of legal aid and in a qualified manner under QOCS.

costs shifting   court order that one party pays the legal costs of another party.

damages-based agreement   an agreement between a legal representative and a client under which the legal representative's fee is determined by reference to the amount of the financial benefit obtained by the client in the litigation.

disbursements   payments made by a legal representative for goods or services other than items to enable the legal representative to provide its service to the client.

docketing   system of assigning a case to one judge from issue up to and including trial.

implementation lectures   series of 16 lectures on the Jackson reforms delivered by Jackson LJ, Lord Neuberger MR, and Ramsey J in 2011 and 2012. Full details of those referred to in this book are in the List of Abbreviations.

indemnity principle   the principle that costs are disallowed to the extent that the receiving party (the winner) is not under an obligation to pay those costs to its lawyers.

Jackson reforms   changes made by LASPO 2012, part 2, and (to the CPR and PDs) by the Civil Procedure (Amendment) Rules 2013 (SI 2013/262) and the 60th Update issued by the Ministry of Justice.

Ministerial Statement of 24 May 2012   Ministerial Statement by the Parliamentary Under-Secretary of State, Ministry of Justice (Jonathan Djanogly) on 24 May 2012 on the Implementation of Part 2 of the Legal Aid, Sentencing and Punishment of Offenders Act 2012: Civil Litigation Funding and Costs.

Ministerial Statement of 17 July 2012   Ministerial Statement by the Parliamentary Under-Secretary of State, Ministry of Justice (Jonathan Djanogly) on 17 July 2012 on the Implementation of Part 2 of the Legal Aid, Sentencing and Punishment of Offenders Act 2012: Civil Litigation Funding and Costs.

party and party costs order   order that one party pays the legal costs of another party. It means the same thing as 'costs shifting'.

paying party   party paying costs under a court order for costs.

proportionality   only reasonable and proportionate costs will be recoverable from the losing party.

qualified one-way costs shifting   a system under which in normal circumstances party and party costs orders (costs shifting) only take place in one direction (usually with the defendant paying the costs of the claimant), but if certain exceptions (qualifications) apply, costs protection (for the claimant) is lost.

receiving party   party being paid its costs under a court order for costs.

success fee   percentage increase that a legal representative may charge for their work on a case.

supplementary legal aid scheme   funding arrangement that runs in parallel with an existing legal aid scheme, but is available to litigants just outside the financial eligibility criteria, and is administered by the legal aid authority.

third-party funding   a method of funding litigation by investing money under a litigation funding agreement usually on the basis that the funder will be paid out of the proceeds recovered in the litigation, often as a percentage of the recovered sum; and that the funder is not entitled to any payment if the litigation is unsuccessful.

time costs   solicitor's charges for work done on a case, usually charged on an hourly rate basis.

Woolf reforms   the original CPR 1998, which were based on the *Woolf Report.*

Table of Cases

Table of Statutes and International Legislation

Table of Secondary Legislation, Rules, Orders, Court Guides, and Codes

SIs shown as SI 2013/XXXX had not been assigned numbers when this book went to press

Parts 44 to 48 are listed twice: as they were before 1 April 2013 and as they are from 1 April 2013. Tables 10.1 and 10.2 show origins and destinations of these provisions.

1

INTRODUCTION: THE JACKSON REFORMS

The *Review of Civil Litigation Costs: Final Report* by Sir Rupert Jackson (Lord **1.01** Justice Jackson)[1] is dated 21 December 2009 and was published on 14 January

---

[1] London: TSO, 2010. In this book it will be referred to simply as *Final Report*.

2010. Its main recommendations will come into force on 1 April 2013, and will have profound effects on the conduct of litigation and the remuneration of lawyers. Without doubt it was the most important report in the area of civil law since Lord Woolf's report on *Access to Justice* in 1996.[2] Sir Rupert recognized that systemic problems cannot be cured by single big point remedies. Accordingly, the approach has been to implement a wide range of reforms which together are intended to result in substantial improvements in the civil justice system.

1.02 The terms of reference for the Review were to look into the rules and principles relating to costs and to make recommendations to promote access to justice at proportionate cost. Sir Rupert Jackson cannot be accused of shirking his responsibilities. The *Final Report* is a tour de force stretching to 557 pages with 10 appendices. Rather than repeating detail to be found in his *Interim Report*, which itself was about 600 pages long, the *Final Report* builds on the evidence from the *Interim Report*, buttresses it with further evidence, and then makes its recommendations. Each issue is analysed on the basis of evidence from experts and practitioners. Meetings were held around the country with interested organizations and groups of practitioners, and records were kept of votes taken at those meetings on all the main issues. The result is that the 109 recommendations were backed up by an impressive array of evidence, unlikely to be surpassed for many years.

1.03 Statistical analysis forming part of the Review found, for example, that in libel claims under conditional fee agreements (CFAs) claimant costs were on average 314 per cent of damages, and that in medium-value clinical negligence cases claimant costs were 30 per cent of damages for self-funded cases but 75 per cent for CFA-funded cases. Not all areas were found to be affected by excessive or disproportionate costs, with the Commercial Court and the Technology and Construction Court emerging very well from the Review.

1.04 Major themes of the *Final Report* include:

- the underlying problems can be tackled only by recognizing that the costs payable in a case are connected with the funding arrangements;
- court procedures and pre-action protocols have a direct impact on the amount of costs;
- complex rules lead to satellite litigation and increased costs; and
- the viability of different funding models depends on the amount of damages available to the claimant in a successful case.

1.05 All these areas were addressed in the Review. The recommendations have to be seen as a balanced package, covering everything from the initial retainer through the protocols to the litigation process and case management, hearings, and the assessment of costs.

---

[2] Lord Woolf, *Access to Justice. Final Report* (London: HMSO, 1996).

A. AIMS AND CONCERNS

In addition to controlling costs to ensure they are proportionate, general aims **1.06** of the Review included:

- Access to justice. This includes ensuring that middle-income individuals and small and medium-sized enterprises (SMEs) have funding options available to them so that they can have access to the court system.
- Providing a range of funding options, based on a free market, choice, and proper advice to clients on funding options.
- Support for the Civil Procedure Rules (CPR) and their overriding objective of dealing with cases justly.
- Protection of vulnerable litigants.
- Concern to ring-fence damages for pain, suffering, and loss of amenity and future care in personal injuries claims.

B. OVERALL GOAL

This was succinctly stated by Sir Rupert Jackson in his 5th Implementation **1.07** Lecture:[3]

The goal of the present round of reforms is to enable both practitioners and the courts to deliver the best possible service to civil litigants at the lowest possible cost.

C. KEY RECOMMENDATIONS

Party and party cost orders

Making costs orders on the principle that costs follow the event is referred to **1.08** as 'costs shifting' in the Review. Even this fundamental principle was examined critically, but Sir Rupert Jackson accepted the arguments of policy and principle underlying the principle, and concluded that it should be retained in civil proceedings.[4]

---

[3] 5th Implementation Lecture, para 5.5. Details of the Implementation Lectures are given in the List of Abbreviations.
[4] *Final Report*, ch 4, para 3.25.

Qualified one-way costs shifting

1.09 In order to promote access to justice, the Review recommended modifying the principle that costs follow the event so as to protect vulnerable parties against adverse costs orders. Identifying who is a 'vulnerable party' for this purpose may need further work, but the idea is that they are parties in asymmetric relationships, such as claimants in personal injuries cases, and probably individual litigants in housing, police, judicial review, and defamation or privacy cases. The Review proposed that the protection should operate in much the same way as the cost protection rules in the Access to Justice Act 1999, s 11(1), which have existed for many years for publicly funded litigants.

Indemnity principle

1.10 Sir Rupert Jackson recommended that the indemnity principle should be abrogated.[5] Under this principle (which arises when costs are being assessed) costs are disallowed to the extent that the receiving party (the winner) is not under an obligation to pay those costs to its lawyers. It lies at the root of most of the technical objections raised in satellite litigation over funding arrangements. Abolishing the indemnity principle is of fundamental importance as it opens the way to a whole range of funding options becoming effective. What is of great concern is that the reforms of 1 April 2013 do not include a clear statement revoking the indemnity principle,[6] and certain provisions are retained which are only relevant if the principle remains.[7]

CFA success fees and ATE

1.11 While CFAs (including those with success fees) are not abolished by the 1 April 2013 reforms, a key recommendation in the Review is that success fees and after-the-event (ATE) insurance premiums should no longer be recoverable from the losing party.[8] Recoverability of success fees and ATE premiums has become a problem because, since 2000, they have dramatically increased the amounts that defendants must pay. The most telling example is the emergence of the 'super-claimant', ie, a litigant who has a CFA, ATE insurance, and third-party funding.[9] Such a package enables a litigant to hedge much of the risk involved in litigation and to pursue a claim at relatively modest cost. While this is beneficial for the so-called super-claimant, it is at the expense of the other side, who has none of the benefits, runs all the risks, and potentially pays all the bills. Other abuses

---

[5] *Final Report*, recommendation 4.
[6] See 10.51 to 10.60.
[7] See 10.53 and 10.59.
[8] *Final Report,* ch 10, para 4.20.
[9] *Final Report*, ch 10, para 2.9.

have included extortionate success fee percentages, which were hard to control on assessment, and the fact that CFAs were open to all litigants, even those rich enough not to need them.

Under the main proposals a lawyer's success fee in a successful case will in future have to be met by the client rather than being recovered from the other side. Secondary recommendations included capping success fees in personal injuries claims to 25 per cent of damages (excluding the damages for future care and expense), and in effect ring-fencing damages for pain, suffering, and loss of amenity by increasing damages under that head by 10 per cent across the board. The 10 per cent increase in damages was proposed to ensure that lawyers could continue to take a success fee in a CFA-funded case, but without financial detriment to the client. **1.12**

Contingency fees: damages-based agreements

Sir Rupert Jackson recommended that contingency fees, which are now known as damages-based agreements (DBAs), should be allowed, but the contingency fee element would not be recoverable from the other side.[10] It was recognized that DBAs would need regulation, and funding by contingency fee should only be valid if the client has received independent advice from a solicitor.[11] **1.13**

New test for proportionality

The *Final Report* took the view that the test for proportionality in assessments of costs on the standard basis that had developed under the CPR did not go far enough to reflect the intention of disallowing disproportionate costs. There will therefore be a new proportionality test, under which only reasonable and proportionate costs will be recoverable from the losing party. **1.14**

The importance of proportionality is emphasized under the 1 April 2013 reforms by adding it to CPR, r 1.1(1), the fundamental definition of the overriding objective. It is also reflected in a wide range of more detailed reforms of the case management powers of the court. **1.15**

D. CONSULTATION ON IMPLEMENTING CHANGES

Many of the key ideas put forward by the Jackson Review were put out to public consultation by the Ministry of Justice in its *Proposals for Reform of Civil Litigation Funding and Costs in England and Wales—Implementation of Lord Justice Jackson's Recommendations*.[12] Sixty areas of possible reform were covered by the **1.16**

---

[10] *Final Report*, recommendation 14.
[11] *Final Report*, recommendation 15.
[12] 15 November 2010.

consultation. Responses were given by a wide range of interested parties, including the Bar Council, the Law Society, the Bar Standards Board, firms of solicitors, various bar associations and chambers, and the insurance industry. *Reforming Civil Litigation Funding and Costs in England and Wales—Implementation of Lord Justice Jackson's Recommendations: The Government Response*[13] was the government's response to the consultation exercise, and confirmed a commitment to implement the main elements of the recommendations from the *Final Report*.

E. LEGAL AID, SENTENCING AND PUNISHMENT OF OFFENDERS ACT 2012

1.17 Changing the funding arrangements for civil proceedings has required primary legislation, mainly because the legal foundations of CFAs are in the Courts and Legal Services Act 1990, ss 58 to 58C, and the Access to Justice Act 1999. These changes were made by part 2 of the Legal Aid, Sentencing and Punishment of Offenders Act 2012 (LASPO 2012), which received royal assent on 1 May 2012. Part 1 of LASPO 2012 enacts a new legal aid system to replace the Community Legal Service system set out in the Access to Justice Act 1999, and part 2 deals with a number of other topics such as DBAs and Part 36 offers. The relevant provisions of the Act extend to England and Wales only,[14] and come into effect on dates to be appointed by order of the Lord Chancellor or Secretary of State.[15] The civil litigation provisions in LASPO 2012 come into force on 1 April 2013.[16]

F. CIVIL PROCEDURE (AMENDMENT) RULES 2013

1.18 The rule-making powers in LASPO 2012, ss 45(8) and 55, were brought into force on 1 October 2012,[17] to provide power to make new rules on DBAs and claimants' Part 36 offers. Power to make other changes to the CPR to implement the 1 April 2013 reforms is already provided by the Civil Procedure Act 1997, s 2.

1.19 The Civil Procedure (Amendment) Rules 2013,[18] together with amendments to practice directions made by the 60th Update, come into force on 1 April 2013 to coincide with the commencement of the relevant provisions of LASPO 2012.

---

[13] Cm 8041, March 2011. In this book referred to as the *Government Response*.

[14] LASPO 2012, s 152(1).

[15] LASPO 2012, s 151(1).

[16] Legal Aid, Sentencing and Punishment of Offenders Act 2012 (Commencement No 5 and Saving Provision) Order 2013 (SI 2013/77).

[17] Legal Aid, Sentencing and Punishment of Offenders Act 2012 (Commencement No 2 and Specification of Commencement Date) Order 2012 (SI 2012/2412).

[18] SI 2013/262.

These instruments make a wide range of changes to the rules governing civil proceedings. Among the most important changes are the following.

Directions questionnaires replace allocation questionnaires

Allocation questionnaires in the old forms N150 and N151 are discontinued from 1 April 2013, and are replaced by new directions questionnaires in forms N180 and N181. This reflects a change of focus from track allocation to case management directions.

1.20

Costs management

A new PD 3E on costs management comes into effect from 1 April 2013. It will apply to all multi-track claims. Part of the process set out in PD 3E is the production of costs budgets, which will enable the court to manage the costs to be incurred by the parties in multi-track claims.

1.21

Costs capping

There is also a new PD 3F on costs capping orders. This is more a matter of reorganizing existing provisions, but the intention is to give greater prominence to an important case management tool for controlling litigation costs.

1.22

Costs rules

The whole of the former CPR, Parts 43 to 48, together with the costs practice direction in PD 43–48, is replaced by new provisions in CPR, Parts 44 to 48 and PD 44 to PD 48. Part 43 is revoked. There has been a great deal of reorganization of material within these provisions, as well as amendments to reflect the changes to the funding system and the costs reforms recommended by the *Final Report*.

1.23

G. DAMAGES IN TORT CLAIMS ETC

The need to increase damages in personal injuries claims to implement recommendation 10 of the *Final Report* has been addressed by the Court of Appeal.[19] The increase applies to a wide range of claims in tort involving personal injuries, distress, or suffering, and extends to cases involving similar heads of damage even if the cause of action is not in tort.

1.24

---

[19] See chapter 14.

H. RECOMMENDATIONS NOT IMPLEMENTED

1.25 While a substantial number of the recommendations made in the *Final Report* are being brought into effect on 1 April 2013, there are many that are not. Among the most prominent are the following.

Costs Council

1.26 Recommendation 5 in the *Final Report* was that the Advisory Committee on Civil Costs (ACCC), which was set up in 2007, should be disbanded, and a Costs Council should be established in its place. The proposed Costs Council was intended to review hourly rates, matrices for fixed costs and fast track trial costs on an annual basis. It was also hoped that the Costs Council would take on wider responsibilities, for example, in setting or giving guidance on hourly rates and recoverable fees for counsel. On 30 October 2012 the Justice Minister, Helen Grant, said that the ACCC was to be disbanded, but there will be no Costs Council. Instead, the ACCC's responsibilities are being transferred to the Civil Justice Council.

Fixed costs on fast track claims

1.27 While fixed trial costs in fast track claims remain,[20] recommendation 18 of the *Final Report*, that the recoverable costs of cases in the fast track should be fixed, has not been implemented. Setting fixed costs across a range of cases in a just way remains an extraordinarily difficult project.

Extension of QOCS

1.28 The 1 April 2013 reforms introduce qualified one-way costs shifting (QOCS) for personal injuries claims. Strictly, this is consistent with the terms of recommendation 19 of the *Final Report*, which said that QOCS should be introduced for personal injuries claims. It was also mentioned in the Executive Summary of the *Final Report* that QOCS should be considered for other categories of claim, particularly those where traditionally there is an inequality of arms between claimants and defendants, such as judicial review and defamation claims. Extending QOCS to other areas is for consideration in the future.

Jury trial

1.29 Among the detailed recommendations in the *Final Report* dealing with the litigation process, which were aimed to reduce costs in different categories of case, was

---

[20] See new CPR, rr 45.37 to 45.40, which are in the same terms as the provisions in the old Part 46.

recommendation 67 that the retention of jury trial in defamation claims needs to be reconsidered. This reform is not going ahead on 1 April 2013. Despite the widely held belief in the importance of being tried by a tribunal of one's peers, the vulnerability of jury trial in the medium term in defamation claims is obvious given the expense involved.

Non-compliance with pre-action protocols

Recommendation 85 was to the effect that pre-action applications should be permitted in respect of breaches of pre-action protocols. The *Final Report* recognized that primary legislation was required to implement this recommendation.[21] While this has not been implemented in LASPO 2012, Sir Rupert Jackson has indicated a prospect of it being included in future legislation.[22]   **1.30**

Case management appeals to include district judge as assessor

Recommendation 88 of the *Final Report*, on district judges sitting as assessors on case management appeals to the Court of Appeal, is not being adopted at present for logistical reasons.[23]   **1.31**

---

[21] Page 472.
[22] 5th Implementation Lecture, para 5.1.
[23] 5th Implementation Lecture, para 5.2.

2

TRANSITIONAL PROVISIONS

A. MAIN COMMENCEMENT DATE

1 April 2013 is the commencement date for the following: **2.01**

(a) LASPO 2012, parts 1 and 2.[1]

(b) Civil Procedure (Amendment) Rules 2013[2] (see r 2).

---

[1] Legal Aid, Sentencing and Punishment of Offenders Act 2012 (Commencement No 5 and Saving Provision) Order 2013 (SI 2013/77).
[2] SI 2013/262.

(c) Amendments to practice directions, pre-action protocols and forms introduced by the 60th Update.

(d) Conditional Fee Agreements Order 2013.[3]

(e) Damages-Based Agreements Regulations 2013.[4]

(f) Recovery of Costs Insurance Premiums in Clinical Negligence Proceedings Regulations 2013[5] (see reg 1).

(g) Civil Legal Aid (Procedure) Regulations 2012[6] (see reg 1).

(h) Civil Legal Aid (Merits Criteria) Regulations 2013[7] (see reg 1).

(i) Civil Legal Aid (Costs) Regulations 2013.[8]

B. LASPO COMMENCEMENT ORDERS

2.02   While the main provisions of LASPO 2012, parts 1 and 2, on legal aid and funding of litigation, come into force on 1 April 2013, rule-making powers in relation to DBAs[9] and Part 36 offers to settle[10] were brought into force on 1 October 2012.[11]

2.03   The extension to the Supreme Court of the power to make pro bono costs orders under the Legal Services Act 2007[12] was also brought into force on 1 October 2012.[13]

C. CFA AND ADDITIONAL LIABILITIES
TRANSITIONAL PROVISIONS

2.04   The broad principle is that the old recoverability regime in the CLSA 1990, s 58, in relation to CFA success fees, and in the Access to Justice Act 1999, ss 29 and 30, in relation to ATE premiums and membership liabilities, will continue to apply after 1 April 2013 to funding agreements entered into up to and including

---

[3] SI 2013/(number not assigned when this Guide went to press).

[4] SI 2013/(number not assigned when this Guide went to press).

[5] SI 2013/92.

[6] SI 2012/3098.

[7] SI 2013/104.

[8] SI 2013/(number not assigned when this Guide went to press).

[9] LASPO 2012, s 45(1) and (8).

[10] LASPO 2012, s 55.

[11] Legal Aid, Sentencing and Punishment of Offenders Act 2012 (Commencement No 2 and Specification of Commencement Date) Order 2012 (SI 2012/2412).

[12] LASPO 2012, s 61.

[13] Legal Aid, Sentencing and Punishment of Offenders Act 2012 (Commencement No 2 and Specification of Commencement Date) Order 2012.

31 March 2013. Any funding arrangement entered into on or after 1 April 2013 will be subject to the new regime as laid down by LASPO 2012.

Abolition of recoverability

Recoverability of CFA success fees under the old legislation was dealt with by the CLSA 1990, s 58A(6), which said that a costs order in any proceedings may include provisions requiring the payment of any fees payable under a CFA which provides for a success fee. That subsection is repealed by LASPO 2012, s 44(4), which has substituted a new CLSA 1990, s 58A(6), which now says: **2.05**

A costs order made in proceedings may not include provision requiring the payment by one party of all or part of a success fee payable by another party under a conditional fee agreement.

Recoverability of ATE insurance premiums was provided by the Access to Justice Act 1999, s 29, which has been repealed with effect from 1 April 2013.[14] Membership organization liabilities were recoverable under the Access to Justice Act 1999, s 30, which has also been repealed with effect from 1 April 2013.[15] **2.06**

Pre-LASPO 2012 CFAs

While the new no-recoverability rule[16] applies to CFAs entered into from 1 April 2013, continuation of the recoverability regime for CFAs entered into before 1 April 2013 is provided by LASPO 2012, s 44(6), which provides: **2.07**

The amendment made by subsection (4) does not prevent a costs order including provision in relation to a success fee payable by a person ('P') under a conditional fee agreement entered into before the day on which that subsection comes into force ('the commencement day') if—

(a) the agreement was entered into specifically for the purposes of the provision to P of advocacy or litigation services in connection with the matter that is the subject of the proceedings in which the costs order is made, or

(b) advocacy or litigation services were provided to P under the agreement in connection with that matter before the commencement day.

This position is confirmed by the transitional provisions in the Conditional Fee Agreements Order 2013, art 7, and by new CPR, r 48.1(1), which provides: **2.08**

The provisions of CPR Parts 43 to 48 relating to funding arrangements, and the attendant provisions of the Costs Practice Direction, will apply in relation to a pre-commencement funding arrangement as they were in force immediately before 1 April 2013, with such modifications (if any) as may be made by a practice direction on or after that date.

---

[14] LASPO 2012, s 46(2).
[15] LASPO 2012, s 47(1).
[16] LASPO 2012, s 44(4), inserting new CLSA 1990, s 58A(6).

2.09 In relation to CFAs, for the purposes of r 48.1(1) a pre-commencement funding arrangement is by r 48.2(1) a funding arrangement as defined by r 43.2(1)(k)(i) (CFAs with success fees), as in force before 1 April 2013, where:

(a) the agreement was entered into before 1 April 2013 specifically for the purposes of the provision to the person by whom the success fee is payable of advocacy or litigation services in relation to the matter that is the subject of the proceedings in which the costs order is to be made; or

(b) the agreement was entered into before 1 April 2013 and advocacy or litigation services were provided to that person under the agreement in connection with that matter before 1 April 2013.[17]

CFAs and pre-action conduct

2.10 Paragraph 9.3 of PD Pre-action Conduct has been retained. This imposes a duty to inform other parties as part of the pre-action protocol process about any funding arrangement,[18] and contains a cross-reference to CPR, r 44.3B(1)(c), as in force before 1 April 2013. It may be that failing to delete PD Pre-action Conduct, para 9.3, is simply an oversight, but the reason presumably is that it has been retained to cover cases where the funding arrangement was entered into before 1 April 2013. Provided the courts realize the references to provisions in the CPR in para 9.3 are to the rules in force before 1 April 2013 there is no harm in retaining para 9.3.

Pre-LASPO 2012 ATE premiums

2.11 As with pre-commencement CFAs, the recoverability regime continues to apply to pre-commencement ATE policies. The omission of the CLSA 1990, s 29, by LASPO 2012, s 46(2), does not apply in relation to a costs order made in favour of a party to proceedings who took out a costs insurance policy in relation to the proceedings before 1 April 2013.[19]

2.12 New CPR, r 48.1(1),[20] also applies to pre-commencement ATE policies. For this purpose a pre-commencement ATE funding agreement is a funding arrangement as defined by r 43.2(1)(k)(ii) (ATE insurance premiums), as in force before 1 April 2013, where the party seeking to recover the insurance premium took out the insurance policy in relation to the proceedings before 1 April 2013.[21]

---

[17] CPR, r 48.2(1)(a)(i).
[18] Within the meaning of CPR, r 43.2(1)(k).
[19] LASPO 2012, s 46(3).
[20] See 2.08.
[21] CPR, r 48.2(1)(a)(ii).

Pre-LASPO 2012 membership organization liabilities

Pre-commencement arrangements in respect of additional liabilities to member- **2.13**
ship organizations likewise continue to be recoverable on and after 1 April 2013.
The Access to Justice Act 1999, s 30, was repealed by LASPO 2012, s 47(1), but
the section goes on to provide that the repeal does not apply in relation to a costs
order made in favour of a person to whom the membership organization gave
an undertaking before 1 April 2013 if the undertaking was given specifically in
respect of the costs of other parties to proceedings relating to the matter which
is the subject of the proceedings in which the costs order is made.[22]

New CPR, r 48.1(1),[23] also applies to pre-commencement membership organi- **2.14**
zation liabilities. For this purpose a pre-commencement agreement is a funding
arrangement as defined by r 43.2(1)(k)(iii) (agreement with a membership organization to meet a person's legal costs), as in force before 1 April 2013, where the
agreement with the membership organization to meet the costs was made before
1 April 2013 specifically in respect of the costs of other parties to proceedings
relating to the matter which is the subject of the proceedings in which the costs
order is to be made.[24]

Mesothelioma claims

It is provided by LASPO 2012, s 48, that the provisions abolishing the recover- **2.15**
ability of CFA success fees and other additional liabilities[25] are not to be brought
into force in relation to diffuse mesothelioma claims until after the publication of
a report commissioned by the Lord Chancellor reviewing the likely effect of the
abolition of recoverability. For this purpose diffuse mesothelioma has the same
meaning as in the Pneumoconiosis etc (Workers' Compensation) Act 1979.[26]

In a Ministerial Statement of 24 May 2012, Jonathan Djanogly, the Parlia- **2.16**
mentary Under-Secretary of State at the Ministry of Justice, said that because
the review required by LASPO 2012, s 48, had not yet commenced, ss 44 to 46
will not come into effect for mesothelioma claims for the time being. Further
details on content and timing relating to how ss 44 to 46 will apply to mesothelioma claims will be released in due course.

This delay in implementing non-recoverability in mesothelioma claims is **2.17**
confirmed by CPR, r 48.2(1)(b).[27] This means that success fees and insurance

---

[22] LASPO 2012, s 47(2).

[23] See 2.08.

[24] CPR, r 48.2(1)(a)(iii).

[25] LASPO 2012, ss 44 to 46.

[26] LASPO 2012, s 48(2). The Pneumoconiosis etc (Workers' Compensation) Act 1979, s 1(3), provides that the diseases to which the Act applies are pneumoconiosis, byssinosis, and diffuse mesothelioma and any other disease which is specified by the Secretary of State for the purposes of this Act
by order made by statutory instrument.

[27] See also Conditional Fee Agreements Order 2013, art 6, and PD 48, para 2.1.

premiums will remain recoverable beyond April 2013, although the fixed recoverable success fees in respect of employer's liability disease claims in CPR, Part 45, Section V, as in force before 1 April 2013, will continue to apply in respect of mesothelioma claims.

Insolvency cases

2.18 The Ministerial Statement of 24 May 2012 said that insolvency cases bring substantial revenue to the taxpayer, as well as other creditors, and encourage good business practice which can be seen as an important part of the growth agenda with wider benefits for the economy. These features were felt to merit a delayed implementation of non-recoverability to allow time for those involved to adjust and implement such alternative arrangements as they consider will allow these cases to continue to be pursued. Like mesothelioma claims, this has been implemented by the Conditional Fee Agreements Order 2013, art 6, and CPR, r 48.2(1)(b).[28]

Publication and privacy proceedings

2.19 Publication and privacy proceedings were not mentioned in the Ministerial Statement of 24 May 2012, but nevertheless implementation of the non-recoverability regime has also been delayed for these cases.[29] For this purpose 'publication and privacy proceedings' means[30] claims for:

(a) defamation;

(b) malicious falsehood;

(c) breach of confidence involving publication to members of the public;

(d) misuse of private information; or

(e) harassment, where the defendant is a news publisher.[31]

2.20 How the delay in the revocation of recoverability in defamation and privacy proceedings relates to the 10 per cent increase in damages in these claims made by *Simmons v Castle*[32] has not been resolved. Presumably implementation of the 10 per cent increase in these cases should be postponed until recoverability is removed.

---

[28] A full definition of insolvency proceedings for this purpose can be found in Conditional Fee Agreements Order 2013, art 6(2)(c) to (f). See also PD 48, para 3.1.

[29] CPR, r 48.2(1)(b), and PD 48, para 3.2.

[30] CPR, r 48.2(2)(c).

[31] As defined in CPR, r 48.2(2)(b).

[32] [2012] EWCA Civ 1039, [2012] EWCA Civ 1288, [2013] 1 All ER 334; see chapter 14.

Clinical negligence

As discussed in chapter 4,[33] from 1 April 2013 while recoverability will have   **2.21**
been abolished for most purposes, recoverability of ATE premiums to cover
experts' reports in clinical negligence cases will continue. The regulations dealing with ATE premiums[34] for these experts' reports apply only to clinical negligence cases where the costs insurance policy is taken out on or after 1 April
2013.[35]

D. DBA TRANSITIONAL PROVISIONS

LASPO 2012, s 45(13), provides that the amendments made to CLSA 1990,   **2.22**
s 58AA, on DBAs by LASPO 2012, s 45(1) to (11), do not apply in relation to a
DBA entered into before s 45 came into force. The Damages-Based Agreements
Regulations 2013 come into force on 1 April 2013.[36]

E. CPR TRANSITIONAL PROVISIONS

Proportionality in standard-basis assessments

The new proportionality test in standard-basis assessments[37] does not apply   **2.23**
in relation to cases commenced before 1 April 2013. In relation to such cases,
CPR, r 44.4(2)(a), as it was in force immediately before 1 April 2013 will apply
instead.[38]

Qualified one-way costs shifting

The provisions on one-way costs shifting[39] do not apply to proceedings where the   **2.24**
claimant has entered into a pre-commencement funding arrangement.[40]

---

[33] See 4.46 to 4.51.
[34] Recovery of Costs of Insurance Premiums in Clinical Negligence Proceedings Regulations 2013
(SI 2013/92).
[35] PD 48, para 4.2.
[36] Damages-Based Agreements Regulations 2013, reg 1(1). Transitional provisions in the regulations apply to pre-1 April 2013 employment cases.
[37] CPR, r 44.3(2)(a) and (5); see 10.68.
[38] CPR, r 44.3(7).
[39] See 10.07.
[40] CPR, r 44.17. Pre-commencement funding arrangements are defined by r 48.2; see 2.08 to 2.14.

Relief from sanctions

2.25 The amendments made to CPR, rr 3.8 and 3.9(1),[41] do not apply to applications made before 1 April 2013 for relief from any sanction imposed for a failure to comply with any rule, practice direction, or court order.[42]

Directions questionnaires

2.26 Directions questionnaires and related case management provisions in CPR, rr 3.7, 3.7A and Part 26 do not apply where a defence is received before 1 April 2013.[43]

Small claims limit

2.27 Raising the small claims limit from £5,000 to £10,000 does not apply to claims issued before 1 April 2013.[44]

Agreement of multi-track directions

2.28 The amendment substituting CPR, r 29.4,[45] does not apply where any case management conference takes place or is due to take place before 9 April 2013.[46]

Disclosure

2.29 The amendment to CPR, r 31.5,[47] does not apply where the first case management conference takes place or is due to take place before 16 April 2013.[48]

Experts

2.30 The amendments made to CPR, r 35.4,[49] do not apply in relation to an application for permission made before 1 April 2013.[50]

Part 36 offers

2.31 The amendments made to CPR, r 36.14,[51] do not apply in relation to a claimant's Part 36 offer which was made before 1 April 2013.[52]

---

[41] See 5.85.
[42] Civil Procedure (Amendment) Rules 2013, r 22(2).
[43] Civil Procedure (Amendment) Rules 2013, r 22(12) and (14).
[44] Civil Procedure (Amendment) Rules 2013, r 22(3).
[45] See 5.67.
[46] Civil Procedure (Amendment) Rules 2013, r 22(4).
[47] See 8.21.
[48] Civil Procedure (Amendment) Rules 2013, r 22(5).
[49] See 9.11.
[50] Civil Procedure (Amendment) Rules 2013, r 22(6).
[51] See 11.28.
[52] Civil Procedure (Amendment) Rules 2013, r 22(7) and see 15.08.

Costs

In relation to costs: **2.32**

(a) The provisions in CPR, rr 45.41 to 45.44, dealing with Aarhus Convention claims, do not apply in relation to a claim commenced before 1 April 2013.[53]

(b) The provision concerning when time for appealing against an assessment starts to run in new r 47.14(7) does not apply where the final hearing was concluded before 1 April 2013.[54]

(c) Liability for costs of detailed assessment proceedings in new r 47.20 does not apply to detailed assessments commenced before 1 April 2013, and in relation to such detailed assessments, rr 47.18 and 47.19, as in force before 1 April 2013, continue to apply.[55]

(d) Interest on the costs of detailed assessment proceedings in new r 47.20(6) does not apply where the date of the default, interim, or final costs certificate is before 1 April 2013.[56]

(e) Any defamation proceedings commenced before 1 April 2013 within the scope of the Defamation Proceedings Costs Management Scheme provided for by PD 51D will proceed and be completed in accordance with that scheme.[57]

(f) Detailed assessments under the County Court Provisional Assessment Pilot Scheme[58] commenced before 1 April 2013 will proceed and be completed in accordance with that scheme.[59]

F. DAMAGES FOR PSLA, SUFFERING, AND DISTRESS

The 10 per cent increase in damages for physical inconvenience and discomfort, **2.33** social discredit, mental distress, and loss of society of relatives,[60] does not apply where there is a funding arrangement, which was entered into before 1 April 2013, falling within the ambit of LASPO 2012, s 44(6).[61]

---

[53] Civil Procedure (Amendment) Rules 2013, r 22(8).
[54] Civil Procedure (Amendment) Rules 2013, r 22(9).
[55] Civil Procedure (Amendment) Rules 2013, r 22(10).
[56] Civil Procedure (Amendment) Rules 2013, r 22(11).
[57] Civil Procedure (Amendment) Rules 2013, r 22(12).
[58] Under PD 51E.
[59] Civil Procedure (Amendment) Rules 2013, r 22(13).
[60] *Simmons v Castle* [2012] EWCA Civ 1039, [2012] EWCA Civ 1288, [2013] 1 All ER 334; see chapter 14.
[61] For which, see 2.07.

3

LEGAL AID

A. INTRODUCTION

LASPO 2012 repeals the provisions in the Access to Justice Act 1999 on the **3.01** Community Legal Service.[1] They are replaced by a new system of legal aid to be administered on behalf of the Lord Chancellor by a civil servant known as the Director of Legal Aid Casework.[2] Many of the concepts of the old legal aid and Community Legal Service systems are retained in the new provisions. The most notable change is that legal aid for clinical negligence has largely been removed.[3] In relation to clinical negligence, legal aid under LASPO 2012 will only be available for claims for severely disabled infants.[4]

It might be thought that the legal aid provisions in LASPO 2012 are part **3.02** of the Jackson reforms, not least because they appear in the same statute that makes the necessary legislative changes needed for the funding changes recommended by the *Final Report*. In fact, it was simply legislative convenience that put the legal aid and Jackson reforms into the same statute, a point made by Sir Rupert Jackson in his first implementation lecture.[5] As was made clear in that lecture, abolition of public funding for most clinical negligence claims runs counter to the views expressed in the *Final Report*, which were to the effect that

---

[1] LASPO 2012, s 39(1), and sch 5, para 51.

[2] LASPO 2012, ss 1 and 4.

[3] LASPO 2012, s 9 and sch 1.

[4] As defined in LASPO 2012, sch 1, para 23.

[5] Cambridge Law Faculty, Legal Aid and the Costs Review Reforms (Legal Aid etc Lecture 5), A Talk by Lord Justice Jackson to the Cambridge Law Faculty on 5 September 2011.

maintenance of legal aid at no less than the existing levels makes sound economic sense and is in the public interest.[6]

3.03   Nevertheless, the changes to the legal aid system do come into force on the same day as the Jackson reforms, and public funding has traditionally played an important role in promoting access to justice. With modern constraints on the public finances, that role will be an attenuated one for the foreseeable future.

B. ABOLITION OF THE LEGAL SERVICES COMMISSION

3.04   Following the recommendations of the Magee Report,[7] the Legal Services Commission is abolished[8] and, with effect from 1 April 2013, is replaced by the Legal Aid Agency. This is an executive agency of the Ministry of Justice. The day-to-day administration of legal aid is transferred to the Lord Chancellor,[9] who is required to designate a civil servant as the Director of Legal Aid Casework.[10] The Director is obliged to comply with directions from, and must have regard to guidance given by, the Lord Chancellor about the carrying out of the Director's functions under the Act, but the Lord Chancellor is not permitted to give directions or guidance in relation to individual cases.[11]

C. CIVIL LEGAL AID

3.05   The Lord Chancellor is under a duty to secure that legal aid ('civil legal services') is made available in accordance with LASPO 2012, part 1.[12] This does not include a duty to provide those services by the means selected by the legally aided person,[13] so services could be provided by telephone or electronic means.[14] Likewise, in civil cases there is no general obligation for the legal services to be provided by the lawyer selected by the legally aided person,[15] who will usually, in effect, be forced to accept the services from a provider who has entered into a contract with the Legal Aid Agency.

3.06   Civil legal services are to be made available to individuals for cases covered by LASPO 2012, sch 1, part 1, unless excluded or modified by sch 1, parts 2, 3,

---

[6] *Final Report*, ch 7, para 4.2.
[7] Sir Ian Magee, *Review of Legal Aid Delivery and Governance* (March 2010).
[8] LASPO 2012, s 38(1).
[9] LASPO 2012, ss 1 to 3.
[10] LASPO 2012, s 4(1).
[11] LASPO 2012, s 4(4).
[12] LASPO 2012, s 1(1).
[13] LASPO 2012, s 27(1).
[14] LASPO 2012, s 27(2).
[15] LASPO 2012, s 27(3).

or 4.[16] Schedule 1 runs to 31 pages, and covers various family, immigration, and other categories of proceedings, often with detailed exclusions. Included within the scheme are judicial review claims,[17] habeas corpus,[18] abuse of position or power by public authorities,[19] breach of ECHR rights by public authorities,[20] clinical negligence claims for severely disabled infants,[21] and various other categories.[22] Most of these are subject to exclusions. There continues to be a list of excluded services,[23] including the familiar exclusions for claims relating to personal injuries and death, defamation, and matters relating to company and partnership law, but now joined by most clinical negligence claims.

There is provision for civil legal services to be made available on an exceptional **3.07** case determination by the Director of Legal Aid Casework where this must be done to avoid a breach of an individual's rights under the ECHR, or where any rights of the individual to the provision of legal services are enforceable EU rights.[24] An exceptional case determination must be made in accordance with the provisions of the Civil Legal Aid (Procedure) Regulations 2012[25] which apply to the form of civil legal services which is the subject of the application.[26]

There continue to be financial qualifications for legal aid[27] and other criteria **3.08** which are set out in regulations.[28] Those additional criteria are based on factors such as cost-benefit considerations, the availability of resources to provide legal services, and the importance of the matter.[29] Generally, civil legal aid is only available to individuals, although corporations may be covered if the Director has made an exceptional case determination.[30]

Individuals will continue to be protected from having to pay for the provision **3.09** of legal services which are provided under the Act other than as provided in regulations.[31] Those regulations may, as with the Community Legal Service, provide for the payment of contributions, or even the whole cost of the services,[32] by way of periodical payments, one or more lump sums, and out of income or capital.[33]

---

[16] LASPO 2012, s 9.
[17] LASPO 2012, sch 1, para 19.
[18] LASPO 2012, sch 1, para 20.
[19] LASPO 2012, sch 1, para 21.
[20] LASPO 2012, sch 1, para 22.
[21] LASPO 2012, sch 1, para 23.
[22] LASPO 2012, sch 1, paras 24 to 46.
[23] LASPO 2012, sch 1, part 2.
[24] LASPO 2012, s 10.
[25] SI 2012/3098.
[26] Civil Legal Aid (Procedure) Regulations 2012, reg 66(2).
[27] LASPO 2012, ss 11(1)(a) and 21.
[28] LASPO 2012, s 11(1)(b); Civil Legal Aid (Merits Criteria) Regulations 2013 (SI 2013/104).
[29] LASPO 2012, s 11(3).
[30] LASPO 2012, s 31, and sch 3, para 3.
[31] LASPO 2012, s 23(1). See 3.11.
[32] LASPO 2012, s 23(2).
[33] LASPO 2012, s 23(8).

D. FORMS OF CIVIL LEGAL SERVICES

3.10 Civil legal services may take any of the following forms:[34]

(a) legal help;

(b) help at court;

(c) family help;

(d) family mediation;

(e) help with family mediation;

(f) legal representation; and

(g) other legal services.

3.11 Different procedures apply for making and withdrawing different categories of public funding, as set out in the Civil Legal Aid (Procedure) Regulations 2012. For example, applications for legal representation which is not controlled work or special case work come within what is known as licensed work, and are governed by regs 29 to 49. Applications must be made in the prescribed form, which must be signed by the individual and the proposed provider.[35] There are detailed procedural requirements to be followed.[36] Different merits criteria apply to each of the different forms of civil legal services.[37] If the Director makes a determination that an individual qualifies for licensed work, the Director is under a duty to issue and send a certificate recording the determination to the individual with a copy to the provider.[38] The determination must specify any contributions payable by the individual,[39] and the certificate must specify the proceedings to which the determination relates and any conditions or limitations on the cover.[40]

3.12 Individuals have a reporting obligation if there is any change in circumstances which might affect their qualification for civil legal services.[41] Providers have duties to report various matters, such as any refusal to accept an offer to settle or an offer to use alternative dispute resolution, or any information which might affect the client's continued qualification for civil legal services.[42]

---

[34] Civil Legal Aid (Procedure) Regulations 2012, reg 3, as more fully defined in the Civil Legal Aid (Merits Criteria) Regulations 2013 (SI 2013/104), rr 12 to 19.

[35] Civil Legal Aid (Procedure) Regulations 2012, reg 31.

[36] In the Civil Legal Aid (Procedure) Regulations 2012.

[37] Civil Legal Aid (Merits Criteria) Regulations 2013 (SI 2013/104), rr 11 and 32 to 46.

[38] Civil Legal Aid (Procedure) Regulations 2012, reg 37(1).

[39] Civil Legal Aid (Procedure) Regulations 2012, reg 36.

[40] Civil Legal Aid (Procedure) Regulations 2012, reg 37(2).

[41] Civil Legal Aid (Procedure) Regulations 2012, reg 40(1).

[42] Civil Legal Aid (Procedure) Regulations 2012, reg 40(3).

E. FIRST CHARGE

Where civil legal services have been provided, there continues to be a first charge   **3.13**
on any property recovered or preserved by the assisted person (including any
compromise or settlement of the dispute), in respect of the amounts expended
by the Lord Chancellor in securing the provision of the services.[43] Regulations
may provide for exceptions.[44]

F. COSTS PROTECTION

LASPO 2012, s 26, substantially reproduces the costs protection rules in favour   **3.14**
of assisted individuals previously found in Access to Justice Act 1999, s 11. Costs
ordered against an individual in relevant civil proceedings must not exceed the
amount (if any) which it is reasonable for the individual to pay having regard to
all the circumstances, including:

(a) the financial resources of all of the parties to the proceedings; and

(b) their conduct in connection with the dispute to which the proceedings
relate.[45]

For this purpose, the term 'relevant civil proceedings' means the whole or part   **3.15**
of proceedings for which civil legal services have been made available to an individual under LASPO 2012, part 1.[46]

G. LEGAL AID COSTS ORDERS

Regulations may make provision about costs in relation to proceedings for the   **3.16**
purposes of which civil legal services are made available under LASPO 2012,
part 1.[47] Such regulations may make provision requiring the payment by the
Lord Chancellor of the whole or part of any costs incurred by an unassisted
party, which can be found in the Civil Legal Aid (Costs) Regulations 2013.[48]
Costs orders against publicly funded parties are made by considering whether,

---

[43] LASPO 2012, s 25.

[44] LASPO 2012, s 25(3).

[45] LASPO 2012, s 26(1); Civil Legal Aid (Costs) Regulations 2013, rr 5 to 8 and 11 to 20.

[46] LASPO 2012, s 26(2).

[47] LASPO 2012, s 26(5), which is expressed to be subject to the costs protection provisions in
s 26(1) to (4).

[48] At rr 9 and 10. Conditions that must be satisfied are set out in r 10(3) and are similar to those
that previously applied in applications under Access to Justice Act 1999, s 11. There continues to be
a three-month time limit, unless there is a good reason for the delay.

but for costs protection, a costs order would have been made against the publicly funded party[49] and then by considering the application of costs protection.[50] The general principle is that the amount of costs to be paid under a legally aided party's costs order or costs agreement must be determined as if that party were not legally aided.[51]

---

[49] Civil Legal Aid (Costs) Regulations 2013, r 15(1).
[50] Rules 15 and 16.
[51] LASPO 2012, s 26(6) and Civil Legal Aid (Costs) Regulations 2013, r 21.

4

FUNDING

A. INTRODUCTION

4.01 The Review of Civil Litigation Costs was initiated by Sir Anthony Clarke, then Master of the Rolls. Its purpose was to look into ways of tackling what was recognized as the unacceptable cost of litigation with a view to making recommendations that would promote access to justice at a proportionate cost. The *Final Report* notes that litigation is a labour-intensive activity which is carried out by professional people in an adversarial environment in the face of skilled opposition.[1] This means that litigation costs will always be substantial. It does not mean they also have to be disproportionate.

4.02 An idea underpinning much of the *Final Report* is that funding methods and costs rules impact on each other, and neither topic can be considered in isolation. Some methods of funding tend to drive up costs, and some methods of funding have the opposite effect.[2] A central finding of the report was that the recoverability regime applying to additional liabilities in conditional fee agreements (CFAs) imposed substantial and unnecessary costs on taxpayers, motorists, and the public generally.

4.03 Sir Rupert Jackson's solution to the problem of disproportionate costs which has afflicted certain areas of civil litigation is a multifaceted one, with a range of interlocking proposals designed both to keep costs under control and to preserve a fair balance in the system between the interests of claimants and defendants.

4.04 Achieving this in a world with limited provision of legal aid for civil litigants was always going to be a major challenge. CFAs, and the recoverability regime, were introduced to balance the withdrawal of legal aid from most areas of civil litigation. Access to justice implies that litigants with meritorious claims or defences should not be prevented from bringing their cases before the courts on purely financial grounds. The system has to provide measures which enable

---

[1] *Final Report*, ch 4, para 1.1.
[2] *Final Report*, ch 4, para 2.6.

litigants, especially litigants with limited means, to litigate on an affordable basis. Parties who do not have adequate access to funding for litigation must either drop their claim or defence or allow judgment to be entered against them regardless of the legal merits of their case.

At the same time, parties and their insurers should not be exposed to dispro- **4.05** portionate costs liabilities, compounded by the pre-Jackson system (if they lost) of having to pay the success fees of opponents funded under CFAs, together with after-the-event (ATE) insurance premiums which gave protection against their own costs risks if they lost. It was to ensure there will be a balanced system that the Review recommendations, such as abolishing the recoverability of CFA success fees and ATE insurance premiums, were combined with recommendations for an uplift in personal injuries damages awards and a system of qualified one-way costs shifting (QOCS).

Maintaining access to justice with the restrictions on legal aid and the abolition **4.06** of recoverable success fees means that alternative methods of funding need to be available. In fact, the *Final Report* makes the point that it is desirable that as many funding methods as possible should be available to litigants.[3] It is for this reason that the *Final Report* considered alternative sources of funding, including:

(a) contingency fees, which are now known as damages-based agreements (DBAs), see 4.62 to 4.72;

(b) third-party funding, which is also known as litigation funding, see 4.73 to 4.79;

(c) a supplementary legal aid scheme (SLAS), see 4.80; and

(d) contingent legal aid funds (CLAFs), see 4.81.

A large number of concerns have been raised about the effects of various ele- **4.07** ments in the package of reforms proposed in the *Final Report*. An example is when the Legal Aid, Sentencing and Punishment of Offenders Bill was discussed by the SCCO Costs Practitioners Group on 17 November 2011.[4] Concerns were minuted about the abolition of legal aid for much civil litigation (which is not technically part of the Jackson reforms), making ATE premiums irrecoverable, and the implementation of QOCS in personal injury cases. It was felt these reforms would lead to a severe retraction in the ATE market, and in non-personal injury cases few litigants would be able to afford or even obtain ATE cover. It was predicted that fewer clinical negligence cases and housing disrepair cases would be started in future.

The view expressed in the *Government Response*[5] was that some weaker cases **4.08** which were being brought under the existing system would be deterred. The

---

[3] *Final Report*, ch 12, para 4.2.
[4] Minutes at <http://www.justice.gov.uk/downloads/courts/senior-courts-costs-office/cpp-minutes-nov11.pdf>.
[5] Cm 8041, March 2011, para 33.

Government Response went on to say that defendants should benefit from more proportionate total legal expenses, with legal costs for the NHS falling by around a third.

4.09   A point made several times in the *Final Report* is that its 109 recommendations are a balanced package, which is the best way forward given the realities of the present position. Sir Rupert Jackson has said that any attempt to unpick the package distorts the balance and has knock-on consequences.[6] The *Government Response* stated that, taken as a whole, the package of measures is intended to restore a much-needed sense of proportion and fairness to the current regime— not by denying access to justice, but by restoring fair balance to the system.

B. SRA CODE OF CONDUCT

4.10   The proliferation of funding mechanisms will add to the burden on legal representatives of providing information and advising clients on the most suitable method of funding for their case. The Solicitors Regulation Authority (SRA) Code of Conduct 2011 says that clients must receive the best possible information about the likely overall cost of their matter, both at the time of engagement and when appropriate as it progresses.[7] A review may be needed, for example, when significant disbursements such as counsels' or experts' fees are about to be incurred. Advice may need to cover:

(a) hourly rates and other charges that may be made;

(b) the basis on which the rates may be increased, such as annual rate increases;

(c) liability for disbursements and any other payments;

(d) billing arrangements;

(e) the range of funding options available. Legal aid should not be forgotten, nor should before-the-event (BTE) cover, or the possibility of the firm's charges being met by an employer or trade union, as well as the more obvious options such as paying personally or using CFAs and DBAs, and possibly third-party funding;

(f) where the client will be entering into a fee arrangement governed by statute, such as a CFA or DBA, giving the client all relevant information relating to that arrangement;[8]

(g) any arrangements, such as fee-sharing or referral arrangements, which are relevant to the client's instructions;[9]

---

[6] 3rd Implementation Lecture, para 1.3.
[7] SRA Code of Conduct 2011, O 1.13.
[8] SRA Code of Conduct 2011, IB 1.17.
[9] SRA Code of Conduct 2011, IB 1.4.

(h) the client's potential liability for the other side's costs;

(i) where the solicitor is acting for a publicly funded client, explaining how their publicly funded status affects the costs.[10] There will be a similar obligation to explain the effect of QOCS;

(j) whether liability for the other side's costs may be covered by BTE or ATE insurance; and

(k) the possibility of the firm exercising a lien.

4.11 The purpose of these requirements is to ensure the client is given relevant costs information which is expressed clearly and in a way appropriate for the client.[11] The length of the above list means that firms will need good documentation to show that the requirements have been met. Documentation that should be considered includes:

(a) information sheets giving general information about the different funding methods available;

(b) checklists for use in initial interviews with clients; and

(c) ensuring client care letters comply with the above requirements.

4.12 All costs information should be given in writing and updated when necessary. The duty to advise means that the client must be informed of the implications involved in the various options available. It is often impossible to advise on the overall costs at the outset. In such cases the client should be given as much information as possible, given an explanation of why more information on costs cannot be given at that stage, and given either a ceiling or a review date. As the case progresses, the client should be given updates on costs. Particular care is needed when advising a client on an offer to settle under CPR, Part 36, to ensure the client understands the costs implications of the different options available.[12]

4.13 The actual terms of the retainer are a matter for negotiation between the firm and the client. A solicitor may only enter into fee agreements with clients that are legal, and which the solicitor considers are suitable for each client's needs and take account of the client's best interests.[13] There is no need for the client to be separately advised on a fee arrangement unless the agreement is unusual (such as the firm receiving a non-monetary consideration for its services).

---

[10] SRA Code of Conduct 2011, IB 1.18.
[11] SRA Code of Conduct 2011, IB 1.19.
[12] SRA Code of Conduct 2011, IB 1.13.
[13] SRA Code of Conduct 2011, O 1.6.

C. LASPO 2012, PART 2

4.14 Primary legislation to give effect to the main recommendations in the *Final Report* is in LASPO 2012, part 2, at ss 44 to 48 and 55 to 61. The provisions amending the law on CFAs, ATE insurance, and DBAs can only be understood by reading the sections in LASPO 2012 together with the amended provisions of the Courts and Legal Services Act 1990 (CLSA 1990). In this book:

(a) LASPO 2012, ss 44 to 48 and 55 to 61, can be found in appendix 1; and

(b) CLSA 1990, ss 58 to 58C, as amended by LASPO 2012 can be found in appendix 2.

D. CONDITIONAL FEE AGREEMENTS AND ATE INSURANCE

Problems with CFAs

4.15 As discussed in chapter 1 and earlier in this chapter, a key finding of the *Final Report* was that the recoverability of success fees in litigation funded with CFAs has been a major contributing factor in the escalation of civil litigation costs.[14] The *Final Report* identified four crucial flaws with the CFA system as it was in 2009:[15]

(a) It was not targeted at the people who needed it most. Unlike legal aid, with its financial eligibility tests, CFAs were available to rich and poor alike. The Naomi Campbell case[16] caused a great deal of controversy, partly because of the inhibition on the right to freedom of speech caused by the level of costs exposure faced by newspapers when sued over what they publish, but also because, being an internationally well-known model, the claimant did not appear to need to enter into a CFA in order to gain access to justice. As pointed out by Sir Rupert Jackson,[17] it can be far worse than this. There is nothing to stop a business entering into a CFA and ATE insurance in litigation against a consumer.

(b) The client had in practical terms no interest in the level of costs being incurred on his or her behalf. If the case was successful, the costs would generally be paid by the other side. If the claim was unsuccessful, the client had no liability to his or her own lawyer, and would generally be protected against an adverse costs order by ATE insurance. As a result, the client was

---

[14] *Final Report*, Executive Summary, para 4.2.6.
[15] *Final Report*, ch 10, paras 4.7 to 4.19.
[16] See 4.16.
[17] 1st Implementation Lecture.

unlikely to play any significant role in restraining the costs of litigating the dispute.

(c) The costs burden on opposing parties was excessive. Analysis in the *Final Report* indicated that by looking at a block of cases with CFA funding, some of which would win, others lose, the total costs payable by the opposing parties would be higher than the total base costs of all the parties. This was caused by a combination of overestimating the necessary success fee uplifts, ATE premiums, and other inefficiencies and expenses, such as referral fees, commissions, and administrative expenses. For individual cases fought through to an unsuccessful trial the costs liability of the opposing party could be grossly disproportionate, potentially amounting to a denial of justice.

(d) It gave lawyers the opportunity to cherry-pick cases with a high prospect of success while rejecting or dropping less promising cases. The *Final Report* was at pains to point out that the legal profession generally does not succumb to such temptations, but it cannot be healthy to have a system which rewards anyone who adopts such a demeaning approach.

Campbell v MGN Ltd (No 2)[18] was fought over whether the claimant's £850,000 **4.16** base costs together with the £365,000 in success fees were so disproportionate as to infringe the defendant's ECHR, art 10, rights. It was held by the House of Lords that the fees were proportionate to the legitimate aim of providing litigants with access to justice. The European Court of Human Rights disagreed,[19] finding that the success fees were disproportionate and exceeded even the broad margin of appreciation accorded to the governments of contracting States in these matters. Interestingly, the European Court of Human Rights found support for its view in the detailed discussion of the flaws in the old CFA system as set out in the *Final Report*.

Final Report solutions

The *Final Report*'s solution is to abolish the recoverability of CFA success fees, **4.17** in effect reverting to the position on CFAs before recoverability was introduced in April 2000. This was seen to be desirable as part of a balanced package of associated measures. In relation to personal injuries claims, these were set out[20] as comprising:

(a) raising the level of general damages for pain, suffering and loss of amenity by 10 per cent (see chapter 14);

---

[18] [2005] UKHL 61, [2005] 1 WLR 3394.
[19] *MGN Ltd v United Kingdom* (application 39401/04) (2011) 53 EHRR 5.
[20] *Final Report*, ch 10, para 5.3.

(b) capping success fees that legal representatives can seek from their clients to 25 per cent of the damages awarded, excluding damages referable to future care or future losses (see 4.35);

(c) enhancing the rewards available for making a successful claimant's Part 36 offer (see chapter 11); and

(d) providing protection against adverse costs orders in unsuccessful claims by the introduction of QOCS (see chapter 10).

4.18 It was also recommended that the 10 per cent increase be extended to other categories of claim, such as nuisance, defamation, and any other tort that causes suffering to individuals.[21]

Final Report recommendations on CFAs

4.19 There were two recommendations in the *Final Report* that dealt specifically with CFAs:

(a) that CLSA 1990, s 58A(6), and all rules made pursuant to that provision should be repealed;[22] and

(b) that the level of damages for personal injuries, nuisance, and all other civil wrongs to individuals should be increased by 10 per cent.[23]

Consultation

4.20 After the consultation on the implementation of the Jackson reforms the government agreed with the abolition of the recoverability of success fees in line with Sir Rupert Jackson's recommendations. It is to be noted that the idea is not to abolish success fees, which continue to be available as between the client and the lawyer. As before, success fees are subject to a maximum 100 per cent uplift. The proposal has always been simply to abolish recoverability against the losing party as an element of the usual order for costs to follow the event.

4.21 Likewise, following the consultation the government decided to press ahead with the abolition of the recoverability of ATE insurance premiums.

---

[21] *Final Report*, ch 10, para 5.6.
[22] *Final Report*, recommendation 9.
[23] *Final Report*, recommendation 10.

E. CFAS AND LASPO 2012

Amendments to CLSA 1990, ss 58 and 58A

LASPO 2012, s 44, amends CLSA 1990, ss 58 and 58A, in line with recommen- **4.22**
dations made by the *Final Report*. The amendments provide:

(a) that CFAs remain legal, provided they comply with the requirements set out
in s 58(3);

(b) where a CFA provides for a success fee and relates to proceedings specified
by order made by the Lord Chancellor, the agreement must comply with the
additional conditions that will be provided by s 58(4B);

(c) that a costs order may not include payment of any part of a success fee.[24]

This means that while any success fee will no longer be recoverable from the **4.23**
other side, a success fee may be recovered from the lawyer's own client. However,
the extent of such recovery from the lawyer's own client may be restricted by
statutory instrument.

Requirements for effective CFAs

A CFA that complies with the requirements of the CLSA 1990, s 58, shall not be **4.24**
unenforceable by reason only that it is a CFA, but any other CFA is unenforceable.[25]
The requirements that must be satisfied for a CFA to be effective if entered into
on or after 1 April 2013 are laid down by the amended CLSA 1990, s 58(3), (4A),
and (4B), and fall into two categories: those for non-personal injury CFAs and
those for personal injury CFAs.

Non-personal injury CFAs
There are no changes to the requirements for CFAs concerning claims other than **4.25**
for personal injury (nor for personal injury claims where the CFA does not include
a success fee). In these cases CFAs must comply with the following conditions:[26]

(1) the agreement must be in writing;[27]

(2) it must not relate to proceedings which cannot be the subject of an enforceable CFA;[28]

---

[24] CLSA 1990, s 58A(6) as amended, reversing the position under s 58A(6) as it was before
amendment.
[25] CLSA 1990, s 58(1).
[26] CLSA 1990, s 58(3) and (4).
[27] CLSA 1990, s 58(3)(a).
[28] CLSA 1990, s 58(3)(b). See 4.26.

(3) it must comply with any requirements which may be prescribed by the Lord Chancellor (at present there are none);[29] and

(4) if the agreement includes a success fee, it must:

    (a) relate to proceedings of a description specified by statutory instrument[30] (all civil proceedings which can be the subject of an enforceable CFA are currently specified[31]); and

    (b) state the percentage uplift ('success fee'),[32] which must not exceed the percentage prescribed by statutory instrument[33] (currently 100 per cent[34]).

4.26 The only type of civil proceedings which cannot be the subject of an enforceable CFA is family proceedings.[35] For the purposes of these provisions, the term 'proceedings' includes any sort of proceedings (whether commenced or contemplated) for resolving disputes, and not just proceedings in a court.[36]

Personal injury CFAs

4.27 A CFA in a claim for personal injuries[37] must comply with the following conditions:

(1) the agreement must be in writing;[38]

(2) it must not relate to proceedings which cannot be the subject of an enforceable CFA;[39]

(3) it must comply with any requirements which may be prescribed by the Lord Chancellor (at present there are none);[40] and

(4) if the agreement includes a success fee, it must:

    (a) relate to proceedings of a description specified by statutory instrument[41] (all civil proceedings which can be the subject of an enforceable CFA are currently specified[42]);

---

[29] CLSA 1990, s 58(3)(c).
[30] CLSA 1990, s 58(4)(a).
[31] Conditional Fee Agreements Order 2013, art 2.
[32] CLSA 1990, s 58(4)(b).
[33] CLSA 1990, s 58(4)(c).
[34] Conditional Fee Agreements Order 2013, art 3.
[35] CLSA 1990, 58A(1)(b). The term 'family proceedings' is defined in s 58A(2).
[36] CLSA 1990, s 58A(4).
[37] This expression has the same meaning for the purposes of the CLSA 1990, s 58, and the Conditional Fee Agreements Order 2013, art 4, by virtue of art 1(2), as it does in CPR, r 2.3. This provides that a 'claim for personal injuries' means proceedings in which there is a claim for damages in respect of personal injuries to the claimant or any other person or in respect of a person's death, and 'personal injuries' includes any disease and any impairment of a person's physical or mental condition.
[38] CLSA 1990, s 58(3)(a).
[39] CLSA 1990, s 58(3)(b). See 4.26.
[40] CLSA 1990, s 58(3)(c).
[41] CLSA 1990, s 58(4)(a).
[42] Conditional Fee Agreements Order 2013, art 2.

(b) state the percentage uplift ('success fee'),[43] which must not exceed the percentage prescribed by statutory instrument[44] (currently 100 per cent[45]);

(c) provide that the success fee is subject to a maximum limit,[46] which must be expressed as a percentage of the descriptions of damages awarded in the proceedings that are specified in the agreement.[47] These are:

   (i) general damages for pain, suffering and loss of amenity; and

   (ii) damages for pecuniary loss, other than future pecuniary loss, net of any sums recoverable by the Compensation Recovery Unit of the Department for Work and Pensions;[48] and

(d) the maximum limit must not exceed 25 per cent in respect of first instance proceedings,[49] or 100 per cent in respect of appeal proceedings.[50]

Professional conduct obligations

Given the abolition of the recoverability rule, the nature of CFAs has changed, **4.28** and advice given to clients about their effect will necessarily have to change in order to comply with the requirements of the SRA Code of Conduct 2011. Obligations under the Code of Conduct include only entering into fee agreements which are suitable for the client's needs and which take account of the client's best interests,[51] and giving clients the best possible information about the likely overall cost of their matter.[52]

No need to notify the other side of CFA

Abolition of the recoverability of success fees and other additional liabilities **4.29** means there is no need to notify the other side or the court that a case is being funded under a CFA. Consequently, the old CPR, r 44.3B, which was to the effect that, unless the court ordered otherwise, additional liabilities were not recoverable if the receiving party failed to provide information about the funding arrangement in accordance with a rule, practice direction, or court order, has not been reproduced in the new rules. Likewise, the old r 44.15 and the old PD 43–48, paras 19.1 to 19.6, imposing a duty to provide that information, have not been retained in the new CPR, Parts 44 to 48, or PD 44 to PD 48.

---

[43] CLSA 1990, s 58(4)(b).

[44] CLSA 1990, s 58(4)(c).

[45] Conditional Fee Agreements Order 2013, art 3.

[46] CLSA 1990, s 58(4A) and (4B)(a).

[47] CLSA 1990, s 58(4A) and (4B)(b). Those descriptions of damages may only include descriptions of damages specified by order made by the Lord Chancellor in relation to the proceedings (s 58(4B)(d)).

[48] Conditional Fee Agreements Order 2013, art 5(2).

[49] CLSA 1990, s 58(4A) and (4B)(c); Conditional Fee Agreements Order 2013, art 5(1)(a).

[50] Conditional Fee Agreements Order 2013, art 5(1)(b).

[51] SRA Code of Conduct 2011, O 1.6. See 4.13.

[52] SRA Code of Conduct 2011, O 1.13. See 4.10 and 4.11.

4.30   Paragraph 9.3 of PD Pre-action Conduct, which imposes a duty to inform other parties about funding arrangements, has been retained but should be seen as a transitional provision.[53]

Dangers of satellite litigation over CFAs

4.31   Given that the statutory requirements for non-personal injury CFAs are unchanged, the same risks of satellite litigation over their effectiveness remain despite the implementation of the Jackson reforms. There are rather more requirements for CFAs in personal injuries claims which include success fees.[54] Increasing the requirements, combined with the failure to remove the indemnity principle, which was recommendation 4 of the *Final Report*, means CFAs will continue to be a minefield for the unwary. This is considered further in chapter 10.

Assessment of costs in CFA cases

Party and party assessments

4.32   Abolition of the recoverability of success fees and other additional liabilities means that it has been possible to delete all the provisions in CPR, Parts 43 to 48, and the Costs Practice Direction (PD 43–48) that dealt with party and party assessment of additional liabilities. Many of the costs provisions that have not been carried forward into the new CPR, Parts 44 to 48, and their associated practice directions have been deleted for this reason. So, in a post-1 April 2013 party and party assessment of costs which is not caught by the transitional provisions, all that needs to be assessed are the base costs in the same way as in non-CFA cases.

Solicitor and own client assessments

4.33   The old rule that on a solicitor and own client assessment of costs the solicitor cannot seek to recover a greater success fee than that agreed or assessed, unless the court orders otherwise,[55] has been revoked.[56] One of the few vestiges of the provisions on CFAs remaining in the costs provisions in the CPR is r 46.9(4) (the former r 48.8(3)). This provides that where the court is considering a percentage increase on the application of the client, the court will have regard to all the relevant factors as they reasonably appeared to the solicitor or counsel when the conditional fee agreement was entered into or varied. The former r 48.8(4), which defined 'conditional fee agreement' for the purposes of the former r 48.8

---

[53] See 2.10.
[54] See 4.27.
[55] Conditional Fee Agreements Regulations 2000 (SI 2000/692), reg 3(2)(b).
[56] Conditional Fee Agreements Regulations Order 2013, art 7.

as meaning an agreement which is enforceable under the CLSA 1990, s 58, has been omitted from the new rules, as have the old PD 43–48, paras 54.3, 54.5, 54.6, 54.7, and 54.8.

The only remaining provisions on solicitor and client costs are now to be **4.34** found in CPR, rr 46.9 and 46.10, and PD 46, which preserves the old PD 43–48, paras 54.1, 54.2, and 54.4 at PD 46, paras 6.1 to 6.3. These make limited provision for solicitor and own client assessment of CFAs, omitting, for example, the list of relevant factors previously set out in PD 43–48, para 54.7. They do say that a client and solicitor may agree whatever terms they consider appropriate about the payment of the solicitor's charges.[57] It follows from the various provisions that the client can challenge the success fee on a detailed assessment, but the court will only intervene if it considers it was unreasonable in amount on the basis of the risk analysis and all other relevant considerations as they appeared at the date it was agreed.[58]

Success fees limited to 25 per cent of damages

As mentioned above,[59] the *Final Report* recommended that successful lawyers **4.35** in personal injuries CFA-funded cases should have their CFA success fees limited to 25 per cent of the damages awarded (other than those for future care and loss). Without a rule to this effect claimants might find that even with a costs order against the defendant, a significant part of the damages awarded would have to be used to pay their legal representatives' success fees. Obviously, whether this is so will depend on the amount of the claimant's base costs, the percentage of the agreed success fee, and the breakdown of the damages award between pain, suffering, and loss of amenity (PSLA), other past losses, and future care and loss.

This will cause a moral dilemma for many solicitors who take the view (based **4.36** on providing a service for their clients rather than treating litigation purely as a business) that the client should be paid all the compensation awarded (with the firm covering any shortfall on costs). These solicitors will need to decide whether to break with their principles and make use of the 10 per cent additional damages to cover their CFA success fees rather than paying it over to the client, or to use CFAs without success fees. The latter means running litigation at a loss, given that every firm will have a number of cases that are unsuccessful.

---

[57] PD 46, para 6.2.
[58] Applying the indemnity basis burden of proof in CPR, r 44.3(3) (PD 46, para 6.2).
[59] See 4.17.

CFAs and counsel's fees

4.37 The *Final Report* recognized that if solicitors were allowed to enter into CFAs, then so should counsel.[60] There will still be a choice between:

(a) counsel's fees being a disbursement to be paid by the client or solicitor;

(b) counsel also on a CFA and entitled to a specified proportion of the success fee; or

(c) counsel being retained on a DBA and entitled to a specified percentage of any sum recovered.

4.38 In practical terms, though, this will almost certainly mean the end of CFA success fees in personal injuries cases for the Bar. With solicitors limited to 25 per cent of the non-future loss damages as the fund to pay their success fees, and with solicitors entering into CFAs with their clients before instructing counsel, there will often be nothing left for any CFA success fee for the barrister instructed on the case. This in turn will mean that barristers' fees will often be treated as disbursements, with clients facing problems in funding counsel's fees.

General effect of the reforms relating to CFAs

4.39 Perhaps the most significant effect of the reforms is the major rebalancing of the advantages and disadvantages of litigating for and against parties with CFAs. There will be a substantial reduction in the costs exposure of defendants and those funding defendants (who are the side most likely to face paying the other side's success fees under the pre-Jackson system).

4.40 From the claimant's point of view, this means that any success fee and ATE insurance premium has to come out of the damages recovered in the proceedings, or out of the client's other resources. It means running a profitable business will become a great deal more difficult for claimant solicitors and claims processing companies, because they will no longer be able to offer packages to potential claimants promising litigation and the prospect of an award of damages at no risk to the client. Potential claimants will no doubt think twice about bringing claims, which is likely to result in a downturn in the volume of civil claims that are brought.

---

[60] *Final Report*, ch 12, para 4.8.

F. AFTER-THE-EVENT INSURANCE

Use of ATE insurance

ATE insurance is intended to provide an insured with cover against the risk of **4.41** having to pay the costs of an opponent in the event of an adverse costs order being made in litigation. It can also be used to provide cover for the insured's own disbursements, such as the fees of experts or counsel. Typically, it is taken out by claimants, but there is no restriction in this regard, and a defendant who is able to find a willing insurer is also able to take out ATE cover. Such insurance is not necessarily cheap. Under the pre-Jackson system the premium for an ATE policy was recoverable as part of an order for party and party costs.[61]

ATE cover is not necessarily efficient. Figures compiled for the *Final Report*[62] **4.42** showed that approximately 65 per cent of the premiums paid for ATE cover was applied to the insured risk; 15 to 20 per cent was devoted to brokerage; and 15 to 20 per cent to administration and profit. It meant that it would be substantially cheaper for defendants to pay their own costs in every case, whether they won or lost, than to be required to pay their opponents' ATE premiums in cases they lost.[63]

Repudiation of ATE policy by insurer

An inherent risk in ATE insurance is that, because it is a contract of insur- **4.43** ance, the usual principles of insurance law apply. This means, for example, that the insurer can repudiate liability under the policy if there has been a material non-disclosure by the assured. This principle is applied fairly rigorously. It is not unheard of for a litigant who has taken out ATE insurance to find, if the litigation is unsuccessful, that the insurer then scrutinizes the reasons given in the judgment to find some non-disclosure in the application for the policy to justify repudiating liability on the policy. An example of this[64] is where a defendant had been refused security for costs in a commercial dispute on the basis that the claimant had ATE insurance, which meant there was little risk on costs. The claimant then lost the claim, and the insurer avoided the policy on the basis of non-disclosure as revealed by the facts found at the trial, meaning the defendant had no secure fund for its costs.

---

[61] Access to Justice Act 1999, s 29.
[62] *Final Report*, ch 9, para 3.16.
[63] *Final Report*, ch 9, para 4.1.
[64] *Final Report*, ch 9, para 3.14.

ATE premiums and the *Final Report*

4.44   Similar flaws to those afflicting the recoverability of CFA success fees[65] apply also to recoverability of ATE insurance premiums.[66] In particular, recovery of ATE premiums was not targeted to those who needed it, and it removed the incentive for clients to keep their own costs under control. It follows that similar recommendations were made in respect of ATE insurance, namely:

(a) that the Access to Justice Act 1999, s 29, and all rules made pursuant to that provision should be repealed;[67] and

(b) the categories of litigants who merit protection against adverse costs liability on policy grounds should be given the benefit of QOCS.[68]

Repeal of recoverability

4.45   ATE insurance premiums are no longer in general recoverable under a costs order.[69] All the related provisions in the CPR and practice directions have also been deleted. Subject to an exception in relation to clinical disputes (see 4.46 to 4.51), it means that a party taking out ATE insurance after 1 April 2013 does so for its own peace of mind, but cannot recover the premium from the other side.

Clinical disputes: ATE premiums for experts' reports

Circumstances in which premiums may be recovered

4.46   A refinement of the *Final Report* recommendations that was advanced by the Ministry of Justice is a limited power to allow for the recoverability of ATE insurance premiums to cover the cost of expert reports in clinical dispute claims. It was intended that the regulations allowing this would be tightly drawn to prevent abuse, but the underlying concern was that some provision had to be made for experts' reports in these cases, which are often very expensive, and which litigants often cannot reasonably be expected to fund themselves.

4.47   Provisions to create such an exception are contained in LASPO 2012, s 58C(2) to (5). The provisions apply to clinical negligence proceedings. These are defined[70] as proceedings which include a claim for damages in respect of clinical negligence, and proceedings may be any type of proceedings, whether commenced or contemplated, for resolving disputes, and are not limited to court proceedings.

---

[65] See 4.15.

[66] *Final Report*, ch 9, para 4.4.

[67] *Final Report*, recommendation 7.

[68] *Final Report*, recommendation 8.

[69] CLSA 1990, s 58C(1), inserted by LASPO 2012, s 46(1).

[70] LASPO 2012, s 58C(5).

Regulations may be made permitting costs orders to include provision requiring **4.48** the payment of a sum in respect of all or part of the premium for a costs insurance policy insuring against the risk of incurring a liability to pay for one or more expert reports.[71] For this purpose an expert report means a report by a person qualified to give expert advice on all or most of the matters covered by the report.[72]

Requirements for the recovery of clinical disputes ATE premiums
Recovery of ATE premiums for experts' reports is only available where: **4.49**

(a) a costs order is made in favour of a party to clinical negligence proceedings of a prescribed description,[73] provided the costs of the relevant report or reports are not disallowed.[74]

(b) the party has taken out a costs insurance policy insuring against the risk of incurring a liability to pay for one or more expert reports in respect of clinical negligence in connection with the proceedings (or against that risk and other risks);[75]

(c) the policy is of a prescribed description;[76]

(d) the policy states how much of the premium relates to the liability to pay for an expert report or reports in respect of clinical negligence;[77]

(e) the report or reports were in the event obtained;[78]

(f) the report or reports relate to liability or causation, not quantum;[79]

(g) the amount is to be paid in respect of the relevant part of the premium.[80]

Concerns about recoverability of ATE premiums in clinical dispute claims
The provisions discussed at 4.47 to 4.49 were severely criticized by Sir Rupert **4.50** Jackson in his 1st Implementation Lecture. Among the concerns were:

(a) difficulty in finding insurers prepared to take on this type of business;

(b) costs, and the inefficiency of funding through ATE premiums as identified in the *Final Report*;

---

[71] LASPO 2012, s 58C(2).

[72] LASPO 2012, s 58C(5).

[73] CLSA 1990, s 58C(2)(a). There is no further refinement in the Recovery of Costs Insurance Premiums in Clinical Negligence Proceedings Regulations 2013 (SI 2013/92), which simply applies to clinical negligence proceedings.

[74] Recovery of Costs Insurance Premiums in Clinical Negligence Proceedings Regulations 2013, r 2(2)(c).

[75] CLSA 1990, s 58C(2)(b).

[76] CLSA 1990, s 58C(2)(c).

[77] CLSA 1990, s 58C(2)(d).

[78] Recovery of Costs Insurance Premiums in Clinical Negligence Proceedings Regulations 2013, r 2(2)(a).

[79] Recovery of Costs Insurance Premiums in Clinical Negligence Proceedings Regulations 2013, r 2(2)(b).

[80] CLSA 1990, s 58C(2)(e).

(c) lack of targeting. Like old-style CFAs, it seems the exception will apply to all litigants, regardless of their financial resources; and

(d) complexity: it was anticipated that of necessity the supporting regulations would be far from simple.

Jointly instructed experts in clinical disputes

4.51 The Ministry of Justice took the view that recoverable ATE premiums would not be necessary where joint expert reports are commissioned. With respect, halving the cost by commissioning jointly instructed experts does not provide a real answer: half of what are often totally unaffordable experts' fees are still unaffordable for many claimants in clinical dispute claims.

G. MEMBERSHIP ORGANIZATIONS

4.52 Access to Justice Act 1999, s 30, applied where a membership organization undertook to meet (in accordance with arrangements satisfying prescribed conditions) liabilities which members of the body or other persons who are parties to proceedings may incur to pay the costs of other parties to the proceedings. For the purpose of the pre-Jackson recoverability system relating to CFAs and ATE premiums, 'additional liability' extended to any additional amount in respect of any provision made by a membership organization to meet the costs of other parties to litigation.[81]

4.53 Similar objections to those raised against the recoverability of ATE insurance premiums apply also to the recovery of these membership organization contributions. Accordingly, Access to Justice Act 1999, s 30, has been repealed with effect from 1 April 2013 by LASPO 2012, s 47(1).

H. BEFORE-THE-EVENT INSURANCE

Definition

4.54 BTE insurance, which is sometimes known as legal expenses insurance (LEI), is insurance cover that protects against the risk of the assured being involved in future litigation. Often BTE cover is part of a wider insurance policy, such as in many standard motor and household insurance policies.

---

[81] Access to Justice Act 1999, s 30(2); CPR, r 43.2(1)(o).

Cover provided by BTE policies

The nature of the cover will depend on the terms of the policy. It may be that **4.55** the BTE policy will cover the assured's own costs, and may extend to the costs of the other side. There may well be a merits element to the continuation of the cover. Insurers often seek to ensure that panel solicitors are used, which gives the insurer some control over the quality of the service provided, but also often because they have agreed special rates with those solicitors.

Persons insured under an LEI policy must be free to choose a lawyer to repre- **4.56** sent them and that right must be expressly recognized in the policy.[82] In *Brown-Quinn v Equity Syndicate Management Ltd*[83] the insurer maintained a panel of solicitors to represent clients with the relevant BTE cover. It was held that any term in the BTE policy to the effect that the insurer had an absolute right to refuse to accept a substitute solicitor in a situation where the insured wanted to change to a non-panel solicitor would be a breach of the insured's right to choose a lawyer.

Perhaps the more substantial question in *Brown-Quinn v Equity Syndicate* **4.57** *Management Ltd* was whether a non-panel solicitor was restricted to the relatively modest non-panel rate for the work done in the case. It was held that an LEI insurer may limit its liability for payments to solicitors not on its panel provided the insured's freedom of choice was not rendered meaningless. Whether the rates payable to non-panel solicitors are so paltry as to preclude the insured from choosing another lawyer is a question of fact. Evidence of no more than the rates charged by the one solicitor actually chosen by the insured is unlikely to be sufficient for this purpose.

BTE and the *Final Report*

The *Final Report* recognized the value of BTE insurance as a means of funding **4.58** litigation. In practical terms there is nothing the rules can do to require more litigants to be covered by BTE policies: the horse has already bolted by the time rules of court kick in. However, *Final Report*, recommendation 6, is to the effect that positive efforts should be made to encourage the take-up of BTE insurance by SMEs in respect of business disputes, and by householders as an add-on to household insurance policies. The reality may be that the revocation of the recoverability of CFA success fees and ATE premiums may remove the pre-Jackson inclination of many insurers to include BTE as add-ons to other policies as a way of reducing the insurance industry's exposure to success fees.

---

[82] Insurance Companies (Legal Expenses Insurance) Regulations 1990 (SI 1990/1159), reg 6, implementing what is now Directive 2009/138/EC, art 201.
[83] [2012] EWCA Civ 1633, LTL 12/12/2012.

I. REFERRAL FEES

4.59   One of the things picked up in the Executive Summary of the *Final Report*[84] is what Sir Rupert Jackson aptly described as a regrettably common feature of civil litigation, that solicitors were paying referral fees to claims management companies, BTE insurers, and other organizations to 'buy' cases. Sir Rupert commented that referral fees add to the cost of litigation without adding any real value to it.

4.60   Historically, it was a rule of professional conduct for both solicitors and barristers that they were not permitted to advertise or tout for business. Since 1987, the relevant Codes of Conduct for the profession have relaxed this position, and in 2004 the Solicitors' Practice Rules 1990 were amended to allow solicitors to pay referral fees, provided certain safeguards were adhered to. These included ensuring nothing was done to compromise the independence of the solicitor paying the referral fee, that the referral agreement was in writing, and that the client was fully informed. As Sir Rupert Jackson pointed out in the 1st Implementation Lecture, at that time in low-value cases referral fees could amount to more than half the costs received, and in high-value cases referral fees could be £10,000 or more.

4.61   *Final Report* recommendation 20 was to the effect that the payment of referral fees for personal injury claims should be banned. This has been implemented by LASPO 2012, ss 56 to 60, which are aimed at prohibiting the use of referral fees involving regulated persons. The expression 'regulated person' is defined in s 59, and covers both legal professionals and claims management companies and persons regulated by the Financial Services Authority. The scheme of the provisions is that paying referral fees for business that involves the provision of legal services to a client is a breach of s 56. Relevant regulators must ensure they have appropriate arrangements for monitoring and enforcing the restriction on referral fees, with enforcement taking place through the relevant regulator.[85]

J. DAMAGES-BASED AGREEMENTS

Nature of a damages-based agreement

4.62   A DBA is an agreement between a legal representative and a client under which the legal representative's fee is determined by reference to the amount of the financial benefit obtained by the client in the litigation. Until recently DBAs were known as contingency fees and were illegal in contentious litigation. Entering

---

[84] *Final Report*, Executive Summary, para 2.5.
[85] LASPO 2012, s 57.

into such an arrangement was also contrary to the requirements of the codes of conduct regulating the legal profession. Prior to the enactment of LASPO 2012, DBAs were permitted in relation to employment matters.[86] Changes made by LASPO 2012, s 45, have the effect that DBAs are now widely available as a means of funding civil litigation.

Opposition to DBAs

The Bar has opposed contingency fees for many decades, going back well before **4.63** CFAs were even thought of. A key principle in the Bar's Code of Conduct has, until now, been that it is serious professional misconduct to accept instructions in litigation on a contingency fee basis. The key objection is that contingency fees, which give the lawyer an interest in the outcome of litigation, have a tendency to undermine the integrity of the independence that the lawyer has to bring when advising a client.

Arguments against the introduction of contingency fees for contentious work **4.64** were decisively rejected in the *Final Report*. The sting of the objections has been met by the success of CFAs. The profession has no problems with CFAs, which are a particular form of contingency fee arrangement. There has been very little suggestion that the professional integrity of legal advisers has been compromised by CFAs, despite the no win, no fee, character of these arrangements. If the profession can work ethically under CFAs, it can do so under DBAs. The Bar is going to have to face up to a future where contingency fees, based on a percentage of the damages recovered, are a reality in contentious litigation.

Response to the consultation

The introduction of DBAs was taken forward in the *Government Response* of **4.65** March 2011 to the Jackson implementation consultation, which stated an intention to lift the restriction on the use of DBAs in civil litigation.[87] DBAs were said to be a useful additional form of funding for claimants, particularly in commercial claims.

The *Final Report* recommended that a DBA should only be valid if the cli- **4.66** ent receives independent advice from a solicitor.[88] This was rejected by the *Government Response*, which took the view that the formal requirements for DBAs need not be more restrictive than those for CFAs. These are primarily that the agreement must be in writing and must relate to a type of case where this type of funding is permitted.[89]

---

[86] CLSA 1990, s 58AA.
[87] Cm 8041, para 13.
[88] *Final Report*, recommendation 15.
[89] See 4.24 to 4.27.

DBAs and LASPO 2012

4.67 CLSA 1990, s 58AA, has been substantially amended by LASPO 2012, s 45, to give effect to recommendation 14 of the *Final Report*. References in CLSA 1990, s 58AA, to employment matters have been deleted, with the effect that DBAs are now legal and enforceable in most types of civil proceedings provided certain preconditions are satisfied. DBAs may, however, be banned in categories of cases prescribed by the Lord Chancellor.[90]

4.68 LASPO 2012, s 45(8), which inserts a new s 58AA(6A) into CLSA 1990, was brought into force on 1 October 2012.[91] This enabled rules of court to be made with respect to the assessment of costs in cases where the receiving party is funded by a DBA, and had to be brought into force in advance of 1 April 2013 to ensure the relevant rules could be made in time. Rules of court may provide for the assessment of any costs order in favour of a party funded under a DBA.[92]

Requirements for DBAs

4.69 A DBA will be legal and enforceable if:

(a) it is in writing;[93]

(b) it does not relate to proceedings which cannot be the subject of an enforceable CFA[94] or to proceedings of a description prescribed by the Lord Chancellor;[95]

(c) it does not provide for a payment above a prescribed amount or for a payment above an amount calculated in a prescribed manner;[96]

(d) its terms and conditions comply with any prescribed requirements.[97] These terms must specify:[98]

    (i) the claim or proceedings or parts of them to which the agreement relates;

    (ii) the circumstances in which the representative's payment,[99] expenses[100] and costs, or part of them, are payable; and

    (iii) the reason for setting the amount of the payment at the level agreed; and

---

[90] CLSA 1990, s 58AA(4)(aa).

[91] Legal Aid, Sentencing and Punishment of Offenders Act 2012 (Commencement No 2 and Specification of Commencement Date) Order 2012 (SI 2012/2412).

[92] CLSA 1990, s 58AA(6A).

[93] CLSA 1990, s 58AA(4)(a).

[94] See 4.26.

[95] CLSA 1990, s 58AA(4)(aa).

[96] CLSA 1990, s 58AA(4)(b). See 4.70.

[97] CLSA 1990, s 58AA(4)(c).

[98] Damages-Based Agreements Regulations 2013, reg 3. There are further requirements for DBAs in employment matters.

[99] The 'payment' is the part of the sum recovered in the claim that the client agrees to pay the legal representative (see Damages-Based Agreements Regulations 2013, reg 1(2)).

[100] 'Expenses' means disbursements, but not counsel's fees (Damages-Based Agreements Regulations 2013, reg 1(2)).

(e) the person providing services under the agreement has complied with any prescribed requirements concerning the provision of information.[101]

Prescribed amounts and payments for the purposes of para (c) above only apply to claims at first instance.[102] First instance matters fall into two categories in non-employment proceedings:[103]   **4.70**

(a) In respect of non-personal injuries claims, a DBA must not require an amount to be paid by the client other than the agreed payment, net of any costs and expenses which have been paid by another party to the proceedings.[104] The amount to be paid by the client must not exceed an amount which, including VAT, is equal to 50 per cent of the sums ultimately recovered by the client.[105] These costs and expenses may include disbursements in respect of counsel's fees as well as other types of disbursements.[106] 'Costs' means the total of the representative's time reasonably spent, in respect of the claim or proceedings, multiplied by the reasonable hourly rate of remuneration of the representative.[107]

(b) In a claim for personal injuries[108] a DBA must not provide for a payment above an amount which, including VAT, is equal to 25 per cent of the combined sums in sub-paras (i) and (ii) below which are ultimately recovered by the client.[109] The only sums recovered by the client from which the agreed payment may be met are:

(i) general damages for PSLA; and

(ii) damages for pecuniary loss other than future pecuniary loss, net of any sums recoverable by the Compensation Recovery Unit of the Department for Work and Pensions.[110]

Dangers of satellite litigation over DBAs

Provided a DBA complies with the above requirements,[111] there should be no problems in using a DBA. How secure the word 'should' is in the preceding   **4.71**

---

[101] CLSA 1990, s 58AA(4)(d). Requirements to provide information in the Damages-Based Agreements Regulations 2013, reg 5, only apply to employment matters.

[102] Damages-Based Agreements Regulations 2013, reg 4(4).

[103] For which, see Damages-Based Agreements Regulations 2013, reg 7.

[104] Damages-Based Agreements Regulations 2013, reg 4(1).

[105] Damages-Based Agreements Regulations 2013, reg 4(3).

[106] Damages-Based Agreements Regulations 2013, regs 1(2) and 4(1)(a)(ii).

[107] Damages-Based Agreements Regulations 2013, reg 1(2).

[108] Damages-Based Agreements Regulations 2013, regs 1(2) and 4(2). For this purpose 'claim for personal injuries' has the same meaning as in CPR, r 2.3, for which see n 37.

[109] Damages-Based Agreements Regulations 2013, reg 4(2)(b).

[110] Damages-Based Agreements Regulations 2013, reg 4(2)(a).

[111] See 4.69.

sentence is open to doubt. Failure to remove the indemnity principle[112] means in fact this will be a minefield for the unwary. This is considered further in chapter 10.

Recoverability of costs in DBA-funded cases

4.72 A successful claimant with a DBA will recover costs from the unsuccessful defendant in the traditional way under a normal costs order[113] (based on hourly rates plus disbursements). The *Final Report* recognized that if solicitors are allowed to enter into DBAs, then so should counsel. It suggested that counsel's fees would be payable either as a disbursement to be paid by the solicitors, or with counsel also on a contingency fee and entitled to a specified percentage of any sum recovered.[114] The costs recoverable from the losing party will be set off against the client's liability to its lawyers under the DBA. So the client will be left with a liability to pay its lawyers any shortfall between the costs recovered from the losing party and the amount stipulated as the DBA payment.[115] Limitations on the amount of the 'payment' the client can be required to pay to the legal representative are set out in the Damages-Based Agreements Regulations 2013.[116]

K. THIRD-PARTY FUNDING

Description

4.73 Third-party funding is also known as 'litigation funding'. This latter term is a little regrettable, because it is used by the CLSA 1990, s 58B, to describe very different types of funding arrangements known as SLAS and CLAFs (see 4.80 and 4.81). As described in the Code of Conduct for Litigation Funders, a funder has access to funds immediately within its control, or acts as the exclusive investment adviser to an investment fund which has access to funds immediately within its control. Those funds are invested to finance litigation under the terms of a litigation funding agreement (LFA) to enable a litigant to meet the costs of resolving a dispute by litigation or arbitration. An LFA can be entered into before proceedings are commenced.

4.74 Usually the LFA will provide that the funder will receive a share of the proceeds of the claim if the litigation is successful. Under the Code of Conduct the funder should not seek any payment from the litigant in excess of the proceeds of the dispute being funded, unless the litigant is in material breach of the terms

---

[112] *Final Report*, recommendation 4.
[113] CPR, r 44.18.
[114] *Final Report*, ch 12, para 4.8.
[115] *Government Response* (Cm 8041, March 2012), para 13.
[116] See 4.70.

of the LFA. The LFA should state to what extent the funder is liable to the litigant to meet the liability for any adverse costs orders, to meet any ATE premium, provide security for costs, or meet any other financial liability. It should also state the extent to which the funder may provide input to the litigant's decisions in relation to settlement, and whether the funder may terminate the LFA, for example, if the funder reasonably believes the dispute is no longer commercially viable.

Arkin v Borchard Lines Ltd (Nos 2 and 3)[117] is widely regarded as having estab-   **4.75**
lished that a properly structured LFA does not infringe the rules against maintenance and champerty. Maintenance involves supporting litigation by a stranger for no just cause. Champerty is an aggravated form of maintenance where the person providing support obtains a financial interest in the outcome. LFAs were regarded as supporting the public policy of ensuring access to justice, and will be effective provided suitable safeguards are included in the LFA. Whether LFAs are quite as secure as this supposes is considered further in chapter 10.

The *Final Report* recognized that the nature of LFAs means they are usually   **4.76**
only feasible in monetary claims.[118] Further, the funding arrangements inherent in LFAs mean that, at present, they are only likely to be viable in high-value claims with good prospects of success.

Final Report recommendations on third-party funding

There were three recommendations in the *Final Report* on third-party funding: **4.77**

(a) A satisfactory voluntary code should be drawn up, to which all litigation funders should subscribe. There should be provisions in the code dealing with effective capital adequacy, and restrictions upon the ability of funders to withdraw from ongoing litigation.[119]

(b) The question of statutory regulation should be revisited if and when the third-party funding market expands.[120]

(c) Third-party funders should potentially be liable for the full amount of adverse costs, subject to the discretion of the judge.[121]

Future of third-party funding

The Code of Conduct for Litigation Funders referred to at 4.73 was drawn up   **4.78**
by a working party appointed by the Civil Justice Council chaired by Michael Napier CBE, QC. It incorporates the safeguards set out in recommendation 11

---

[117] [2005] EWCA Civ 655, [2005] 1 WLR 3055.
[118] *Final Report*, ch 11, para 1.5.
[119] *Final Report*, recommendation 11.
[120] *Final Report*, recommendation 12.
[121] *Final Report*, recommendation 13.

of the *Final Report*, and was warmly commended by Sir Rupert Jackson in his 6th Implementation Lecture. An Association of Litigation Funders of England and Wales was founded in 2011. Its Rules provide that every member of the Association must abide by the Code of Conduct for Litigation Funders, with the result that litigants who enter into an LFA with an Association member should obtain the protections contemplated by the *Final Report*.

Costs orders against third-party funders

4.79 Costs orders in cases funded by LFAs were considered by *Arkin v Borchard Lines Ltd (Nos 2 and 3)*.[122] At present there is no specific legislative framework governing LFAs, so the general law applies. This means the jurisdiction to make costs orders against LFA funders derives from the power to make third-party costs orders under the Senior Courts Act 1981, s 51.[123] If an LFA-funded claim is defeated, the court needs to balance the public interest in promoting access to justice with the rule that costs usually follow the event.[124] Performing this balance, Lord Phillips of Worth Matravers MR[125] said that a professional funder should potentially be liable for the costs of the opposite party to the extent of the funding provided. This potential liability is likely to be incorporated in the share of the proceeds of the litigation that will be demanded by the funder under the terms of the LFA if the claim is successful.

L. SLAS AND CLAFs

Supplementary legal aid scheme

4.80 A supplementary legal aid scheme (SLAS) is a proposal advanced by the General Council of the Bar. A SLAS would run in parallel with an existing legal aid scheme, but would be available to litigants just outside the financial eligibility criteria for legal aid, and would be administered by the legal aid authority. A SLAS is a self-funding scheme under which a percentage of any award in litigation that it funds is ploughed back into the SLAS.

Contingent legal aid funds

4.81 Contingent legal aid funds (CLAFs) have been promoted by the Bar as an alternative method of funding litigation. A CLAF is a self-funding scheme which requires seed capital, with funds being generated from successful cases, which

[122] [2005] EWCA Civ 655, [2005] 1 WLR 3055.
[123] See *Aiden Shipping Co Ltd v Interbulk Ltd* [1986] AC 965.
[124] CPR, r 44.2(2)(a), from 1 April 2013.
[125] *Arkin v Borchard Lines Ltd (Nos 2 and 3)* at [41].

are used to cover the costs of both sides in unsuccessful cases. A substantial preponderance of successful cases is necessary to ensure such a scheme is successful. Equivalent schemes in other jurisdictions tend to be relatively small scale. There was more support for CLAFs than a SLAS, but the *Final Report* gave only muted support, doubting the financial viability of such schemes.

CLSA 1990, s 58B

CLSA 1990, s 58B (which has never been brought into force),[126] has the title **4.82** 'Litigation funding agreements'. However, it is not concerned with the type of funding arrangement discussed at 4.73 to 4.79. Instead, it is concerned with the types described at 4.80 and 4.81.

For the purposes of CLSA 1990, s 58B, a litigation funding agreement is an **4.83** agreement under which:

(a) a person ('the funder') agrees to fund (in whole or in part) the provision of advocacy or litigation services (by someone other than the funder) to another person ('the litigant'); and

(b) the litigant agrees to pay a sum to the funder in specified circumstances.[127]

While this definition seems sufficiently wide to cover the type of third-party **4.84** funding described at 4.73 to 4.76, it is plain from the requirements laid down by CLSA 1990, s 58B,[128] that the structure of LFAs as described at 4.73 to 4.76 does not fit the scheme laid down by s 58B. According to Sir Rupert Jackson,[129] s 58B was intended to make provision for CLAFs and a SLAS.[130]

Requirements under CLSA 1990, s 58B

A litigation funding agreement[131] which satisfies all of the following conditions shall **4.85** not be unenforceable by reason only of its being a litigation funding agreement:[132]

(a) the funder must be a person, or person of a description, prescribed by the Secretary of State;

(b) the agreement must be in writing;

(c) the agreement must not relate to proceedings which cannot be the subject of an enforceable CFA[133] or to proceedings of any such description as may be prescribed by the Secretary of State;

---

[126] Section 58B is inserted in CLSA 1990 by the Access to Justice Act 1999, s 28.

[127] CLSA 1990, s 58B(2).

[128] See 4.85 and 4.86.

[129] 2nd Implementation Lecture, para 2.2.

[130] See 4.80 and 4.81.

[131] As defined in CLSA 1990, s 58B(2); see 4.83.

[132] CLSA 1990, s 58B(1) and (3).

[133] See 4.26.

(d) the agreement must comply with such requirements (if any) as may be so prescribed;

(e) the sum to be paid by the litigant must consist of any costs payable to him or her in respect of the proceedings to which the agreement relates together with an amount calculated by reference to the funder's anticipated expenditure in funding the provision of the services; and

(f) that amount must not exceed such percentage of that anticipated expenditure as may be prescribed by the Secretary of State in relation to proceedings of the description to which the agreement relates.

4.86 Prescribed requirements may include providing prescribed information to the litigant before the agreement is made.[134]

Possible implementation of a SLAS

4.87 In June 2011, the Ministry of Justice announced that it intended to introduce a SLAS, but in December 2012 Ministers decided not to proceed with the scheme for the time being. Under the Ministry's proposals a fixed contribution of 25 per cent of the funded client's damages (excluding any damages for future care and loss) would be repayable to the legal aid fund.

4.88 In any event, it was surprising that the contribution under the proposed SLAS was as high as 25 per cent. Similar schemes in other jurisdictions operate with lower contributions from funded parties. Sir Rupert Jackson has quoted the 6 per cent deduction that applies under the Hong Kong SLAS if a case settles before delivery of the trial brief, and 10 per cent if the claim goes beyond that stage.[135] Certainly, for claims that settle early, because the 25 per cent is a fixed percentage regardless of the costs actually incurred, it will usually be more advantageous for a client to enter into a CFA with a success fee.

Costs orders in cases with s 58B litigation funding

4.89 A costs order made in any proceedings may, subject in the case of court proceedings to rules of court, include provision requiring the payment of any amount payable under a litigation funding agreement.[136] Rules of court may make provision with respect to the assessment of any costs which include fees payable under a litigation funding agreement.[137]

---

[134] CLSA 1990, s 58B(5).
[135] 2nd Implementation Lecture.
[136] CLSA 1990, s 58B(8).
[137] CLSA 1990, s 58B(9).

5

CASE MANAGEMENT

A. INTRODUCTION

5.01 Part of the terms of reference for the Review of Civil Litigation Costs was to establish the effect case management procedures have on costs, and to consider whether changes in process and/or procedure could bring about more proportionate costs. All the feedback received during the costs review was to the effect that, despite academic criticism, both costs and time are saved by good case management.[1] Accordingly, implementation of the Jackson reforms requires judges to have an active role, and to be interventionist when required.

5.02 Robust case management was summarized, by Sir Rupert Jackson, as consisting of the following:[2]

(a) delivery of effective case management directions by a judge with relevant expertise who is on top of the case;

(b) moving the claim along swiftly to settlement or trial; and

(c) firm enforcement of directions once they are given, applying a 'no nonsense' approach.

---

[1] *Final Report*, ch 39, para 5.5.
[2] 5th Implementation Lecture, para 1.5.

Achieving real savings in costs is heavily dependent on effective and propor- **5.03** tionate case preparation. Left to their own devices, history tells us that lawyers tend to devote as much time as they have available with a view to winning a case. While a successful outcome is obviously in most cases the whole point of going to law, getting there at any price is not. In an article appropriately called 'No expense spared',[3] Geoffrey Bindman explained how costs escalation often comes about. First, some lawyers have realized that the more work they do the more they are paid. Secondly, if an opponent has a tendency to overindulge in correspondence or any other aspect of the litigation, it is hard not to respond. Unanswered letters often attract criticism at a later stage. If one barrister takes ever more technical points, they have to be answered or the risk is that the case will be lost on those points. So, 'however much money one side chose to invest in the case, the other side had to match it or go to the wall'.

Breaking this cycle of escalating costs, or the even more disreputable practice **5.04** of costs building, requires a change of culture.

Effective case management

In the 9th Implementation Lecture, Lord Neuberger of Abbotsbury MR **5.05** approved[4] three essential elements of effective case management as originally formulated by the former Senior Master, Robert Turner:[5]

(a) a proactive judiciary who engage with the litigation from a very early stage;

(b) lawyers who are prepared to put aside during the pre-trial stages the adversarial attitudes of the old regime and adopt a cooperative stance with the courts and with their opponents; and

(c) a well-resourced court staff who, at all levels, are well trained and experienced in the work required of them at all stages of the life of the litigation.

Good case management is widely accepted as being effective in reducing delays **5.06** and restraining costs. There are dissenting voices. Sir Rupert Jackson referred to the literature set out in the final chapter of Michael Legg, *Case Management and Complex Civil Litigation*,[6] where the contrary arguments are set out. Such contrary views have been considered and were taken into account in the Review of Civil Litigation Costs, but Sir Rupert Jackson reiterated the conclusion that good case management saves both time and costs to the benefit of both the parties and the court.[7]

---

[3] (1992) 142 NLJ 1618.

[4] 9th Implementation Lecture, para 13.

[5] Robert Turner, '"Actively": the word that changed the civil courts' in *The Civil Procedure Rules Ten Years On,* ed Déirdre Dwyer (Oxford: OUP, 2009), 77–88.

[6] Sydney: Federation Press, 2011.

[7] 5th Implementation Lecture, para 1.9.

5.07 Proportionality is seen as the key to good case management. As stated in the 5th Implementation Lecture, the package of reforms affecting case management seeks to steer a middle course between officious intermeddling by the courts that would needlessly drive up costs, and a laissez-faire approach which leaves the parties in uncontrolled, directionless litigation.[8]

Will history repeat itself?

5.08 Effecting a culture change was also the intention of the Woolf reforms that led to the introduction of the Civil Procedure Rules (CPR) in 1999. Lord Neuberger's stark conclusion in the 9th Implementation Lecture was that in this respect the Woolf reforms have failed.[9] Lord Neuberger pointed to three causes:

(a) The Woolf reforms were not fully implemented. Lord Neuberger particularly pointed to the failure to implement Lord Woolf's recommendation on fixed costs for fast track claims.

(b) The Woolf reforms required a complete change in culture. While there was change, it was not as complete as had been hoped.

(c) The Woolf reforms were completely undermined by the maelstrom of satellite costs litigation generated by CFAs.

5.09 Depressingly, a similar confluence of factors can be seen as a real danger to the Jackson reforms. Like Woolf, the Jackson recommendation on fixed costs in fast track claims is not being implemented. Although there is a real determination to ensure there is a complete culture change with the introduction of the Jackson reforms, resource constraints may undermine their practical effectiveness. Part of the reason for holding back certain changes to create a 'big bang' on 1 April 2013 was to ensure the reforms were taken seriously by the profession. Whether the rule changes and judicial determination are enough remains to be seen. One risk factor is whether sufficient resources will be provided by the Ministry of Justice to enable full active case management by the judiciary. In times of fiscal restraint this is a real danger. Finally, while the primary source feeding the welter of satellite costs litigation over the last 12 years (recoverability of CFA success fees) has gone, the indemnity principle has not. This will be discussed further in chapter 10, but it is this principle that provides the starting point for almost all the arguments raised in the burgeoning case law on costs. Whether the Jackson reforms will also be lost in the crossfire of satellite litigation remains to be seen.

---

[8] 5th Implementation Lecture, para 1.10.
[9] 9th Implementation Lecture, para 3.

B. *FINAL REPORT*: CASE MANAGEMENT RECOMMENDATIONS

There were 12 recommendations on case management and court administration **5.10** in the *Final Report*:

(a) 'Proportionate costs' should be defined in the CPR by reference to sums in issue, value of non-monetary relief, complexity of litigation, conduct, and any wider factors, such as reputation or public importance; and the test of proportionality should be applied on a global basis.[10]

(b) Measures should be taken to promote the assignment of cases to designated judges with relevant expertise ('docketing').[11]

(c) A menu of standard paragraphs for case management directions for each type of commonly occurring case should be made available to all district judges both in hard copy and online.[12]

(d) Case management conferences (CMCs) and pre-trial reviews (PTRs) should either:

   (i) be used as occasions for effective case management (with the judge having proper time for pre-reading); or

   (ii) be dispensed with and replaced by directions on paper.[13]

(e) In multi-track cases the entire timetable for the claim, including the trial date or trial window, should be drawn up at as early a stage as is practicable.[14]

(f) Pre-action applications should be permitted in respect of breaches of pre-action protocols.[15]

(g) The courts should be less tolerant than hitherto of unjustified delays and breaches of orders. This change of emphasis should be signalled by amendment of CPR, r 3.9. If and in so far as it is possible, courts should monitor the progress of the parties in order to secure compliance with orders and pre-empt the need for sanctions.[16]

(h) The Master of the Rolls should designate two lords justices, at least one of whom will, so far as possible, be a member of any constitution of the Civil Division of the Court of Appeal which is called upon to consider issues concerning the interpretation or application of the CPR.[17]

---

[10] *Final Report*, recommendation 1.
[11] *Final Report*, recommendation 81.
[12] *Final Report*, recommendation 82.
[13] *Final Report*, recommendation 83.
[14] *Final Report*, recommendation 84.
[15] *Final Report*, recommendation 85.
[16] *Final Report*, recommendation 86.
[17] *Final Report*, recommendation 87.

(i) Consideration should be given to the possibility of the Court of Appeal sitting with an experienced district judge as assessor when case management issues arise.[18]

(j) Most county court claims should be issued at regional centres.[19]

(k) Only if cases are defended should they be transferred to county courts with staff trained in the administration of contested cases.[20]

(l) The Association of Her Majesty's District Judges and Her Majesty's Courts and Tribunals Service should together draw up a scheme for increased delegation of routine work from district judges to proper officers within the court service.[21]

C. OVERRIDING OBJECTIVE

5.11 To emphasize the culture change required by the Jackson reforms, the statement of the overriding objective of the CPR has been amended by adding the words 'and at proportionate cost' after 'justly'. So, from 1 April 2013 the overriding objective in r 1.1(1) is:

These Rules are a new procedural code with the overriding objective of enabling the courts to deal with cases justly and at proportionate cost.

5.12 A similar amendment is made to r 1.1(2), together with a new para (f), which now says:

Dealing with a case justly and at proportionate cost includes, so far as is practicable—

(a) ensuring that the parties are on an equal footing;

(b) saving expense;

(c) dealing with the case in ways which are proportionate—

    (i) to the amount of money involved;

    (ii) to the importance of the case;

    (iii) to the complexity of the issues; and

    (iv) to the financial position of each party;

(d) ensuring that it is dealt with expeditiously and fairly;

(e) allotting to it an appropriate share of the court's resources, while taking into account the need to allot resources to other cases; and

(f) enforcing compliance with rules, practice directions and orders.

---

[18] *Final Report*, recommendation 88.
[19] *Final Report*, recommendation 95.
[20] *Final Report*, recommendation 96.
[21] *Final Report*, recommendation 97.

D. ABOLITION OF ALLOCATION QUESTIONNAIRES

With effect from 1 April 2013 allocation questionnaires will be replaced by forms **5.13**
giving notice of proposed allocation to the relevant track and directions questionnaires. This reflects a change from allocation being primarily a judicial decision to a system of court officials making provisional allocation decisions which
may be revisited at a later stage. Accordingly:

(a) Old forms N149 (Allocation Questionnaire (small claims track)), N150
(Allocation Questionnaire), and N151 (Allocation Questionnaire (amount
to be decided by the court)) are discontinued.

(b) From 1 April 2013, the court staff will use the following forms:

(i) N149C, notice of proposed allocation to the small claims track;

(ii) N149A, notice of proposed allocation to the fast track; and

(iii) N149B, notice of proposed allocation to the multi-track.

(c) Also from 1 April 2013, the parties will use the following forms:

(i) N181 Directions Questionnaire (small claims track);

(ii) N180 Directions Questionnaire (fast track and multi-track); and

(iii) N151 Directions Questionnaire (amount to be decided by the court).

All references in the CPR and PDs to allocation questionnaires have been **5.14**
changed to refer to directions questionnaires.

E. TRACK ALLOCATION

Prior to the Jackson reforms track allocation was a judicial decision based on con- **5.15**
sideration of the court file, the completed allocation questionnaires filed by the parties, and, if necessary, a case management conference (CMC) or allocation hearing.
Concern was expressed in the *Final Report* that there were instances where CMCs
were ritualistic occasions where district judges issued standard directions without
getting to grips with the case. *Final Report* recommendation 83 is to the effect that
CMCs should be dispensed with if they will not perform a valuable function. Going
further than this, track allocation, which is one of the key decisions typically made at
CMCs, will now be made, on a provisional basis, by court staff rather than a judge.

Provisional track allocation

As from 1 April 2013, CPR, r 26.3(1), now says: **5.16**

If a defendant files a defence—
(a) a court officer will—
   (i) provisionally decide the track which appears to be most suitable for the claim; and
   (ii) serve on each party a notice of proposed allocation; and

   (b) the notice of proposed allocation will—

      (i)   specify any matter to be complied with by the date specified in the notice;

      (ii) require the parties to file a completed directions questionnaire and serve copies on all other parties;

      (iii) state the address of the court or the court office to which the directions questionnaire must be returned;

      (iv) inform the parties how to obtain the directions questionnaire; and

      (v)   if a case appears suitable for allocation to the fast track or multi-track, require the parties to file proposed directions by the date specified in the notice.

5.17   The old r 26.3(1), (1A), and (5) have been removed by Civil Procedure (Amendment) Rules 2013, r 8(c)(ii), (iii), and (viii).[22] The court will continue to serve unrepresented parties with the appropriate directions questionnaire.[23] The time when the court does so may be varied by a practice direction in respect of claims issued by the Production Centre,[24] although at present no such variation has been made in PD 7C.

5.18   CPR, r 26.3(2), has a simple paragraph cross-reference change, but it means that where there are two or more defendants the court will serve the new notice of proposed allocation under r 26.3(1) when all the defendants have filed a defence, or when the period for filing the last defence has expired, whichever is the sooner.

5.19   Where either r 14.5 (admission of part of a claim for a specified amount of money) or r 15.10 (claimant's notice where the defence is that the money claimed has been paid) applies, the new r 26.3(4) says the court will not serve the notice of proposed allocation under r 26.3(1) until the claimant has filed a notice requiring the proceedings to continue.

Filing directions questionnaires

5.20   The date for filing directions questionnaires will be specified in the notice of proposed allocation served by the court under CPR, r 26.3(1).[25] Once a notice of proposed allocation has been served:[26]

   (a) each party must file at court, and serve on all other parties, the documents required by the notice by no later than the date specified in it; and

   (b) the date specified will be—

      (i) if the notice relates to the small claims track, at least 14 days; or

      (ii) if the notice relates to the fast track or multi-track, at least 28 days,

   after the date when it is deemed to be served on the party in question.

---

[22] SI 2013/262.
[23] CPR, r 26.3(1B).
[24] CPR, r 26.3(7), as in force from 1 April 2013.
[25] See 5.16.
[26] CPR, r 26.3(6), as in force from 1 April 2013.

Documents that need to be filed and served under r 26.3(6)(a) will usually include **5.21** the appropriate directions questionnaire.

The parties are not permitted to vary the date for complying with the notice of **5.22** proposed allocation by agreement.[27]

Completion of directions questionnaires

The parties must consult one another and cooperate in completing the directions **5.23** questionnaires and giving other information to the court.[28] They must try to agree the case management directions which they will invite the court to make.[29] The process of consultation must not delay the filing of the directions question- naire or, where required, the proposed directions (whether or not agreed).[30]

Specimen directions for multi-track claims[31] should be used where applicable, **5.24** and are available on the Ministry of Justice website at: <http://www.justice.gov .uk/courts/procedure-rules/civil>.

If a party wishes to give the court further information which is believed to **5.25** be relevant to allocation or case management it shall be given when the party files the directions questionnaire and must be copied to all other parties.[32] The general rule is that the court will not take such information into account unless the document containing it either confirms that all parties have agreed that the information is correct and that it should be put before the court, or confirms that the party who has sent the document to the court has delivered a copy to all the other parties.[33] Examples of information likely to assist the court are given by PD 26, para 2.2(3), which remains unchanged.

Dispensing with directions questionnaires

Where a court hearing takes place (for example, on an application for an **5.26** interim injunction or for summary judgment under CPR, Part 24) before the claim is allocated to a track, the court may at that hearing dispense with the need for the parties to file directions questionnaires, treat the hearing as an allocation hearing, make an order for allocation, and give directions for case management.[34]

---

[27] CPR, r 26.3(6A), as in force from 1 April 2013.
[28] PD 26, para 2.3(1), as in force from 1 April 2013.
[29] PD 26, para 2.3(2), as in force from 1 April 2013.
[30] PD 26, para 2.3(3), as in force from 1 April 2013.
[31] See 5.70 and 5.71.
[32] PD 26, para 2.2(1), as in force from 1 April 2013.
[33] PD 26, para 2.2(2).
[34] PD 26, para 2.4(1), as in force from 1 April 2013.

Fixing date for directions questionnaires at an interim hearing

5.27 Where there is an interim hearing the court also has the power to fix a date for filing directions questionnaires and may give other directions.[35]

Failure to file directions questionnaires

5.28 Paragraphs (8) to (10) of CPR, r 26.3, were inserted by the Civil Procedure (Amendment No 2) Rules 2012,[36] with effect from 1 October 2012. As originally made they dealt with sanctions for default in filing allocation questionnaires. They have been amended by Civil Procedure (Amendment) Rules 2013, r 8(c) (xiii) to (xv), by omitting what was r 26.3(9), and making changes to paras (8) and (10). The omitted r 26.3(9), which dealt with designated money claims, has been replaced by a new r 26.3(7A). The old r 26.5(5), which also dealt with failing to file allocation questionnaires, has also been omitted.[37]

Designated money claims: automatic striking out

5.29 The new CPR, r 26.3(7A), provides:

> If a claim is a designated money claim and a party does not comply with the notice served under rule 26.3(1) by the date specified—
>
> (a) the court will serve a further notice on that party, requiring them to comply within 7 days; and
>
> (b) if that party fails to comply with the notice served under subparagraph (a), the party's statement of case will be struck out without further order of the court.

5.30 This is not the same as the notorious County Court Rules (CCR), ord 17, r 11(9), under the pre-CPR rules, in that under the new provision there are two reminders from the court before striking out takes effect. However, recent satellite litigation on costs issues was as nothing compared with the avalanche of satellite litigation over CCR, ord 17, r 11(9). Rather like the new CPR, r 26.3(7A), the CCR paragraph was only three lines long, but at one stage over half the pending appeals to the Court of Appeal were generated by this one provision.

5.31 Avoiding satellite litigation is a key component of the Jackson reforms, and the fear must be that this provision is likely to generate its own industry of that kind. It is also likely to attract attention over whether it complies with the European Convention on Human Rights (ECHR), art 6(1), on two grounds:

(a) whether it is both necessary and a proportionate response to the perceived public need; and

---

[35] PD 26, para 2.4(2), as in force from 1 April 2013.
[36] SI 2012/2208.
[37] Civil Procedure (Amendment) Rules 2013, r 8(e)(ii).

(b) striking out under CPR, r 26.3(7A)(b), without any judicial involvement may be difficult to justify under ECHR, art 6.

The answer to these points may be that because striking out under CPR, **5.32** r 26.3(7A), takes place without a hearing, the defaulting party may apply to set aside or vary the striking out of its statement of case. This is plainly what is assumed by r 26.3(10): see below. There are a number of problems with this. One is that there is no 'order' under r 26.3(7A). Striking out takes effect automatically, with no judge making any order, so there is no order that can be set aside or varied. The wording of r 26.3(10), although plainly aimed at r 26.3(7A), does not therefore seem to hit the intended target. Secondly, it is possibly the case that r 26.3(10) is contemplating the use of the power to set aside or vary under r 3.3(5). Again, this depends on the court having made an order on its own initiative (r 3.3(4)). For similar reasons, the jurisdiction to set aside or vary under r 23.10 does not readily apply, partly because there is no prior interim application under Part 23 when r 26.3(7A) comes into operation, and partly because there is no order by a judge, just automatic striking out.

Where striking out occurs under r 26.3(7A), the more natural approach for the **5.33** defaulting party is to apply for relief from sanctions under r 3.9. As discussed at 5.86, a defaulting party is unlikely to meet with a tolerant response from the court.

By the amended r 26.3(10), where an order has been made under r 26.3(7A)(b), **5.34** a party who was in default will not normally be entitled to an order for the costs of any application to set aside or vary that order nor of attending any CMC and will, unless the court thinks it unjust to do so, be ordered to pay the costs that the default caused to any other party.

Non-designated money claims: default in filing directions questionnaire
From 1 April 2013, CPR, r 26.3(8), provides that if a claim is not a designated **5.35** money claim and a party does not comply with the notice served under r 26.3(1) by the date specified, the court will make such order as it considers appropriate, including:

(a) an order for directions;
(b) an order striking out the claim;
(c) an order striking out the defence and entering judgment; or
(d) listing the case for a CMC.

As with designated money claims, where an order has been made under r 26.3(8), **5.36** a party who was in default will not normally be entitled to an order for the costs of any application to set aside or vary that order nor of attending any CMC and will, unless the court thinks it unjust to do so, be ordered to pay the costs that the default caused to any other party.[38]

---

[38] CPR, r 26.3(10).

Stay to allow for settlement

5.37   CPR, r 26.4(1), on including a written request for a stay while the parties try to settle the case by alternative dispute resolution (ADR), remains almost unchanged except that the request will now be made in the directions questionnaires. Rule 26.4(2) on what happens where all parties make such a request has been replaced, and there is also a new para (2A). The new paragraphs provide:

> (2) If all parties request a stay the proceedings will be stayed for one month and the court will notify the parties accordingly.
> (2A) If the court otherwise considers that such a stay would be appropriate, the court will direct that the proceedings, either in whole or in part, be stayed for one month, or for such other period as it considers appropriate.

5.38   The rest of r 26.4, on extending the stay, notifying the court if the claim settles, and directions if the court is not notified (r 26.4(3) to (5)), remain unchanged.

Allocating the claim to a track

5.39   The old CPR, r 26.5(1), on when track allocation will occur, is replaced with the following provision:

> The court will allocate the claim to a track—
>
> (a)   when all parties have filed their directions questionnaires; or
>
> (b)   when giving directions pursuant to r 26.3(8),
>
> unless it has stayed the proceedings under r 26.4.

5.40   Accordingly, the provisional track allocation that takes place under r 26.3 is no more than a temporary state of affairs. While r 26.5(1) is primarily about timing, it also makes clear that it is the decision made by the judge that is the actual decision on track allocation.

F. SMALL CLAIMS TRACK

Raising the small claims track limit

5.41   With effect from 1 April 2013 the small claims limit is raised from £5,000 to £10,000. The relevant track allocation rule can be found in CPR, r 26.6. Rule 26.6(1) to (3) has been amended to read:

> (1)   The small claims track is the normal track for—
>
> (a)   any claim for personal injuries where—
>
> (i)   the value of the claim is not more than £10,000; and
>
> (ii)   the value of any claim for damages for personal injuries is not more than £1,000;

   (b) any claim which includes a claim by a tenant of residential premises against a landlord where—

      (i) the tenant is seeking an order requiring the landlord to carry out repairs or other work to the premises (whether or not the tenant is also seeking some other remedy);

     (ii) the cost of the repairs or other work to the premises is estimated to be not more than £1,000; and

    (iii) the value of any other claim for damages is not more than £1,000.

(2) For the purposes of paragraph (1) 'damages for personal injuries' means damages claimed as compensation for pain, suffering and loss of amenity and does not include any other damages which are claimed.

(3) Subject to paragraph (1), the small claims track is the normal track for any claim which has a value of not more than £10,000.

Consequential changes are made to the note after r 27.1(2). There is also an increase in the amount that may be ordered in respect of experts' fees under r 27.14(2)(f) from £200 to £750 (PD 27, para 7.3).   **5.42**

Effect of raising the small claims limit

At a stroke the change to CPR, r 26.6(3), has moved thousands of claims out of the costs shifting system that applies to the fast track into the broadly non-costs regime that applies to the small claims track. It will have little effect on low-value personal injuries claims, which are frequently allocated to the fast track because of r 26.6(1)(a)(ii), which has this result where the damages for pain, suffering, and loss of amenity exceed £1,000. It means that the majority of claims affected by the change will be contract claims and non-personal injury tort claims.   **5.43**

    Removing these cases from the fast track should free up district judge time in the county courts for effective case management. That is on the assumption that the time saved in case managing claims with values between £5,000 and £10,000 will exceed the time involved in deciding the cases that do not settle and which go to a small claims hearing. Without the discipline imposed by fast track directions, it may be anticipated that a larger number of these cases will progress to hearings than before the Jackson reforms, so the savings in judicial time may not be that great.   **5.44**

Small claims costs after reallocation

After a case is reallocated to a new track, unless the court otherwise orders, any special rules about costs applying to the first track will apply up to the date of reallocation, and any special costs rules applying to the second track apply thereafter.[39] Proceedings in *Tibbles v SIG plc*[40] were at first allocated to the small   **5.45**

---

[39] Former CPR, r 44.11, which is replaced by the new r 46.13 as from 1 April 2013.
[40] [2012] EWCA Civ 518, [2012] 1 WLR 2591.

claims track, but were later transferred to the fast track. Both the judge and the legal representatives overlooked the effect of the former r 44.11, and no special order was made concerning the costs of the claim prior to reallocation. About 11 months later the claimant realized this would mean that about £20,000 of costs incurred before reallocation would be irrecoverable, and applied to vary the original order to allow those costs to be assessed as if they were incurred on the fast track.

5.46   It was held that while it would be wrong to attempt to provide an exhaustive list of situations where the court could appropriately vary an order under CPR, r 3.1(7), the primary situations were where there had been a material change of circumstances and where the facts on which the original decision was based were misstated. At root this was a case where a provision in the CPR had simply been overlooked, which, given the time that had elapsed since the order, made it inappropriate to exercise the power under r 3.1(7). It might have been different if the application had been made the day after the original order.

G. REMOVING PARTY VETO ON TRACK ALLOCATION

Former veto removed

5.47   Before 1 April 2013, CPR, r 26.7(3), said that the court would not allocate proceedings to a track if the financial value of the claim exceeded the limit for that track unless all the parties consented. Rule 26.7(3) has been removed from the CPR by the Civil Procedure (Amendment) Rules 2013, r 8(g).

5.48   This means that the court can insist on a claim being allocated to a lower track than indicated by its value regardless of the wishes of the parties. It may do so where the claim is a straightforward one and suitable for a lower track despite its financial value.

Effect of revocation of r 26.7(3) on low-value claims

5.49   While removal of CPR, r 26.7(3), means, for example, that cases above £25,000 can be allocated to the fast track and that claims with a value over £10,000 can be allocated to the small claims track, the rule change has a particular significance where it is used for the latter purpose.

5.50   The former r 27.14(5) and (6) and PD 26, para 8.1(2), dealt with cases where the parties consented to a case above the small claim limits being allocated to the small claims track. These provisions could not be preserved given the revocation of CPR, r 26.7(3). There is a new PD 26, para 8.1(2), which says the court will not normally allow more than one day for the hearing of a claim which is allocated to the small claims track even though it has a financial value above the small claims track limits set out in CPR, r 26.6(2). The implication is that if a claim needs more than a day for the hearing, normally it will not be allocated to the small claims track.

H. ACTIVE CASE MANAGEMENT

Two innovations introduced by the CPR, both of which are central to effective **5.51**
case management and which complement each other, are:

(a) the overriding objective of dealing with cases justly, which in turn includes
dealing with cases proportionately; and

(b) active case management.

As explained by the former Senior Master, Robert Turner,[41] including active case **5.52**
management as part of the court's overriding objective effected a revolution in
English civil procedure. This single change wrested control of litigation from the
parties, and gave it to the judiciary. Instead of judges influencing litigation in a
reactive way, under the CPR judges were expected to intervene in a proactive
way.

I. DIRECT CONTACT WITH THE PARTIES

Direct policing of case management directions has been enhanced by the inser- **5.53**
tion of a new CPR, r 3.1(8), with effect from 1 April 2013. This provides:

The court may contact the parties from time to time in order to monitor compliance with
directions. The parties must respond promptly to any such enquiries from the court.

Perhaps it is not surprising that Sir Rupert Jackson found that experience in **5.54**
overseas jurisdictions suggests that a phone call or email from the court enquir-
ing about progress on a case can have a dramatic effect.[42] As Sir Rupert went
on to say, securing compliance with directions is far preferable than imposing
sanctions for breach.

J. DOCKETING

Docketing was defined in the *Final Report* as the system of assigning a case **5.55**
to one judge from issue up to and including trial. It was considered in some
detail by Lord Neuberger in the 9th Implementation Lecture. There have been
docketing schemes in other jurisdictions. According to Lord Neuberger the docketing system used in the United States District Court in the Eastern District
of Virginia was so successful in speeding up litigation that local lawyers had

---

[41] Robert Turner, '"Actively": the word that changed the civil courts' in *The Civil Procedure Rules
Ten Years On,* ed Déirdre Dwyer (Oxford: OUP, 2009), 77–88.
[42] 5th Implementation Lecture, para 3.3.

taken to calling it the 'Rocket Docket'.[43] There have been systems of assignment of masters in the Queen's Bench Division and assignment of judges in the Technology and Construction Court and the Commercial Court in England for some considerable time.

Benefits of docketing

5.56 Under docketing, pre-trial case management deadlines and trial dates are crucial. Once set these dates should stay set.[44] They should be moved only if there are exceptional circumstances beyond the control of the parties. This should mean that the parties concentrate on what is essential in preparing a case, with what is inessential not being pursued. The result should be that costs are reduced, and the early identification of the issues should promote early settlements.

5.57 Lord Neuberger identified the following beneficial effects of docketing:[45]

(a) judicial preparation time is reduced because judges will be familiar with their cases;

(b) pre-trial hearings will be dealt with more efficiently;

(c) it will be the end of formulaic case management directions;

(d) continuity will mean that fewer mistakes are made;

(e) it helps the court to keep track of a claim's progress; and

(f) the court sets the pace, and is able to take active steps to ensure the parties keep to the timetable.

Implementation of docketing

5.58 Having a system for implementing docketing is mainly a matter of court administration and resourcing, and so does not feature in the revisions to the CPR. However, legal representatives should also play a role in identifying cases suitable for docketing, and there may be directions dealing with docketing in individual cases, so it would be helpful if guidance[46] were to be included in a practice direction.

Cases suitable for docketing

5.59 Normally, small claims and fast track cases will not be suitable for docketing.[47] It is likely that in these cases having a single managing judge would increase costs.

---

[43] 9th Implementation Lecture, para 17.
[44] Lord Neuberger, 9th Implementation Lecture, para 19.
[45] 9th Implementation Lecture, paras 22–4.
[46] Which was promised in the 9th Implementation Lecture, para 31.
[47] Lord Neuberger, 9th Implementation Lecture, para 30.

Docketing is not even right for every multi-track claim. Straightforward multi-track cases are unlikely to benefit from docketing. Generally, it will be the more complex and specialist claims which will be the most suitable for docketing. Complexity for this purpose may be based on the law or the facts. Suitable cases will include many Chancery claims, clinical negligence, and complex personal injuries claims.

Both practitioners and the judiciary will have responsibilities in identifying **5.60** cases which are suitable for docketing.[48] This will include a need to review the position if, for example, a case that initially looked reasonably straightforward develops into something rather more complicated.

Practice in docketed claims

The Admiralty and Commercial Courts Guide contains the following provisions **5.61** on the assignment of judges to specific cases in section D4, which were amended in the light of recommendation 50 of the *Final Report* to permit more frequent allocation of appropriate cases to designated judges. They may reasonably be regarded as a guide to the approach in other courts:

D4.1 An application for the assignment of a designated judge to a case may be made in circumstances where any or all of the following factors:

i) the size of or complexity of the case,

ii) the fact that it has the potential to give rise to numerous pre-trial applications,

iii) there is a likelihood that specific assignment will give rise to a substantial saving in costs,

iv) the same or similar issues arise in other cases,

v) other case management considerations,

indicate that assignment to a specific judge at the start of the case, or at some subsequent date, is appropriate.

D4.2 An application for the appointment of a designated judge should be made in writing to the judge in charge of the list at the time of fixing the case management conference. In appropriate cases the court may assign a designated judge regardless of whether an application is made.

D4.3 If an order is made for allocation to a designated judge, the designated judge will preside at all subsequent pre-trial case management conferences and other hearings. Normally all applications in the case, other than applications for an interim payment, will be determined by the designated judge and he will be the trial judge.

D4.4 In all cases the Commercial Court listing office will endeavour to ensure a degree of judicial continuity. To assist in this, where a previous application in the case has been determined by a judge of the Commercial Court whether at a hearing or on paper, the parties should indicate clearly when lodging the papers, the identity of the judge who last considered the matter, so that so far as reasonably practicable, the papers can be placed before that judge.

---

[48] 9th Implementation Lecture, para 31.

K. CASE MANAGEMENT CONFERENCES AND
PRE-TRIAL REVIEWS

5.62 Under the Jackson reforms CMCs, and in particular the first CMC, are seen as crucial events for focusing the case. The first CMC should be a real event at which the court takes hold of the case.[49] Its purpose includes giving directions which will focus the disclosed documents, the factual evidence, and the expert evidence on the real issues between the parties.

5.63 Recommendation 83 of the *Final Report* said:

> CMCs and PTRs should either (a) be used as occasions for effective case management or (b) be dispensed with and replaced by directions on paper. Where such interim hearings are held, the judge should have proper time for pre-reading.

5.64 The comment made in the *Final Report*[50] was that in some instances CMCs (especially initial CMCs) are not used as occasions when the court gets to grip with the case and narrows the issues, but rather as ritualistic occasions when the district judge issues standard directions in his or her standard form. CMCs, even when conducted by telephone, are expensive events. When nothing substantial is achieved, those costs are wasted.

5.65 Combined with docketing, costs management,[51] and a radical change in the culture within which litigation is conducted, what the *Final Report* and also Lord Neuberger in the 9th Implementation Lecture are looking for is good, directed, case management, which is designed to move the case forward with purpose, and at proportionate cost.

Costs budgets and case management

5.66 As discussed more fully in chapter 6, the court will have regard to any available costs budgets, and will take into account the costs involved in taking each procedural step, whenever it is making case management decisions.[52] Information provided by the parties in their costs budgets will be extremely valuable in assessing what steps are required, and in what form, in order to progress the claim in a proportionate manner.

---

[49] Sir Rupert Jackson, 7th Implementation Lecture, para 5.3.
[50] Para 5.1.
[51] See chapter 6.
[52] CPR, r 3.17(1).

Attempts to agree directions

CPR, r 29.4, as in force from 1 April 2013, replaces the former rule dealing with **5.67** taking steps to agree directions. The new r 29.4 states:

The parties must endeavour to agree appropriate directions for the management of the proceedings and submit agreed directions, or their respective proposals to the court at least seven days before any case management conference. Where the court approves agreed directions, or issues its own directions, the parties will be so notified by the court and the case management conference will be vacated.

L. FAST TRACK

There are no specific case management changes to the fast track regime in the **5.68** Jackson reforms, other than increasing the normal minimum financial value of fast track claims from £5,000 to £10,000. This has the effect of reducing the coverage of the fast track to a band between £10,000 and £25,000.

Fixed fast track trial costs as from 1 April 2013 remain unchanged, and the **5.69** relevant rules can be found in CPR, rr 45.37 to 45.40.

M. MULTI-TRACK

Model directions

A new CPR, r 29.1(2), has been inserted with effect from 1 April 2013: **5.70**

When drafting case management directions both the parties and the court should take as their starting point any relevant model directions and standard directions which can be found online at www.justice.gov.uk/courts/procedure-rules/civil and adapt them as appropriate to the circumstances of the particular case.

These were seen as essential by the *Final Report*, to assist practitioners and to **5.71** reduce costs, and also to impose some degree of consistency between courts. Evidence gathered for the Review of Civil Litigation Costs, as is common experience to all court users, was to the effect that many judges have their own standard directions, which are usually very similar to each other, but with individual variations. An obvious costs and time-consuming exercise is where the parties have agreed directions between themselves, but then have to revisit everything because the agreed directions do not match the wording preferred by a local judge. Rule 29.1(2) is a very welcome reform.

Multi-track disclosure

Disclosure through what is known as the menu option is being introduced for **5.72** multi-track claims. This will be considered in chapter 8.

N. WITNESS STATEMENTS

5.73 Over-long witness statements, and occasionally calling more witnesses than are necessary to prove the case, are sources of increased costs. These points are addressed in the new CPR, r 32.2(3), as in force from 1 April 2013, which provides:

The court may give directions—

(a) identifying or limiting the issues to which factual evidence may be directed;

(b) identifying the witnesses who may be called or whose evidence may be read; or

(c) limiting the length or format of witness statements.

O. EXPERTS

5.74 Innovations in relation to expert evidence, including witness conferencing, are considered in chapter 9.

P. ENFORCEMENT OF DIRECTIONS

Ineffective enforcement of directions under the Woolf reforms

5.75 There is no doubt that litigation has proceeded with a great deal more expedition under the Woolf reforms than under the old Rules of the Supreme Court 1965. Judges have taken their active case management responsibilities seriously, and litigators have to an extent taken on board the new ethos sought by the Woolf reforms. But not always. A range of evidence was referred to in the *Final Report*. The Property Bar Association pointed out that one of the central tenets of the CPR was that judges would take much greater procedural control of cases. Its members' experience was that judges, particularly at county court level, did not have the time, inclination, or material to do this properly. Evidence from solicitors was to the effect that there were frequent failures to comply with directions, but very few meaningful penalties were imposed. The Association of Her Majesty's District Judges asked that district judges who are prepared to make unpalatable decisions and impose robust but fair penalties be supported by the appellate courts.

Relief from sanctions under Woolf

5.76 In its original form, CPR, r 3.9(1), provided that on an application for relief from any sanction imposed for a failure to comply with any rule, practice direction, or court order, the court had to consider all the circumstances including the following nine factors:

(a) the interests of the administration of justice;

(b) whether the application for relief has been made promptly;

(c) whether the failure to comply was intentional;

(d) whether there is a good explanation for the failure;

(e) the extent to which the party in default has complied with other rules, practice directions, court orders, and any relevant pre-action protocol;

(f) whether the failure to comply was caused by the party or his legal representative;

(g) whether the trial date or the likely trial date can still be met if relief is granted;

(h) the effect which the failure to comply had on each party; and

(i) the effect which the granting of relief would have on each party.

Early authorities on r 3.9(1) held it was essential for the judge to consider each of   **5.77**
the factors listed in r 3.9(1) systematically, and then to weigh the various factors
in deciding whether granting relief would accord with the overriding objective.[53]
This formalistic approach was disapproved by *Khatib v Ramco International*,[54]
where it was said the judge has to identify the factors from the r 3.9(1) list that
are relevant to the circumstances of the particular case, and conduct an appropriate review and balancing exercise.

Indulging default under r 3.9

A particularly poor example of court control of litigation was provided by *Marine*   **5.78**
Rescue Technologies Ltd v Burchill.[55] In itself, the case is not that remarkable. It
was not regarded as sufficiently important to justify even a bare citation in either
Civil Procedure (the White Book)[56] or *Blackstone's Civil Practice*.[57] Proceedings
had been commenced in 2001. No progress was made in the claim through nine
months in 2002. There was a second period of inactivity for five months in the
middle of 2003. Warren J commented that this second period of delay '[did] not
(to my mind) indicate a claimant who is not seriously pursuing his litigation.
Matters could have moved faster, but this is not anything approaching a wilful
delay which would give rise to any sort of allegations of abuse of process.'[58]

---

[53] See *Woodhouse v Consignia plc* [2002] EWCA Civ 275, [2002] 1 WLR 2558; and *RC Residuals Ltd v Linton Fuel Oils Ltd* [2002] EWCA Civ 911, [2002] 1 WLR 2782.
[54] [2011] EWCA Civ 605, [2011] CP Rep 35
[55] [2006] EWHC 3697 (Ch), LTL 17/5/2007; [2007] EWHC 1976 (Ch), LTL 21/8/2007.
[56] London: Sweet & Maxwell, 2012.
[57] Oxford: OUP, 2013.
[58] [2006] EWHC 3697 (Ch) at [20].

5.79   Additional claims under Part 20 were added in 2003. A direction was made at a CMC in January 2004 giving the defendant permission to serve an amended defence and counterclaim by 10 February 2004. The claimant agreed to a 42-day extension, and the amended defence and counterclaim was served on 13 April 2004. At [22], '... what one sees happening is a piece of litigation that is happening at not the speediest of speeds, but on the other hand, one cannot say that there is any sort of serious, let alone contumelious, delay on the part of either party. It is worth noting at that stage (but I will come back to it) that neither side complied with the witness statement exchange order [made at the CMC].'[59] The case again went quiet for three months until November 2004. A further directions hearing took place on 7 December 2004. Disclosure was attempted in early 2005, but there was then a third period of inactivity for six and a half months from March to September 2005. There was then an application to strike out the claim, which was heard on 26 February 2006.

5.80   A number of Court of Appeal authorities were cited,[60] and the following words of Clarke LJ[61] were quoted:

It is no longer appropriate for the defendants to let sleeping dogs lie: cf *Allen v Sir Alfred McAlpine and Sons Ltd.*[62] A defendant cannot let time go by without taking action and then later rely upon the subsequent delay as amounting to prejudice and say that the prejudice caused by the delay is entirely the fault of the claimant. Such an approach would in my judgment be contrary to the ethos underlying the CPR, quite apart from being contrary to PD 23, para 2.7. One of the principles underlying the CPR is cooperation between the parties.

5.81   Applying the principles from the cited authorities to the facts of the case before him, Warren J had absolutely no hesitation in rejecting the striking-out application. The reasons stated by the judge were:

It seems to me that such delay as there has been in the context of this litigation, the periods cannot individually and even cumulatively be viewed as in any way disgraceful. Things have moved more slowly than they might have, but at each stage it had been open to the defendants to suggest that things move along, but they have never done that; they and their solicitors have apparently been quite happy to let things go on as they did. There is, I think, no prejudice such as that which Mr Burchill now submits he has suffered, but, even if that is wrong, he is largely responsible for it himself.[63]

---

[59] [2006] EWHC 3697 (Ch) at [22].

[60] Including *Walsh v Misseldine* [2000] CPLR 201; *Purdy v Cambran* [1999] CPLR 843; *Annodeus Entertainment v Gibson* (2000) *The Times*, 3 March 2000; *Axa Insurance Co Ltd v Swire Fraser Ltd* [2000] CPLR 142; and *Asiansky Television plc v Bayer-Rosin* [2001] EWCA Civ 1792, [2002] CPLR 111.

[61] From *Asiansky Television plc v Bayer-Rosin.*

[62] [1968] 2 QB 229.

[63] [2006] EWHC 3697 (Ch) at [49].

The claim was eventually struck out. It returned to Warren J in 2007[64] following **5.82** disobedience of an unless order relating to disclosure, and on this occasion the judge refused to grant relief from a striking-out sanction.

Marine Rescue Technologies Ltd v Burchill is important because trenchant **5.83** criticism of the litigation by Professor Adrian Zuckerman was picked up by Sir Rupert Jackson in the *Final Report*[65] and quoted as a wake-up call to the courts and the profession. Professor Zuckerman analysed the history of the case and commented:

> By no stretch of the imagination can this be considered an efficient use of court resources, nor was it fair to other litigants waiting in the queue, nor did it provide effective protection to the defendant from being unnecessarily subjected to 6 years of futile litigation. ... The main responsibility for this state of affairs must be accepted by the Court of Appeal. The Court of Appeal has steadfastly declined to develop a coherent policy for enforcing compliance with rules and case management directions. Its refusal to provide leadership in this regard is nowhere more apparent than in relation to its interpretation of CPR, r 3.9.

The message from the *Final Report* is that all this has to stop. **5.84**

Relief from sanctions

Given the criticism of the approach to CPR, r 3.9, recommendation 86 of the **5.85** *Final Report* was to the effect that the rule should be replaced to signal an end to the previous tolerant approach to procedural default.[66] The new r 3.9(1), as in force from 1 April 2013, simply provides:

> On an application for relief from any sanction imposed for a failure to comply with any rule, practice direction or court order, the court will consider all the circumstances of the case, so as to enable it to deal justly with the application, including the need—
>
> (a) for litigation to be conducted efficiently and at proportionate cost; and
>
> (b) to enforce compliance with rules, practice directions and orders.

Post-Jackson approach to relief from sanctions

Lord Neuberger has said that the rigorous approach taken to compliance in the **5.86** line of cases on extending claims forms culminating in *Hoddinott v Persimmon*

---

[64] [2007] EWHC 1976 (Ch).

[65] *Final Report*, ch 39.

[66] Anticipating the change in approach, in a number of cases in 2012 the Court of Appeal emphasized that it is vital that it should support robust but fair case management decisions made by first instance judges. Examples are *Fred Perry (Holdings) Ltd v Brands Plaza Trading Ltd* [2012] EWCA Civ 224, [2012] FSR 28; *Deripaska v Cherney* [2012] EWCA Civ 1235, [2013] CP Rep 1; and *Stokors SA v IG Markets Ltd* [2012] EWCA Civ 1706, LTL 2/11/2012.

Homes (Wessex) Ltd[67] will become the standard approach under the revised CPR, r 3.9.[68]

5.87   In the discussion that follows, references in the cases to granting an extension to the period of validity of a claim form have been replaced by references (in square brackets) to granting relief from sanctions. A good starting point on the *Hoddinott v Persimmon Homes (Wessex) Ltd* line of cases is *Hashtroodi v Hancock*.[69] In this case the court said:

(a)   the discretion to [grant relief from sanctions] should be exercised in accordance with the overriding objective; and

(b)   the reason for the failure to [comply with the court's directions] within the specified period is a highly material factor. If there is a very good reason for the failure to [comply, relief] will usually be granted. If there is no more than a weak reason, the court is very unlikely to [grant relief from the sanction].[70]

5.88   Rix LJ in *Cecil v Bayat*[71] adopted the following principles:

(a)   [relief from sanctions] can only be granted if there is a good reason for granting [relief from sanctions]; and

(b)   if there is a good reason, the court must consider the balance of hardship between the parties in either granting or refusing [relief from sanctions].

5.89   In relation to extending the period of validity of a claim form, good reasons are almost always based on difficulties in effecting service of the claim form, such as problems in tracing the defendant for the purpose of service, and situations where the defendant is evading service. In relation to sanctions, good reasons are likely to arise from circumstances outside the control of the party in default. Another situation is where the claimant could not have known about the claim until the last moment.[72]

5.90   However, seeking [relief from sanctions] following the negligence or incompetence of the claimant's solicitors in failing to [comply with the court's orders] in time, perhaps because the legal representative simply overlooked the matter, will inevitably be regarded as a bad reason.[73] The following are also regarded as inadequate reasons:

(a)   deliberately not [complying] in order to avoid prejudicing ongoing negotiations. This was the result in *The Mouna*,[74] and would certainly be the same

---

[67] [2007] EWCA Civ 1203, [2008] 1 WLR 806.

[68] Lord Neuberger, 9th Implementation Lecture, para 19.

[69] [2004] EWCA Civ 652, [2004] 1 WLR 3206.

[70] *Collier v Williams* [2006] EWCA Civ 20, [2006] 1 WLR 1945.

[71] [2011] EWCA Civ 135, [2011] 1 WLR 3086 at [109].

[72] [2011] EWCA Civ 135, [2011] 1 WLR 3086 at [108].

[73] *Hastroodi v Hancock* at [20].

[74] [1991] 2 Lloyd's Rep 221.

under the CPR, given r 26.4, which allows the court to grant a stay of the proceedings to allow for settlement of the case by ADR;

(b) awaiting an expert's report for the purposes of drafting the particulars of claim. This is a reason for obtaining an extension for service of the particulars of claim, not [an excuse for not complying with the requirements of the CPR].[75] A claimant in this situation should serve the claim form, and seek an extension of time for service of the particulars of claim from the court;

(c) seeking time to prepare the particulars of claim, schedule of loss and damage, and medical evidence;[76] and

(d) delays while arranging funding for the litigation. This situation should be addressed by seeking a stay of the claim while funding is arranged.[77]

The position was summarized by Dyson LJ in *Hoddinott v Persimmon Homes (Wessex) Ltd*:[78] **5.91**

A key element of the Woolf reforms was to entrust the court with far more control over proceedings than it had exercised under the previous regime. The rules must be applied so as to give effect to the overriding objective: this includes dealing with a case so as to ensure so far as is practicable that cases are dealt with expeditiously and fairly: CPR, r 1.1(2)(d). That is why the court is unlikely to grant [relief from sanctions] if no good reason has been shown for the failure to [comply].

Q. DISTRIBUTION OF BUSINESS

The underlying rules on the distribution of business between the High Court **5.92** and county courts, and between the general and specialist civil courts, remain unchanged. Generally there is a choice between using the High Court or the county courts, but the County Courts Act 1984, ss 15 to 33, and the High Court and County Courts Jurisdiction Order 1991[79] contain detailed rules imposing various limits on the jurisdiction of the civil courts. Among the most important of the rules are:

(a) In money claims other than personal injuries claims, a claimant:

  (i) must use the county court if the value of the claim is up to £25,000; and

  (ii) has a choice between the county court and High Court if the value of the claim exceeds £25,000.[80]

---

[75] *Collier v Williams.*
[76] *Mason v First Leisure Corporation plc* [2003] EWHC 1814 (QB), LTL 26/8/2003.
[77] *Cecil v Bayat.*
[78] At [54].
[79] SI 1991/724.
[80] High Court and County Courts Jurisdiction Order 1991, art 4A.

(b) In personal injuries claims, a claimant:

    (i) must use the county court if the value of the claim is up to £50,000; and

    (ii) has a choice between the county court and High Court if the value of the claim exceeds £50,000.[81]

5.93 In calculating the value of a personal injury claim it is necessary to add together:

- general damages for pain, suffering and loss of amenity;
- past losses (property damage, loss of income, expenses, etc); and
- future losses (through to death or recovery).

5.94 The following must be disregarded in calculating the value of a personal injuries claim:[82]

- interest;
- costs;
- contributory negligence;
- counterclaims; and
- recovery of state benefits under the Social Security (Recovery of Benefits) Act 1997.

R. DESIGNATED MONEY CLAIMS

5.95 Recommendations 95 and 96 of the *Final Report* have been to an extent side-stepped by the amendments to the CPR made by the Civil Procedure (Amendment No 4) Rules 2011[83] with effect from 19 March 2012. These introduced procedures for designated money claims which are similar to those contained in recommendations 95 and 96.

Definition of designated money claim

5.96 A designated money claim is any claim which is started in a county court under CPR, Part 7, which is only a claim for either or both a specified amount of money or an unspecified amount of money and which is not governed by any special procedures laid down by the CPR.[84] This covers a wide range of county court claims, most of which seek a money remedy and are not specialist claims.

---

[81] High Court and County Courts Jurisdiction Order 1991, art 5.
[82] High Court and County Courts Jurisdiction Order 1991, art 9, which applies CPR, r 16.3(6).
[83] SI 2011/3103.
[84] CPR, r 2.3(1).

Commencement of designated money claims

In designated money claims the claim form must be sent to the County Court   **5.97**
Money Claims Centre in Salford, and is issued in Northampton County Court.[85]
Claimants must specify their 'preferred county court' in the claim form to which
the proceedings should be transferred if necessary.[86] Undefended designated
money claims are often transferred to the claimant's preferred county court
(there are a number of technical rules dealing with the situations where this happens, but broadly covering situations where the court has to assess the amount
payable or the rate of payment). Defended designated money claims remain in
the Northampton County Court until the point when all the parties have filed
their directions questionnaires or when the time for filing directions questionnaires has expired.

S. TRANSFERS

General powers to order transfers can be found in the County Courts Act 1984,   **5.98**
ss 40 to 42. The High Court has unlimited power under s 40(2) to transfer cases
to the county court regardless, in a suitable case, of whether the case is outside
the monetary limits of the county court.[87] An application for a transfer from
a county court to a specialist list should be made to the receiving court under
CPR, r 30.5, with notice to the relevant county court,[88] because transfers to and
from specialist lists can only be made by judges dealing with claims in the specialist list.[89] Comments in *Natl Amusements (UK) Ltd v White City (Shepherds
Bush) LP*[90] to the effect that r 30.5 gives any division of the High Court jurisdiction to order transfers are too wide, given that r 30.5(3) requires applications for
transfers to and from specialist lists to be made to the specialist court.

Automatic transfer to home court

Where automatic transfer to the preferred county court under CPR, r 26.2A,   **5.99**
does not apply (see 5.102 at para (f)), defended claims for specified sums of
money against individuals are automatically transferred to the defendant's home
court on receipt by the court of a defence.[91] A claim for a specified amount of
money will also be automatically transferred to the defendant's home court if

---

[85] PD 7A, para 4A.1.
[86] CPR, r 2.3; PD 5A, para 4A.2.
[87] *National Westminster Bank plc v King* [2008] EWHC 280 (Ch), [2008] Ch 385.
[88] *Collins v Drumgold* [2008] EWHC 584 (TCC), [2008] CILL 2585.
[89] CPR, r 30.5(2) and (3).
[90] [2009] EWHC 2524 (TCC), [2010] 1 WLR 1181.
[91] CPR, r 26.2.

the defendant is an individual and applies to set aside a default judgment,[92] or if the court is to determine or redetermine the rate of payment following an admission by a defendant who is an individual.[93]

5.100   Where the claim is a designated money claim for a specified amount and the defendant is an individual, at the relevant time:[94]

(a) the claim will be transferred automatically to the defendant's home court, or, where there are two or more defendants who are individuals, to the home court of the defendant who first files a defence;[95] unless

(b) the defendant specifies another court in his or her directions questionnaire, in which case the transfer will be to that specified court.[96]

5.101   The 'relevant time' is when the first of the following events occurs:[97]

(a) all parties have filed their directions questionnaires;

(b) any stay ordered by the court or period to attempt settlement through mediation has expired; or

(c) if the claim falls within PD 7D (claims for the recovery of taxes and duties):

(i) the defence is filed; or

(ii) enforcement of a default judgment other than by a warrant of execution is requested.

Transfer of designated claims to preferred court

5.102   A designated money claim will be transferred automatically to the preferred county court (the one specified by the claimant on the claim form) where:

(a) the claimant files a request for judgment following an order striking out a statement of case where the request includes an amount of money to be decided by the court in accordance with CPR, r 3.5;[98] or

(b) the claimant files a request for the entry of judgment in default where the request includes an amount of money to be decided by the court in accordance with rr 12.4 and 12.5;[99] or

---

[92] CPR, r 13.4(1).
[93] CPR, rr 14.12(2) and 14.13(3).
[94] As defined by CPR, r 26.2A(6); see 5.101.
[95] CPR, r 26.2A(3).
[96] CPR, r 26.2A(5).
[97] CPR, r 26.2A(6).
[98] CPR, r 3.5A.
[99] CPR, r 12.5A.

(c) the defendant, not being an individual, applies to set aside a default judgment in a claim for a specified amount of money;[100] or

(d) the claimant files a request for judgment following an admission of liability where the request includes an amount of money to be decided by the court in accordance with r 14.6 or r 14.7;[101] or

(e) the court is to determine or redetermine the rate of payment following an admission by a defendant who is not an individual;[102] or

(f) the claim is for a specified amount against a party who is not an individual, or if the claim is a designated money claim but not for a specified amount, unless the claimant specifies another court in his or her directions questionnaire, in which case the transfer will be to that specified court.[103] In this case the transfer takes effect at the 'relevant time' as defined by r 26.2A(6).[104]

Notice of proposed allocation in automatically transferred cases

By the new CPR, r 26.3(3), replacing the old provision, if proceedings are auto- **5.103** matically transferred under rr 26.2 or 26.2A it is the court in which the proceedings were commenced that will serve the notice of proposed allocation, and will do so before the proceedings are transferred. The court will not transfer the proceedings until all parties have complied with the notice of proposed allocation or the time for doing so has expired.

Discretionary transfers

Transfers in other cases are governed by CPR, Part 30, with criteria for deciding **5.104** whether to transfer being set out in r 30.3(2). These criteria include the financial value of the claim, and whether it would be more convenient to try the case in another court. The convenience of the defendant is always a strong factor, because the defendant has not chosen to be sued.[105] Simply inserting a high value on the claim form does not ensure the claim will not be transferred to a county court.[106] For transfers to the Royal Courts of Justice where the Crown is a party, see the Attorney-General's note annexed to PD 66.

Guidance was given on the allocation of cases between the county courts **5.105** and the Technology and Construction Court (TCC) of the High Court by *West*

---

[100] CPR, r 13.4(1A).
[101] CPR, r 14.7A.
[102] CPR, rr 14.12(2A) and 14.13(3A).
[103] CPR, r 26.2A(4) and (5).
[104] See 5.101.
[105] *Pepin v Taylor* [2002] EWCA Civ 1522, LTL 10/10/2002.
[106] *Kohanzad v Derbyshire Police Authority* [2004] EWCA Civ 1387, LTL 8/10/2004, where the amount was £5 million.

Country Renovations Ltd v McDowell.[107] Claims with a value up to £250,000 should usually be commenced in the county court, or will be transferred down if they are commenced in the TCC. The judgment includes a lengthy but non-exhaustive list of exceptions to the general rule. General factors listed by Coulson J in *Collins v Drumgold*[108] were:

(a) whether the dispute arose out of or was connected with a claim suitable for the TCC as set out in PD 60, para 2.1;

(b) the value of the claim and its complexity;

(c) the convenience of the parties; and

(d) any costs implications in proceeding in the High Court rather than the county court (sometimes transferring to a specialist list will save costs).

Transfer to civil trial centre

5.106   Cases commenced in courts that are not civil trial centres (such courts are described as 'feeder courts') are considered by a procedural judge when defences are filed. If it appears that the case is suitable for allocation to the multi-track, the district judge will normally make an order allocating the case to the multi-track, will give case management directions, and transfer the claim to a civil trial centre.[109] A case may be allocated to the multi-track and be retained in a feeder court if it is envisaged that more than one CMC may be required and the parties or their legal advisers are located inconveniently far from the designated civil trial centre[110] or where pressure of work in the trial centre has led to the designated civil judge approving retention of the case by the feeder court. If it is not possible to decide whether a case should be allocated to the fast or multi-track, the procedural judge will either hold an allocation hearing at the feeder court, or transfer the case to a civil trial centre for the allocation decision to be made there.[111] Once a case is transferred, a judge will consider the file when it is received at the civil trial centre and give any further directions that appear necessary or desirable.[112]

---

[107] [2012] EWHC 307 (TCC), [2012] 3 All ER 106.
[108] [2008] EWHC 584 (TCC), [2008] CILL 2585.
[109] PD 26, para 10.2(5).
[110] PD 26, para 10.2(10).
[111] PD 26, para 10.2(6) and (8).
[112] PD 26, para 10.2(9).

6

COSTS MANAGEMENT

A. INTRODUCTION

The purpose of costs management is that the court should manage both the **6.01** steps to be taken and the costs to be incurred by the parties to any proceedings so as to further the overriding objective.[1] This is done on the basis of detailed costs budgets prepared by the parties, which are agreed between the parties or approved by the court, and which are used as the basis for making decisions on the proportionate steps needed for preparing the case for trial.

Chapter 40 of the *Final Report* was devoted to costs management. Costs man- **6.02** agement also featured as a topic within several other chapters in the *Final Report*, and should be seen as the central theme tying together many of the detailed reforms. Under the Jackson reforms the courts need to take on an important role

---

[1] CPR, r 3.12(2).

in managing costs as a necessary part of case management. As Ramsey J said in the 16th Implementation Lecture:

> It is no longer acceptable for questions of costs to be left to the end of litigation when the costs have been spent. Some control on the expenditure of costs needs to be implemented as part of the case management of cases. That control will now be provided by costs management.

B. NEED FOR COSTS MANAGEMENT

6.03 Costs budgeting was considered and rejected by Lord Woolf as part of his review of civil litigation in 1996. Lord Woolf referred to an issues paper by Adrian Zuckerman, which discussed a number of mechanisms for controlling costs in advance, such as budget-setting, fixed fees related to value, fixed fees related to procedural activity, or a mixture of the two. From para 17 of the *Woolf Report* it is plain the suggestion caused considerable controversy:

> The paper occasioned a general outcry from the legal profession. Prospective budget-setting was seen as unworkable, unfair and likely to be abused by the creation of inflated budgets. The ability of judges to be involved in the hard detail of matters such as cost was generally doubted. The imposition of fixed fees, even relating only to *inter partes* costs, was seen as unrealistic and as interference with parties' rights to decide how to instruct their own lawyers. There was widespread concern that these suggestions heralded an attempt to control solicitor and own client costs. The restrictions were generally seen as 'artificial and unworkable'.

6.04 As Sir Rupert Jackson put it: 'Lord Woolf's response was that if budgeting were unacceptable, then the problem of costs would be attacked by case management rather than by orders limiting the expenditure of recoverable costs'.[2]

6.05 Sir Rupert commented[3] that there have been considerable developments since 1996 in the field of costs capping and predictable costs, which now enable mature reflection on whether costs budgeting is a form of costs management that should be developed. He also commented that judges have become more familiar with the assessment of costs than they were at the time of Lord Woolf's Report, given their involvement in summary assessments and in other ways under the CPR.

6.06 Introducing costs management is not without its risks. As Sir Rupert Jackson pointed out,[4] there are two significant negative factors which point against the introduction of the procedure:

(a) Costs management is an exercise that generates additional costs. It will only be worth incurring these additional costs if there are net savings through the better management of the case as a result of the process.

---

[2] *Preliminary Report*, ch 48, para 3.11.
[3] *Preliminary Report*, ch 48, para 3.12.
[4] *Final Report*, ch 40, para 7.1.

(b) Costs management will impose additional demands on the limited resources of the courts.

The counter-argument was first set out in the *Preliminary Report*[5] as follows: **6.07**

(a) Litigation is in many instances a 'project', which both parties are pursuing for purely commercial ends.

(b) Any normal project costing thousands (or indeed millions) of pounds would be run on a budget. Litigation should be no different.

(c) The peculiarity of litigation is that at the time when costs are being run up, no one knows who will be paying the bill. There is sometimes the feeling that the more one spends, the more likely it is that the other side will end up paying the bill. This gives rise to a sort of 'arms race'.

(d) Under the present regime, neither party has any effective control over the (potentially recoverable) costs which the other side is running up.

(e) In truth both parties have an interest in controlling total costs within a sensible original budget, because at least one of them will be footing the bill.

(f) The parties' interests may, in truth, be best served if the court (i) controls the level of recoverable costs at each stage of the action, or alternatively (ii) makes less prescriptive orders (e.g. requiring notification when the budget for any stage is being overshot by, say, 20 per cent or more).

While in many cases litigation may be seen as a purely commercial project, it may **6.08** be objected that in a great many it is not. The model fits well with the approach taken by many businesses, who weigh the expense and time commitment to litigation against its potential benefits. For many other litigants resort to the law is a matter of necessity or compulsion. Injured claimants do not enter litigation for purely commercial reasons, but to obtain the compensation they are entitled to as a matter of law. A business suing on unpaid invoices may do so for commercial purposes, but the main reason is to secure the assistance of the law in enforcing the payment obligations of customers who have not paid.

Point (b) in the list is, however, a compelling reason for having a budget of the **6.09** anticipated costs of the contemplated litigation. The question remains as to how much time and effort should be devoted to developing and agreeing that budget. The force behind point (b) is that it is only fair to clients to ensure they have the information they need to make informed decisions about whether and how to pursue their legal remedies. Solicitors already have professional responsibilities to provide exactly this form of information to their clients.[6] Costs budgeting and costs management go further, because this information has to be shared with the other parties, and is subject to scrutiny and approval by the court.

---

[5] *Preliminary Report*, ch 48, para 3.28. Subsequently reiterated in the *Final Report*, ch 40 at paras 6.8 and 7.2, and in Ramsey J's 16th Implementation Lecture.

[6] SRA Code of Conduct 2011, O 1.12 and O 1.13, and IB 1.14. See 4.10.

6.10   Points (c) to (f) are well made. They do provide a justification for the further intervention of the courts, and are to be balanced against the negative factors mentioned above. There is not a great deal said about the second of those factors, the additional demands on court resources, but the *Final Report* does say[7] it is hoped that there will be a saving of judicial time through some cases settling earlier, given the parties' fuller understanding of their exposure on costs, and in more effective control of some of the present excesses of litigation. Research conducted in preparation for the *Final Report*, together with the experience gained from costs management pilot schemes in defamation claims[8] and in the Birmingham Mercantile Court and the Technology and Construction Court, led to the conclusion that the benefits outweighed the risks.

C. *FINAL REPORT* RECOMMENDATIONS ON COSTS MANAGEMENT

6.11   The *Final Report* made the following recommendations on costs management:

(a)   The linked disciplines of costs budgeting and costs management should be included in CPD training for solicitors and barristers who undertake civil litigation.[9]

(b)   Costs budgeting and costs management should be included in the training offered by the Judicial College to judges who sit in the civil courts.[10]

(c)   Rules should set out a standard costs management procedure, which judges would have a discretion to adopt if and when they see fit, either of their own initiative or upon application by one of the parties.[11]

(d)   Primary legislation should enable the Civil Procedure Rule Committee to make rules for pre-issue costs management.[12]

6.12   Primary legislation on pre-commencement costs management has not yet been enacted, but procedural rules governing costs management have been implemented in amendments to CPR, Part 3. The changes will demand new skills from litigators and judges. Costs budgeting involves the ability to assess and estimate the likely costs in a claim in advance, so is a very different discipline from assessing costs after they have been incurred at the end of a case or on a summary assessment at an interim hearing. It is not even purely an exercise in estimating what costs might be incurred in the future. Costs budgets also need to comply

---

[7] *Final Report*, ch 40, para 7.15.
[8] Pursuant to PD 51D.
[9] *Final Report*, recommendation 89.
[10] *Final Report*, recommendation 90.
[11] *Final Report*, recommendation 91.
[12] *Final Report*, recommendation 92.

with the requirements of reasonableness and proportionality. Developing these skills needs to be a key component of continuing training for legal representatives and judges alike.

D. ESSENTIAL FEATURES OF COSTS MANAGEMENT

The *Final Report*[13] identified the essential elements of costs management as follows: **6.13**

(a) The parties prepare and exchange litigation budgets or, as the case proceeds, amended budgets.

(b) The court states the extent to which those budgets are approved.

(c) So far as possible, the court manages the case so that it proceeds within the approved budgets.

(d) At the end of the litigation, the recoverable costs of the winning party are assessed in accordance with the approved budget.

E. JACKSON REFORMS: CASES GOVERNED BY COSTS MANAGEMENT

Costs management applies to all multi-track cases commenced on or after 1 April 2013 in: **6.14**

(a) a county court; or

(b) the Chancery Division or Queen's Bench Division of the High Court.[14]

Costs management does not normally apply to: **6.15**

(a) claims in the Admiralty and Commercial Courts;

(b) claims which are the subject of fixed costs or scale costs.

The exclusion of Admiralty and Commercial Courts cases reflects the conclusion in the *Final Report*[15] that there is no case as yet for costs management in these cases. The rules on fixed costs are in CPR, Part 45. Scale costs are prescribed for proceedings in a Patents County Court.[16]   **6.16**

---

[13] *Final Report*, ch 40, para 1.4.

[14] CPR, r 3.12(1). It has been announced that r 3.12(1) is to be amended so as to deal with similar cases in the Chancery Division, the Technology and Construction Court and Mercantile Courts. See the end of appendix 3.

[15] *Final Report*, ch 40, para 7.4.

[16] See CPR, rr 45.30 to 45.32, as in force from 1 April 2013.

6.17 The court may make a specific order either:

(a) applying costs management to a case that does not fall within the above categories; or

(b) disapplying costs management from a case that would otherwise come within r 3.12.[17]

F. FILING COSTS BUDGETS

6.18 Unless the court otherwise orders, all parties except litigants in person must file and exchange budgets as required by the rules or as the court otherwise directs.[18] Each party must do so within 28 days after service of any defence. A litigant in person, even though not required to prepare a budget, must nevertheless be provided with a copy of the budget of any other party.[19]

Format of costs budgets

6.19 Unless the court otherwise orders, a budget must be in the form of Precedent H annexed to PD 3E.[20] It must be in landscape format with at least 12 point typeface. It requires each side to provide information on time costs and disbursements for the following stages in the litigation:

(a) pre-action costs;

(b) issue and statements of case;

(c) case management conference;

(d) disclosure;

(e) witness statements;

(f) expert reports;

(g) pre-trial review;

(h) trial preparation;

(i) trial;

(j) ADR/settlement discussions; and

(k) contingencies, such as unlikely but possible interim applications.

6.20 It was objected in the period before the *Final Report* that the above list could be interpreted as providing for the bricks without the mortar. The objection

---

[17] CPR, r 3.12(1).
[18] CPR, r 3.13.
[19] PD 3E, para 2.8.
[20] PD 3E, para 1.

challenged providing for the costs of the key stages of litigation without allowing for the emails to the client, reviews, strategy meetings, etc that are also necessary in properly conducted litigation. It may be assumed that the costs to be included in the budget should include the time costs for attendance of the client, correspondence with the other side, and general project and strategy management for each stage. A note to this effect was included in the documentation used on the defamation proceedings cost management scheme.

A costs budget must be dated and verified by a statement of truth signed by **6.21** a senior legal representative of the party. The form of the statement of truth is as follows:[21]

The costs stated to have been incurred do not exceed the costs which my client is liable to pay in respect of such work. The future costs stated in this budget are a proper estimate of the reasonable and proportionate costs which my client will incur in this litigation.

The opening sentence of the statement of truth reflects the indemnity principle, **6.22** which was supposed to have been abrogated.[22]

Evidence from the Birmingham pilot scheme was to the effect that it took on **6.23** average about two and a half hours to complete the costs budget form.[23] Some firms have developed bespoke software to assist with the process.

In substantial cases, the court may direct that budgets be limited initially to part **6.24** only of the proceedings and subsequently extended to cover the whole proceedings. In cases where a party's budgeted costs do not exceed £25,000, there is no obligation on that party to complete more than the first page of Precedent H.[24]

Failure to file a costs budget

Unless the court otherwise orders, any party which fails to file a budget despite **6.25** being required to do so will be treated as having filed a budget comprising only the applicable court fees.[25] Unfortunately, this automatic sanction is likely to give rise to a substantial body of satellite litigation. This topic is discussed further at 5.29 to 5.34 in relation to automatic striking out for failure to comply with a notice of proposed allocation.[26]

A party who is in default of the requirement to file a costs budget will be able **6.26** to apply under r 3.9 for relief from the sanction prescribed by r 3.14. This is done by making an application in accordance with Part 23 supported by evidence. As discussed at 5.76 to 5.91, r 3.9(1) has been amended by the Jackson reforms by removing the long list of factors that should be taken into account. As in force

---

[21] PD 22, para 2.2A.
[22] *Final Report*, recommendation 4, and see 10.54.
[23] Final Report, ch 40, para 2.7.
[24] PD 3E, para 1.
[25] CPR, r 3.14.
[26] CPR, r 26.3(7A)(b).

from 1 April 2013, r 3.9(1) says that on an application for relief from sanctions the court will consider all the circumstances of the case relevant to enable it to deal justly with the application, including the need:

(a) for litigation to be conducted efficiently and at proportionate cost; and

(b) to enforce compliance with rules, practice directions, and orders.

6.27 Depriving a successful party of all its costs other than court fees is a draconian penalty for failing to comply with the requirement to file a costs budget. Probably this is intended to ensure that, where there is a default, an application for relief from the r 3.14 sanction is made promptly so that effective costs management can be achieved. Where the default is persisted in until trial it becomes increasingly difficult to have sympathy for the defaulting party.

6.28 Simplification of r 3.9(1) by removing the detailed factors set out in the earlier version of the rule implies that in exercising the discretion given by the rule the court should concentrate its attention on the facts and circumstances of the particular case. That said, if an application is made a decent time before trial, it is difficult to see why relief should not be granted. In such cases the next question is on what terms relief should be granted. In addition to paying the costs of and occasioned by the default, it is suggested that consideration should be given to disallowing all or part of the costs, apart from court fees, from the approved costs budget of the defaulting party for the period of the default.

G. COSTS MANAGEMENT ORDERS

Nature of costs management orders

6.29 In addition to exercising its other powers, the court may manage the costs to be incurred by any party in any proceedings.[27] It may do so by making a 'costs management order'.[28] By such order the court will:

(a) record the extent to which the budgets are agreed between the parties; or

(b) in respect of budgets or parts of budgets which are not agreed, record the court's approval after making appropriate revisions.

6.30 Ramsey J has said that there is a presumption in favour of making a costs management order.[29] This applies also to cases outside the normal categories covered by r 3.12(1), because costs management is a necessary adjunct to proper case management and furthering the overriding objective. It seems that complex high-value commercial litigation is an exception, as stated in the *Final Report*,

---

[27] CPR, r 3.15(1).
[28] CPR, r 3.15(2).
[29] 16th Implementation Lecture, para 19.

and there will be circumstances, such as an impending mediation, that may justify postponing the decision to make a costs management order.[30]

Approval of costs budgets

The primary position is that costs budgets should be agreed by the parties. If **6.31** the budgets or parts of the budgets are agreed between all parties, the court will record the extent of such agreement.[31]

In so far as the budgets are not agreed, the court will review them and, after **6.32** making any appropriate revisions, record its approval of the revised budgets.[32] Court approval is a forward-looking process, which deals with future costs yet to be incurred. Accordingly, the court may not approve costs incurred before the date of any budget as part of the costs management process. The court may, however, record its comments on those costs and should take those costs into account when considering the reasonableness and proportionality of all subsequent costs.[33]

Ramsey J has said a court considering disputed costs budgets will look at **6.33** both the total costs and the overall costs of each stage of the proceedings.[34] In doing so:

…whilst the court will consider the underlying time estimate and applicable rate in reviewing the overall cost of a stage, the court is not embarking on a detailed assessment in advance. In this way there is discouragement of a detailed nit-picking approach which can lead, in itself, to increased costs and satellite issues. Rather, there is encouragement for a lighter approach which considers whether the total budgeted costs of each stage fall within the range of reasonable and proportionate costs for a given case.

The last point is important, because in approving a budget the court will apply **6.34** the new proportionality test to the costs budget.[35] The judge carrying out costs management will not only scrutinize the reasonableness of each party's budget, but also stand back and consider whether the total sums on each side are proportionate in accordance with the new definition.[36] If the total figures are not proportionate, the judge will only approve budget figures for each party which are proportionate. Thereafter both parties, if they choose to press on, will be litigating in part at their own expense, unless the conduct of the paying party results in a more generous assessment of costs.

The court's approval will relate only to the total figures for each phase of the **6.35** proceedings, although in the course of its review the court may have regard to

---

[30] 16th Implementation Lecture, para 18.
[31] PD 3E, para 2.3.
[32] PD 3E, para 2.3.
[33] PD 3E, para 2.4.
[34] 16th Implementation Lecture, para 21.
[35] 16th Implementation Lecture, para 16; CPR, r 44.3.
[36] *Final Report*, ch 40, para 7.23.

the constituent elements of each total figure. When reviewing budgets, the court will not undertake a detailed assessment in advance, but rather will consider whether the budgeted costs fall within the range of reasonable and proportionate costs.

6.36 After its budget has been approved, each party is required to re-file its budget in the form approved with re-cast figures, which shall be annexed to the order approving it.[37]

Budgets and case management

6.37 The primary purpose for the introduction of costs budgeting is to provide an effective case management tool for judges when considering the directions that are best suited to the case in hand. When making any case management decision, the court will have regard to any available budgets of the parties and will take into account the costs involved in each procedural step.[38] This is so whether or not a costs budgeting order has been made.[39] This means that in deciding what directions to make, the court will have to consider the costs impact of those steps.[40]

6.38 Examples given by Ramsey J in the 16th Implementation Lecture included:

(a) whether full electronic disclosure will result in disproportionate costs;

(b) whether it is proportionate to have standard disclosure, or whether the costs of more limited disclosure would be more proportionate; and

(c) the impact on costs of expert evidence and witness statements.

6.39 The *Final Report* contains an interesting quotation from Judge Simon Brown based on experience from the Birmingham pilot scheme.[41] It was found that case management conferences took longer to conduct with costs budgets from the parties, but there were considerable advantages. As stated by the judge:

This does not take much extra time in court. It all becomes part of the case management process, which is more thorough than it was before we had the costs management pilot tool to help us come to grips with proportionality. I now rarely just sign off agreed consent orders for directions as I used to. I am able to ask what the preparation plans for the litigation are by each party and how much they really plan to spend in fulfilling them. It does take some extra time but it makes case management much more realistic e.g. I ask about disclosure and how much they really want bearing in mind the costs of doing it e.g. electronic disclosure which may require an expert at some cost. I have increasingly used the cost-benefit analysis here to order iterative specific disclosure rather than blanket

---

[37] PD 3E, para 2.7.
[38] CPR, r 3.17(1).
[39] CPR, r 3.17(2).
[40] 16th Implementation Lecture, para 17.
[41] *Final Report*, ch 40, para 2.11.

standard disclosure. I am also much better able to control experts' costs, and increasingly use a single joint expert if I feel the court will need expertise it does not have e.g. tax or investments experts.

Judicial control of parties' budgets

If a costs management order has been made, the court will thereafter control the **6.40** parties' budgets in respect of recoverable costs.[42] The court may set a timetable or give other directions for future reviews of budgets.[43]

Costs management conferences

The court may convene a hearing which is solely for the purpose of costs man- **6.41** agement (for example, to approve a revised budget). Such a hearing is referred to as a 'costs management conference'.[44] Where practicable, costs management conferences should be conducted by telephone or in writing.[45]

Reviews of costs budgets

Each party shall revise its budget in respect of future costs upwards or down- **6.42** wards, if significant developments in the litigation warrant such revisions.[46] Such amended budgets shall be submitted to the other parties for agreement. In default of agreement, the amended budgets shall be submitted to the court, together with a note of (a) the changes made and the reasons for those changes, and (b) the objections of any other party. The court may approve, vary, or disapprove the revisions, having regard to any significant developments which have occurred since the date when the previous budget was approved or agreed.

The onus is on the parties to put forward revised budgets if significant devel- **6.43** opments in the litigation make this desirable.[47] Solicitors may wish to appoint review dates for this purpose. As with the original budgets, a revised budget should initially be submitted to the other side for approval, and only referred to the court if this is not forthcoming. It may be necessary to hold a costs management conference for this purpose.

Anticipating possible events that will impact on costs estimates, such as **6.44** unwanted interim applications by the other side, and including them in the original costs budget under 'contingencies', will, in some cases, avoid the need to return to court with revised costs budgets.

---

[42] CPR, r 3.15(3).
[43] PD 3E, para 2.5.
[44] CPR, r 3.16(1).
[45] CPR, r 3.16(2).
[46] PD 3E, para 2.6.
[47] Ramsey J, 16th Implementation Lecture, para 22.

H. COSTS RELATING TO COSTS MANAGEMENT

6.45 Ensuring that the costs involved in the process do not themselves add to the problem of excessive litigation costs has always been a concern. Save in exceptional circumstances:

(a) the recoverable costs of initially completing Precedent H shall not exceed the higher of £1,000 or 1 per cent of the approved budget; and

(b) all other recoverable costs of the budgeting and costs management process shall not exceed 2 per cent of the approved budget.[48]

6.46 In so far as such costs exceed these limits they will have to be borne by the client or be absorbed in the firm's overheads.

I. COSTS BUDGETS AND THE COSTS OF THE PROCEEDINGS

6.47 A two-speed approach seems to be contemplated when it comes to costs management and the costs of the proceedings.

6.48 First, there are cases where a costs management order has been made. In these cases, when assessing costs on the standard basis, the court will:

(a) have regard to the receiving party's last approved or agreed budget for each phase of the proceedings; and

(b) not depart from such approved or agreed budget unless satisfied that there is good reason to do so.[49]

6.49 The need to show a good reason for departing from the budget should reduce the area of dispute on the assessment of costs. Because the paying party has seen and considered the receiving party's budget from an early stage there are likely to be fewer disputes than before the Jackson reforms about the amount of costs payable at the end of the process.[50]

6.50 Secondly, there are cases where costs budgets have been used, but there has been no costs management order. In these cases, one of the factors the court to which will have regard is the receiving party's last approved or agreed budget.[51] This applies to all assessments, but the difference is that, in the absence of a costs management order, there is no presumption against departing from the budget.

---

[48] PD 3E, para 2.2.

[49] CPR, r 3.18.

[50] Ramsey J, 16th Implementation Lecture, para 24; *Henry v News Group Newspapers Ltd* [2013] EWCA Civ 19, 163 NLJ 140, at [28].

[51] CPR, r 44.4(3)(h).

7

COSTS CAPPING ORDERS

A. INTRODUCTION

The Jackson reforms have moved the provisions on costs capping orders from **7.01** relative obscurity in CPR, Part 44, to the mainstream of costs management within Part 3. A costs capping order is an order limiting the amount of future costs (including disbursements) which a party may recover pursuant to an order for costs subsequently made.[1] For this purpose 'future costs' are those incurred in respect of work done after the date of the costs capping order, but excluding the amount of any additional liability.[2]

B. PROCEDURE FOR APPLYING FOR A COSTS CAPPING ORDER

An application for a costs capping order may be made at any stage of the **7.02** proceedings,[3] although it should be made as soon as possible and preferably before, at or shortly after the first case management hearing.[4] Where a costs capping order is sought in relation to trust funds, notice of intention to apply for it must be filed with the first statement of case or (for Part 8 claims) with the evidence or, if there is no evidence, acknowledgment of service.[5] The application

---

[1] CPR, r 3.19(1).
[2] CPR, r 3.19(2).
[3] CPR, r 3.19(5).
[4] PD 3F, para 1.2.
[5] PD 3F, para 5.5.

is made using the procedure in CPR, Part 23.[6] The application notice must set out whether the order is sought in respect of the costs of the whole proceedings or on a particular issue which is ordered to be tried separately. It must be accompanied by a costs budget supported by a statement of truth setting out the costs incurred by the applicant to date and the likely future costs.[7] Directions may be made for dealing with the application, which may include filing schedules of costs, time estimates, and whether the judge should sit with an assessor.[8]

C. REQUIREMENTS FOR MAKING COSTS CAPPING ORDERS

7.03   A costs capping order can only be made if:

(a) it is in the interests of justice to make the order;

(b) there is a substantial risk that without the order costs will be disproportionately incurred; and

(c) the risk of disproportionate costs cannot be adequately controlled by case management directions and orders or by the detailed assessment of costs.[9]

7.04   If these conditions are made out, the court has a discretion whether to make the order which it exercises taking into account all the circumstances of the case, but in particular:[10]

(a) whether there is a substantial imbalance between the financial positions of the parties;

(b) whether the costs of determining the amount of the cap are likely to be proportionate to the overall costs of the litigation;

(c) the stage which the proceedings have reached; and

(d) the costs which have been incurred to date and the future costs.

D. DISCRETION TO MAKE COSTS CAPPING ORDER

7.05   The criteria set out in 7.04 demand a restrictive approach, and will be satisfied only in an exceptional case.[11] This is at odds with the statement in the

---

[6] CPR, r 3.20(1).

[7] CPR, r 3.20(2); PD 3F, para 2.

[8] CPR, r 3.20(3).

[9] CPR, r 3.19(5).

[10] CPR, r 3.19(6).

[11] PD 3F, para 1.1; *Barr v Biffa Waste Services Ltd (No 2)* [2009] EWHC 2444 (TCC), [2010] 3 Costs LR 317.

Final Report that the intention was to remove the requirement for 'exceptional circumstances'.[12] Delay weighs against making the order.[13]

Pre-Jackson cases were not very consistent on when costs capping orders **7.06** might be appropriate. In *Smart v East Cheshire NHS Trust*[14] Gage J said:

> The court should only consider making a costs cap order in cases where the applicant shows by evidence that there is a real and substantial risk that without such an order costs will be disproportionately or unreasonably incurred; and that this risk may not be managed by conventional case management and a detailed assessment of costs after a trial.

A different approach was adopted in *King v Telegraph Group Ltd*[15] by Brooke **7.07** LJ who said: '... it would be very much better for the court to exercise control over costs in advance, rather than to wait reactively until after the case is over and the costs are being assessed'. This is consistent with cases such as *Solutia UK Ltd v Griffiths*[16] and *Leigh v Michelin Tyre plc*.[17] The object of the order is to encourage the parties to plan the case in advance so as to ensure that costs are proportionate.[18]

In *Henry v British Broadcasting Corporation*[19] the order was refused because **7.08** the application was made at a very late stage close to the trial. One of the reasons given in *Willis v Nicholson*[20] for refusing a cap beyond limiting the claimant to his latest estimate, rather than by a costs capping order, was a concern about the time and costs that would have been involved in having a costs judge decide what the costs cap should be.

E. FORM OF COST CAPPING ORDERS

The scheme of the order is to avoid an inflexible cap, while enabling the court to **7.09** retain control over the amount of costs at any time. Either party may apply to vary the order, which may be allowed only if there has been a material and substantial change of circumstances or if there is some other compelling reason why a variation should be allowed.[21] An application to vary is made in accordance with CPR, Part 23,[22] and should be supported by evidence and a revised costs budget. Figure 7.1 is a typical costs capping order.

---

[12] *Final Report*, ch 40, para 7.18.
[13] See PD 3F, para 1.2.
[14] [2003] EWHC 2806 (QB), [2004] 1 Costs LR 124 at [22].
[15] [2004] EWCA Civ 613, [2005] 1 WLR 2282 at [92].
[16] [2001] EWCA Civ 736, [2002] PIQR P16.
[17] [2003] EWCA Civ 1766, [2004] 1 WLR 846.
[18] See *Jefferson v National Freight Carriers plc* [2001] EWCA Civ 2082, [2001] 2 Costs LR 313.
[19] [2005] EWHC 2503 (QB), [2006] 1 All ER 154.
[20] [2007] EWCA Civ 199, [2007] PIQR P22.
[21] CPR, r 3.19(7).
[22] CPR, r 3.21.

FIGURE 7.1 Costs capping order

The future base costs of the [Claimant/Defendant] shall not without the permission of the court exceed the sum of £ (save that any costs awarded in favour of a party on any interim application shall not count towards the said £). Either party may apply without notice to increase the figure of £ and any such application shall be supported by a statement addressing the need for the increase and a revised costs estimate calculated to trial.

8

DISCLOSURE

A. INTRODUCTION

Disclosure was recognized as a major source of costs in the *Final Report*. A **8.01** fairly striking recent example was *Al Rawi v Security Service*,[1] which reached the Supreme Court in 2011 on the use of closed material in civil claims. It was a false imprisonment claim that raised national security issues, but the point relevant to this chapter is that the defendants had approximately 250,000 relevant documents, of which about 140,000 were potentially protected by public interest immunity (PII). It was estimated that the volume of documents might mean it

---

[1] [2011] UKSC 34, [2012] 1 AC 531.

would take as long as three years to complete a PII exercise. Not surprisingly, there were dual concerns on the part of the defendants about the likely cost and delays in dealing with disclosure. In the *Final Report*[2] evidence is quoted from a City firm saying:

> ...in 'heavy' commercial litigation, by far the largest costs driver is disclosure. The costs incurred in the disclosure process have significantly increased over recent years, principally because litigants, their advisers and the courts have struggled to grapple with the practical and logistical difficulties involved with e-disclosure.

8.02 It is not just the largest cases that cause concern. Sir Rupert Jackson has said that even in medium-sized claims where all the documents are in paper form (which is nowadays becoming rather rare), disclosure can be a major exercise which generates disproportionate costs. 'It can also result in a formidable bundle, most of which is never looked at during the trial. In larger actions where the relevant documents are electronic the problem is multiplied many times over. That problem is accentuated because relatively few solicitors and even fewer barristers really understand how to undertake e-disclosure in an effective way.'[3]

B. PRE-WOOLF APPROACH TO DISCOVERY

8.03 The existence of the concerns over disclosure under the Civil Procedure Rules (CPR) outlined at 8.01 and 8.02 shows how intractable the problem is of keeping the costs of disclosure of documents under control. One of the principal problems that beset the pre-CPR system of discovery flowed from the decision of the Court of Appeal in *Compagnie Financiere et Commerciale du Pacifique v Peruvian Guano Co,*[4] where Brett LJ said:

> ... every document relates to the matters in question in the action, which not only would be evidence upon any issue, but also which, it is reasonable to suppose, contains information which *may*—not which *must*—either directly or indirectly enable the party [seeking discovery] either to advance his own case or to damage the case of his adversary ... a document can properly be said to contain information which may enable the party [seeking discovery] either to advance his own case or to damage the case of his adversary, if it is a document which may fairly lead him to a train of inquiry, which may have either of these two consequences.

8.04 This concept of the 'train of inquiry' made discovery of documents an extensive and costly process and was a principal cause of complaint by practitioners and

---

[2] *Final Report*, ch 27, para 2.1.
[3] 7th Implementation Lecture, para 2.1.
[4] (1882) 11 QBD 55 at p 63.

litigants alike. In *O Co v M Co*[5] Colman J, perhaps in anticipation of the new approach, and certainly out of frustration with the old, stated:

> The principle was never intended to justify demands for disclosure of documents at the far end of the spectrum of materiality which on the face of it were unrelated to the pleaded case of the plaintiff or defendant and which were required for purely speculative investigation ... That formulation [Brett LJ's 'train of inquiry'] must not, in my judgment, be understood as justifying discovery demands which would involve parties to civil litigation being required to turn out the contents of their filing systems as if under criminal investigation merely on the off-chance that something might show up from which some relatively weak inference prejudicial to the case of the disclosing party might be drawn.

C. DISCLOSURE UNDER THE CPR PRE-JACKSON

By the old version of CPR, r 31.5(1), a court order made before 1 April 2013 **8.05** requiring a party to give disclosure was an order to give standard disclosure, unless the court directed otherwise. By r 31.6, which is unchanged, standard disclosure requires a party to disclose only:

(a) the documents on which it relies; and

(b) the documents which—

    (i)   adversely affect its own case;

    (ii) adversely affect another party's case; or

    (iii) support another party's case; and

(c) the documents which it is required to disclose by a relevant practice direction.

While the categories set out in r 31.6 come close to the concept of relevance, **8.06** that particular word is not used in r 31.6, and is not the test.[6] Strictly, the question is whether an individual document is one on which the disclosing party seeks to rely, or one which affects any of the parties in any of the ways set out in r 31.6. Although these categories do not include 'train of inquiry' documents,[7] they are nevertheless wide ranging, and many clients are surprised at the breadth of documentation that they are required to disclose. With the proliferation of photocopying, emails, and other forms of electronic communication, it is the sheer scale of the potentially disclosable documentation that makes the process so expensive.

---

[5] [1996] 2 Lloyd's Rep 347 at pp 350–1.
[6] *Shah v HSBC Private Bank (UK) Ltd* [2011] EWCA Civ 1154, [2012] Lloyd's Rep FC 105.
[7] See 8.03.

8.07   To ensure the system works fairly between the opposing parties, lawyers are under professional duties to advise their clients on their disclosure obligations, and clients must take personal responsibility by signing a disclosure statement, which typically is incorporated in the standard list of documents.[8]

D. TRAIN OF INQUIRY DOCUMENTS UNDER THE CPR

8.08   Sometimes a party wants to have disclosure of train of inquiry documents from the other side. As such documents are not covered by the definition of standard disclosure, either an order covering train of inquiry documents needs to be obtained at a case management conference (CMC), or an application should be made for specific disclosure.[9] The costs involved in disclosing train of inquiry documents means this is rarely justifiable in fast track claims. It is also comparatively rare for them to be required in multi-track claims, being most typically encountered in commercial fraud claims. Before making such an order the court will take into account all the circumstances of the case with particular regard to the overriding objective.[10]

E. CONTROLLING DISCLOSURE PRE-JACKSON

8.09   In the exercise of its case management powers in furtherance of the overriding objective, even before the Jackson reforms the court could decide to make orders limiting disclosure. Existing provisions within CPR, Part 31, allow for a range of approaches to giving disclosure. They are helpfully summarized in the Admiralty and Commercial Courts Guide at E2.1, which encourages the court to consider a number of alternative orders, including:

(a) ordering standard disclosure;[11]

(b) dispensing with or limiting standard disclosure;[12]

(c) ordering sample disclosure;

(d) ordering disclosure in stages;[13]

---

[8] *Arrow Trading and Investments Est 1920 v Edwardian Group Ltd* [2004] EWHC 1319 (Ch), [2005] 1 BCLC 696.

[9] Under CPR, r 31.12.

[10] PD 31A, para 5.4.

[11] CPR, rr 31.5(1) and 31.6, as in force before 1 April 2013.

[12] CPR, r 31.5(2), as in force before 1 April 2013.

[13] CPR, r 31.13, which remains unchanged.

(e) ordering disclosure otherwise than by service of a list of documents, for example, by service of copy documents;[14] and

(f) ordering specific disclosure.[15]

F. COSTS REVIEW APPROACH TO DISCLOSURE

It was patently clear from the evidence gathered by the Civil Litigation Costs **8.10** Review that the costs of disclosure would have to be addressed if civil costs were to be brought back under control. Sir Rupert Jackson outlined ten possible options for reform.[16] These were:

(a) Maintain the current position with standard disclosure remaining the default disclosure order.

(b) Abolish standard disclosure and limit disclosure to documents relied upon, with the ability to seek specific disclosure.

(c) Introduce 'issues based' disclosure akin to the approach being trialled by the Commercial Court.

(d) Revert to the old system of discovery with the 'trail of inquiry' test.

(e) No default position with the parties and court being required to consider the most appropriate process for disclosure at the first CMC. This option has generally been referred to as the 'menu' option.

(f) More rigorous case management by the court, including greater use of sanctions against parties who provide disclosure in a haphazard manner, or late, or ordering the parties to agree a constructive process and scope.

(g) Use of experienced lawyers as disclosure assessors in 'heavy' cases to identify which categories of documents merit disclosure.

(h) Restrict the number of specific disclosure applications and/or raise the standard to be met.

(i) Reverse the burden of proof in specific disclosure applications, with the costs of the disclosure exercise being met by the requesting party unless documents of real value emerge.

(j) Allocate a single judge at the outset of substantial cases to enable him or her to become more familiar with the facts and procedural history.

---

[14] CPR, r 31.10(8)(a), and PD 31A, para 1.4, which remain unchanged.
[15] CPR, r 31.12, which remains unchanged.
[16] *Final Report*, ch 37, para 1.2.

8.11 The solution adopted is a combination of:

(a) maintaining the current standard disclosure system for fast track claims and also for personal injury claims on the multi-track;

(b) adopting the menu option for other multi-track claims;

(c) introducing docketing to ensure judicial continuity in more complex claims;[17] and

(d) adopting a less tolerant approach to breach of directions.[18]

G. *FINAL REPORT* RECOMMENDATIONS ON DISCLOSURE

8.12 There were two recommendations on disclosure in chapter 37 of the *Final Report*:

(a) E-disclosure as a topic should form a substantial part of:

(i) CPD for solicitors and barristers who will have to deal with e-disclosure in practice; and

(ii) the training of judges who will have to deal with e-disclosure on the bench.[19]

(b) A new CPR, r 31.5A, should be drafted to adopt the menu option in relation to (i) large commercial and similar claims and (ii) any case where the costs of standard disclosure are likely to be disproportionate. Personal injury claims and clinical negligence claims should be excluded from these provisions.[20]

H. IMPLEMENTATION

8.13 There was already a project, under Coulson J, to look into rule changes to make provision for electronic disclosure. This culminated in the introduction of PD 31B on electronic disclosure on 1 October 2010, together with new paras 2A.1 and 2A.2 being inserted into what is now PD 31A.

8.14 Regarding recommendation 78,[21] the Rule Committee set up a subcommittee, also under Coulson J, to consider the amendments that would be needed to introduce the menu option. After full consideration, it was decided that instead of adding a r 31.5A the better course was to introduce the menu option by completely replacing the former r 31.5.

---

[17] See 5.55 to 5.61.
[18] See 5.86 to 5.91.
[19] *Final Report*, recommendation 77.
[20] *Final Report*, recommendation 78.
[21] See 8.12.

I. ELECTRONIC DISCLOSURE

The provisions on the disclosure of electronic documents in PD 31B apply to **8.15** cases likely to be allocated to the multi-track.[22] It provides a comprehensive and up-to-date set of rules governing the disclosure of electronic documents. PD 31B, para 6, sets out the following general principles:

(a) electronic documents should be managed efficiently in order to minimize the cost incurred;

(b) technology should be used in order to ensure that document management activities are undertaken efficiently and effectively;

(c) disclosure should be given in a manner which gives effect to the overriding objective;

(d) electronic documents should generally be made available for inspection in a form which allows the party receiving them the same ability to access, search, review, and display the documents as the party giving disclosure; and

(e) disclosure of electronic documents which are of no relevance to the proceedings may place an excessive burden in time and cost on the party to whom disclosure is given.

Keeping the costs of electronic disclosure in proportion

In order to keep costs in proportion, the parties and their legal advisers are **8.16** required to discuss the use of technology for the purposes of managing disclosure of electronic documents.[23] Particular topics to discuss include the tools to be used to reduce the burden and costs of disclosure, and the need to preserve electronic documents.[24] In *Digicel (St Lucia) Ltd v Cable and Wireless plc*[25] the court ordered the parties' solicitors to meet to discuss the best way of restoring email accounts, in view of the possible cost of doing so.

Electronic documents questionnaire

An electronic documents questionnaire in the form in the schedule to PD 31B **8.17** may be used to provide information relevant to the procedures for the disclosure of electronic documents. If used, the questionnaire has to be verified by a state-

---

[22] PD 31A, para 2A.2.
[23] PD 31B, para 8.
[24] PD 31B, para 9.
[25] [2008] EWHC 2522 (Ch), [2009] 2 All ER 1094.

ment of truth[26] and the questionnaire itself is treated as a disclosed document for the purpose of the collateral use rule.[27]

Case management directions on electronic disclosure

8.18 It is important to obtain appropriate directions for disclosure at the first CMC, which in turn requires cooperation between the parties.[28] This is considered further at 8.28 in relation to the menu option.

Searches for electronic documents

8.19 One of the main difficulties in keeping costs under control in relation to electronic documents is the extent of the duty to make a reasonable search for documents.[29] PD 31B, paras 20 to 27, give guidance which includes a list of factors to be taken into account in deciding on the ambit of a reasonable search for electronic documents. These factors include the nature and complexity of the proceedings, the ease of retrieval, and the availability of the documents or their contents from other sources. In *Fiddes v Channel 4 Television Corporation*,[30] the costs of doing a search of backup tapes for deleted emails was estimated at £10,000. Even in the context of a case where the costs were already estimated at £1 million, and where the relevant respondent had changed her story from saying she had deleted her emails because her email account was full to saying she had not sent any emails in the relevant period, a finding that the documents in the proposed search were unlikely to be significant or relevant meant that a refusal to order the search was not overturned on appeal. PD 31B, paras 25 to 27, deal with keyword searches for electronic documents. A search based on targeted keyword electronic searches was held to be inadequate in *Digicel (St Lucia) Ltd v Cable and Wireless plc*,[31] where email accounts of specified individuals were required. Limited searches for electronic documents were regarded as reasonable in *Abela v Hammonds Suddards*.[32]

Lists of documents and inspection in relation to electronic documents

8.20 Lists of documents may be provided in electronic form in CSV (comma-separated values) or other agreed format.[33] Any supplementary list should run sequentially

---

[26] PD 31B, para 11.
[27] CPR, r 31.22.
[28] PD 31B, paras 14 to 19.
[29] As required by CPR, r 31.7.
[30] [2010] EWCA Civ 516, LTL 24/3/2010.
[31] [2008] EWHC 2522 (Ch), [2009] 2 All ER 1094.
[32] (2008) LTL 9/12/2008.
[33] PD 31B, para 30(2).

from the last numbered entry in the previous list.[34] Inspection may be given in electronic form, and may take the form of the provision of disclosure data electronically, or electronic copies of disclosed documents.[35] Unless otherwise agreed or ordered, electronic documents should be disclosed in their native form (ie, preserving any metadata).[36] If electronic documents are best accessed using technology which is not readily available to the other side, there is a duty to cooperate in making the documents available.[37]

J. STANDARD DISCLOSURE FROM 1 APRIL 2013

As from 1 April 2013 there is a new CPR, r 31.5. The old r 31.5 had three sub-paragraphs which said that an order to give disclosure is an order to give standard disclosure, and providing that the parties may agree, or the court may order, that disclosure be dispensed with or limited. **8.21**

Under the new r 31.5(1), in all claims to which r 31.5(2) does not apply: **8.22**

(a) an order to give disclosure is an order to give standard disclosure unless the court directs otherwise;

(b) the court may dispense with or limit standard disclosure; and

(c) the parties may agree in writing to dispense with or to limit standard disclosure.

Under the new r 31.5(2), unless the court otherwise orders, the detailed rules governing menu option disclosure in r 31.5(3) to (8) apply to all multi-track claims, other than those which include a claim for personal injuries. **8.23**

Putting r 31.5(1), (2), and (7) together, the probable intention is that standard disclosure applies: **8.24**

(a) to all fast track claims unless the court directs otherwise, or the court or parties decide to dispense with or limit disclosure;

(b) to all personal injury claims, subject to the same provisos; and

(c) to non-personal injury multi-track claims if the court otherwise orders.

The way that r 31.5(2) is worded probably means the court cannot make a specific direction in any other situation (for example, applying the menu option to a fast track claim or a personal injuries claim). It seems to say that the menu option is only available in multi-track claims (other than personal injuries claims), with the **8.25**

---

[34] PD 31B, para 30(7).
[35] PD 31B, paras 31 and 32.
[36] PD 31B, para 33.
[37] PD 31B, para 36.

power to order otherwise being limited to taking cases out of the menu option. However, the wording is not entirely free from doubt.

8.26 No changes are made to the means of giving standard disclosure, making reasonable searches etc.

8.27 Small claims track cases remain outside Part 31[38] and so in these cases standard disclosure does not apply. Instead, small claims directions usually provide for advance provision of copies of the documents on which each party intends to rely.[39]

K. MENU OPTION DISCLOSURE

8.28 In non-personal injuries multi-track claims, menu option disclosure applies unless the court otherwise orders.[40] To the extent that the documents to be disclosed are electronic, the provisions of PD 31B also apply.[41] Menu option disclosure takes place in three stages:

Disclosure report

8.29 Not less than 14 days before the first CMC each party must file and serve a disclosure report[42] together with its electronic documents questionnaires if these have been exchanged under PD 31B.[43] A disclosure report must be verified by a statement of truth[44] and must:

(a) describe briefly what documents exist or may exist that are or may be relevant to the matters in issue in the case;

(b) describe where and with whom those documents are or may be located;

(c) in the case of electronic documents, describe how those documents are stored;

(d) estimate the broad range of costs that could be involved in giving standard disclosure in the case, including the costs of searching for and disclosing any electronically stored documents. This ties in with costs budgeting;[45] and

(e) state which of the directions under r 31.5(6) or (7) are to be sought.

---

[38] CPR, r 31.1(2).
[39] CPR, r 27.4(3)(a)(i).
[40] CPR, r 31.5(2).
[41] CPR, r 31.5(9).
[42] CPR, r 31.5(3).
[43] CPR, r 31.5(4).
[44] CPR, r 31.5(3).
[45] See 6.18.

Discussion to agree proposal for disclosure

Not less than seven days before the first CMC the parties must, at a meeting or **8.30**
by telephone, discuss and seek to agree a proposal in relation to disclosure that
meets the overriding objective.[46] A similar discussion must also be held on any
other occasion as the court may direct.[47]

Any agreed proposal should be filed at court. If the parties agree proposals for **8.31**
the scope of disclosure which the court considers are appropriate in all the circumstances, the court may approve them without a hearing and give directions
in the terms proposed.[48]

CMC disclosure orders

Unless disclosure directions have been made without a hearing,[49] at the first or **8.32**
any subsequent CMC the court will decide on the appropriate orders to make
about disclosure. It will do so having regard to the overriding objective and the
need to limit disclosure to that which is necessary to deal with the case justly.[50]
The menu of orders available under CPR, r 31.5(7), comprises:

(a) an order dispensing with disclosure;

(b) an order that a party disclose the documents on which it relies, and at the
same time request any specific disclosure it requires from any other party;

(c) an order that directs, where practicable, the disclosure to be given by each
party on an issue by issue basis;

(d) an order that each party disclose any documents which it is reasonable to
suppose may contain information which enables that party to advance its
own case or to damage that of any other party, or which leads to an inquiry
which has either of those consequences;

(e) an order that a party give standard disclosure;

(f) any other order in relation to disclosure that the court considers
appropriate.

The courts are likely to be heavily influenced by the costs budgets filed by the **8.33**
parties in deciding which type of order from the above menu is most suitable for
the case in hand. The order made at the first CMC sets the tone for the future
conduct of the case, and can have a pivotal effect on the overall costs of the
claim. It is therefore essential that great care is taken over developing proposals
and orders for disclosure.

---

[46] CPR, r 31.5(5).
[47] CPR, r 31.5(5).
[48] CPR, r 31.5(6).
[49] CPR, r 31.5(6).
[50] CPR, r 31.5(7).

Documents on which a party intends to rely

8.34 There have been technical cases on what is meant by the documents on which a party relies.[51] This concept is probably restricted to documents relied upon in support of that party's affirmative case or to rebut the case advanced by the other side. The fact a party does not intend to adduce a document as part of its evidence at trial is probably conclusive that the document does not fall into r 31.6(a).[52] Rule 31.6(a) does not cover documents that may be referred to as a shield in cross-examination.[53]

Train of inquiry documents

8.35 CPR, r 31.5(7)(d), allows the court to make an order for disclosure of train of inquiry documents, for which see 8.03.

Key of the warehouse order

8.36 CPR, r 31.5(7)(f), allows the court to make any other order in relation to disclosure that the court considers appropriate. Sir Rupert Jackson said that this could be used, for example, to make a 'key of the warehouse' order.[54] Such an order requires each party to hand over all its documents after removing any privileged documents, and the other side can then choose which documents it wishes to use in the litigation. Such an order reverses the usual approach of the disclosing party sifting its own documents and deciding which documents are to be disclosed to the other side. Instead, each party devotes its resources to selecting the documents it wants to use from the stock of documents held by the other parties.

8.37 Such an order is only likely to be an efficient way of proceeding in large cases, and probably only when there are not too many parties. In multi-party claims the usual approach to disclosure has the merit of needing to conduct a sifting of all the documentation of a party only once.

8.38 In cases with large numbers of documents the risks of inadvertent disclosure of privileged material is substantially greater if a key of the warehouse order is made. Sir Rupert Jackson suggested that such an order should include a proviso to the effect: 'Any disclosure of privileged documents shall not amount to waiver of privilege in the documents disclosed.'[55]

Attendance at the CMC

8.39 The *Final Report* included a draft of the proposed r 31.5A[56] which included a requirement that the solicitor or other person who will have conduct of giving

---

[51] CPR, r 31.5(7)(b). The phrase also features in r 31.6(a).
[52] *Shah v HSBC Private Bank (UK) Ltd* [2011] EWCA Civ 1154, [2012] Lloyd's Rep FC 105.
[53] *Favor Easy Management Ltd v Wu* [2010] EWCA Civ 1630, [2011] 1 WLR 1803 at [22].
[54] 7th Implementation Lecture, para 4.7.
[55] 7th Implementation Lecture, para 4.8.
[56] See 8.12 and 8.14.

disclosure for a party should be present at the first CMC.[57] While such a require-ment does apply in relation to the person who signs any electronic disclosure questionnaire,[58] there is no similar provision in the new CPR, r 31.5, in force from 1 April 2013. Sir Rupert Jackson is of the view that this is a matter of pro-fessional conduct, and that solicitors should take seriously the need to have the relevant person present at the first CMC.[59]

Disclosure directions

8.40 The court may at any point give directions as to how disclosure is to be given,[60] and in particular may direct:

(a) what searches are to be undertaken, of where, for what, in respect of which time periods and by whom, and the extent of any search for electronically stored documents;

(b) whether lists of documents are required;

(c) how and when the disclosure statement is to be given;

(d) in what format documents are to be disclosed (and whether any identifica-tion is required);

(e) what is required in relation to documents that once existed but no longer exist; and

(f) whether disclosure shall take place in stages.

---

[57] *Final Report*, ch 37, para 3.11.
[58] PD 31B, para 16.
[59] 7th Implementation Lecture, paras 4.4 and 4.5.
[60] CPR, r 31.5(8).

9

EXPERTS

A. INTRODUCTION

9.01 CPR, Part 35, was being reviewed by the Civil Justice Council and the Civil Procedure Rule Committee at the same time as Sir Rupert Jackson was conducting the Civil Litigation Costs Review. Amendments to CPR, Part 35, and PD 35 were made as a result, which came into force on 1 October 2009. Those amendments were warmly welcomed in the *Final Report*, particularly the change to r 35.6(1) to the effect that written questions to experts must be proportionate.[1]

9.02 While some of the evidence referred to in the *Final Report* raised criticisms over, for example, the length of some experts' reports and a failure to adhere to the limits of expert evidence,[2] the overall view was that the existing rules on experts are about right. A very sensible view was expressed by the Council of Her Majesty's Circuit Judges:[3]

Either they are necessary or they are not. If they are, then they have to be paid their market price, which, in the case of eminent people, may be considerable. As has now been recognised, it is not fair to the parties to try to force them to a single expert in many situations, and this tendency in fast track cases can in effect lead to trial by expert, not by

---

[1] *Final Report*, ch 38, para 1.4.
[2] As set out in cases such as *Liddell v Middleton* [1996] PIQR P36 (see 9.08).
[3] Quoted in the *Final Report*, ch 38, para 3.5.

Judge. However, it is frequently the case that parties are often anxious to assemble a larger range of experts than may actually be needed for fair determination of the issues, and this can be dealt with by judicial case management. Sensible trial management, encouraging agreement for example that experts be heard back to back as early in the trial as possible can also save significant sums in attendance fees.

B. ADMISSIBILITY OF EXPERT EVIDENCE

9.03 The Civil Evidence Act 1972, s 3(1), provides:

> Subject to any rules of court … where a person is called as a witness in any civil proceedings, his opinion on any relevant matter on which he is qualified to give expert evidence, shall be admissible in evidence.

Requirements

9.04 For expert evidence to be admissible in civil proceedings, the following requirements must be satisfied:

(a) there must be a matter which is outside the ordinary experience of the tribunal of fact;[4]

(b) it must be a matter on which there is a recognized body of expertise governed by accepted rules and principles;

(c) the witness put forward by the party seeking to rely on expert evidence must be suitably qualified to give expert testimony on the subject; and

(d) the party seeking to rely on the expert's evidence must comply with the relevant rules of court under CPR, Part 35, including obtaining a direction granting permission to rely on the expert's evidence at trial under r 35.4(1).[5]

9.05 Greater latitude is given in small claims track cases, where the strict rules of evidence do not apply.[6]

Matter outside the ordinary experience of the judge

9.06 One of the concerns raised in the *Final Report* was a tendency to instruct experts when expert evidence is not permitted under the law of evidence. As seen above,[7] expert evidence is not admissible unless it addresses a matter of art or science beyond the experience of the tribunal of fact. Medical, engineering, valuation,

---

[4] See 9.06.
[5] See 9.11.
[6] CPR, r 27.8(3).
[7] At 9.04.

and accountancy issues are common examples. The rule is that if the matter is outside the ordinary experience of the tribunal of fact, expert evidence is admissible, and the converse is also true, that the tribunal of fact cannot reach a decision on that matter without the assistance of an expert because the court needs to act on evidence.

As a result, expert evidence is not usually admitted on questions of credibility **9.07** of a witness, even where the witness under consideration is a child.[8] Although an employment consultant may give expert evidence on the employment opportunities in an area, and the claimant's prospects of finding work, expert evidence is not admissible on a claimant's motivation for finding work.[9] In *esure Insurance Ltd v Direct Line Insurance plc*[10] permission was refused to call an expert to give evidence about consumers' confusion over trademarks as the tribunal could form its own view.

Accident reconstruction experts were particularly referred to in the *Final* **9.08** *Report*.[11] Such an expert is permitted to give scientific evidence based on physical evidence of the road layout, vehicle positions, skid marks, and the positions of debris, gouge, and paint marks, and from that evidence to deduce minimum speeds and movements of the vehicles. However, such an expert is not permitted to analyse the witness statements and to draw conclusions as to what the drivers did, whether they should have seen each other, or taken avoiding action, as these are matters on which the trial judge does not need expert assistance.[12]

In ordinary road traffic whiplash injuries cases there is no need for expert evi- **9.09** dence on causation.[13] It is only if the defendant contends that the nature of the collision, for example, at very low speed, makes it very unlikely that any injury was suffered in the accident, that medical evidence dealing with causation will be necessary.

C. *FINAL REPORT* RECOMMENDATIONS ON EXPERTS

There were two recommendations on expert evidence in the *Final Report*: **9.10**

(a) CPR, Part 35, or PD 35 should be amended so as to require that a party seeking permission to adduce expert evidence must provide the court with an estimate of the costs of that evidence.[14]

---

[8] *Re N (A Minor) (Sexual Abuse: Video Evidence)* [1997] 1 WLR 153, but contrast *Re M and R (Minors) (Sexual Abuse: Expert Evidence)* [1996] 4 All ER 239.

[9] *Larby v Thurgood* [1993] ICR 66.

[10] [2008] EWCA Civ 842, [2008] RPC 34.

[11] *Final Report*, ch 38, para 3.1.

[12] *Liddell v Middleton* [1996] PIQR P36.

[13] *Casey v Cartwright* [2006] EWCA Civ 1280, [2007] 2 All ER 78, explaining *Kearsley v Klarfeld* [2005] EWCA Civ 1510, [2006] 2 All ER 303.

[14] *Final Report*, recommendation 79.

(b) The procedure developed in Australia, known as 'concurrent evidence', should be piloted in cases where all parties consent. If the results of the pilot are positive, consideration should be given to amending CPR, Part 35, to provide for use of that procedure in appropriate cases.[15]

D. ESTIMATE OF COSTS OF EXPERT EVIDENCE

9.11 *Final Report* recommendation 79 on requiring an estimate of the cost of proposed expert evidence when seeking permission to rely on it under CPR, r 35.4(1), complements the requirements on costs budgeting discussed in chapter 6. This has been implemented by making some simple amendments to r 35.4, together with some other amendments aimed at focusing expert evidence. As from 1 April 2013, r 35.4(1) and (2) now read:

(1) No party may call an expert or put in evidence an expert's report without the court's permission.
(2) When parties apply for permission they must provide an estimate of the costs of the proposed expert evidence and identify—

(a) the field in which expert evidence is required and the issues which the expert evidence will address; and

(b) where practicable, the name of the proposed expert.

9.12 The relevant amendment is the added requirement in r 35.4(2) to provide an estimate of the costs of the proposed expert evidence. Sir Rupert Jackson expressed the hope[16] that this would not cause any additional work or expense because it is inconceivable that any party would wish to instruct an expert witness without first obtaining an estimate of the expert's fees. Indeed, this is broadly required already in the list of terms of engagement that should be agreed at the outset when instructing an expert.[17]

E. FOCUSING EXPERT EVIDENCE

9.13 Sir Rupert Jackson came to the conclusion, in the light of experience, that a modest sum spent by the parties on case management at an early stage of proceedings would avoid unnecessary expenditure on experts' fees at a later stage. Amendments made to CPR, r 35.4(2) and (3), require the parties to identify the issues that proposed expert evidence will address. This should assist in focusing the expert evidence, which should mean it is confined within a narrower

---

[15] *Final Report*, recommendation 80.
[16] 4th Implementation Lecture, para 3.3.
[17] PD 35, para 7.2.

ambit and should keep costs down. This in turn should help in preparing costs budgets,[18] because there will be greater certainty over what the experts will be covering in their reports.

The revised CPR, r 35.4(2), has been set out at 9.11. In its amended form r 35.4(3) provides: 9.14

If permission is granted it shall be in relation only to the expert named or the field identified under paragraph (2). The order granting permission may specify the issues which the expert evidence should address.

The amendments: 9.15

(a) add (in r 35.4(2)(a)) the requirement to identify the issues which the expert evidence will address; and

(b) add (in r 35.4(3)) the power to specify, in the order granting permission, the issues which the expert evidence should address.

Paragraphs (3A) and (4) of r 35.4 remain unchanged. Paragraph (3A) deals with claims on the small claims and fast tracks, and says that any permission given for expert evidence on these tracks will normally permit only one expert on a particular issue. Rule 35.4(4) enables the court to limit the amount of a party's expert's fees and expenses that may be recovered from any other party.   9.16

F. CONCURRENT EXPERT EVIDENCE

In the *Final Report* Sir Rupert Jackson said[19] that a number of experts, practitioners, and judges have expressed support for the use of concurrent evidence in appropriate cases. Concurrent evidence has been used for both factual and expert evidence in arbitrations for many years.[20] It is also known as witness conferencing, or even colloquially as 'hot-tubbing'.   9.17

Actual practice varies. Typically, the parties will draw up a list of issues or questions to be canvassed with the witnesses at the hearing. At the hearing, the evidence of a number of witnesses will be taken simultaneously. Normally, the tribunal takes the lead in asking questions. The tribunal will have regard to the list (if any) drawn up in advance, but is not bound to those questions. Each witness is asked the same or similar questions. Witnesses are given the opportunity both to respond to the tribunal and to comment on the answers from the other witnesses. Legal representatives for the parties are then given the opportunity to ask their own questions. As much of the ground will have been covered in the questions asked by the tribunal, the expectation is that the parties will not   9.18

---

[18] See 6.18.

[19] *Final Report*, ch 38, para 3.23.

[20] See, for example, *Russell on Arbitration,* 23rd edn (London: Sweet & Maxwell 2007).

engage in traditional cross-examination. It is felt to be particularly effective in valuation and similar disputes. It tends to be highly regarded by judges and arbitrators, less so by advocates.

Manchester pilot

9.19 A concurrent evidence procedure was piloted on a voluntary basis in the Manchester specialist courts (the Mercantile Court, Technology and Construction Court, and Manchester Chancery Court) in 2011. Guidelines were drawn up which dealt with identifying suitable cases, pre-trial procedures, and how the evidence would be taken at the trial.

9.20 Under the pilot, prior to the trial the parties were required to produce an agreed agenda for taking the concurrent evidence. This was to contain a numbered list of the issues on which the experts disagreed following their discussion and joint statement produced under CPR, r 35.12. When they were called at the trial the experts were sworn or affirmed, and took their places at the witness table. The judge would then identify to the experts any significant factual matters that had come out at the trial which might affect their evidence. The judge would then take the experts through the issues on the agenda.

9.21 In relation to each agenda item, the judge would initiate the discussion by asking the witnesses in turn for their views. Once the expert had expressed a view, the judge would ask follow-up questions, and would then invite the other expert to comment or ask his or her own questions. The process would be repeated for each expert. Counsel would then ask their questions. Finally, the judge would summarize the experts' respective positions, and would ask them to confirm or correct the summary.

9.22 A preliminary report on the Manchester pilot[21] was based on a small sample of three cases. The preliminary view was to the effect that the main benefits of the concurrent evidence procedure were to be found in the efficiency of the process, the ease with which differences of views could be examined and assessed.[22] Professor Genn commented that the procedure encouraged representatives, experts, and the judge to focus on the issues prior to the trial and to identify areas of disagreement.

9.23 Counsel seemed to think that the process was less rigorous than traditional cross-examination, while the experts, the judiciary, and solicitors were divided in their opinions. It was also unclear whether there were any costs savings in adopting the procedure.[23]

---

[21] By Professor Dame Hazel Genn (January 2012), available at <http://www.judiciary.gov.uk>.
[22] At para 30 of the report.
[23] At paras 31 to 33 of the report.

Amendment to permit concurrent evidence

Building on the Manchester pilot, new paras 11.1 to 11.4 have been added to PD **9.24**
35 with effect from 1 April 2013. These provide:

11.1 At any stage in the proceedings the court may direct that some or all of the experts
from like disciplines shall give their evidence concurrently. The following procedure shall
then apply.

11.2 The court may direct that the parties agree an agenda for the taking of concurrent
evidence, based upon the areas of disagreement identified in the experts' joint statements
made pursuant to r 35.12.

11.3 At the appropriate time the relevant experts will each take the oath or affirm.
Unless the court orders otherwise, the experts will then address the items on the agenda
in the manner set out in paragraph 11.4.

11.4 In relation to each issue on the agenda, and subject to the judge's discretion to
modify the procedure—

(1) the judge may initiate the discussion by asking the experts, in turn, for their views.
Once an expert has expressed a view the judge may ask questions about it. At one or
more appropriate stages when questioning a particular expert, the judge may invite
the other expert to comment or to ask that expert's own questions of the first expert;

(2) after the process set out in (1) has been completed for all the experts, the parties' representatives may ask questions of them. While such questioning may be designed to
test the correctness of an expert's view, or seek clarification of it, it should not cover
ground which has been fully explored already. In general a full cross-examination or
re-examination is neither necessary nor appropriate; and

(3) after the process set out in (2) has been completed, the judge may summarise the
experts' different positions on the issue and ask them to confirm or correct that summary.

Suitable cases for concurrent evidence

Sir Rupert Jackson said concurrent evidence would be suitable in many cases **9.25**
where there are opposing reports from experts in the same field.[24] Interestingly,
in the 4th Implementation Lecture Sir Rupert uses the phrase 'reputable experts'.
This is because concurrent evidence is a means of getting to the heart of an issue
with the assistance of experts who are cooperating with the tribunal of fact with
that in view. Less reputable experts may be better evaluated through traditional
cross-examination. There is no restriction on the type of case where concurrent evidence may be useful. However, Sir Rupert mentioned that the procedure
should not be attempted unless the judge has time to master the expert reports
properly.

---

[24] 4th Implementation Lecture, para 4.5.

10

COSTS

A. INTRODUCTION

10.01　As Lord Neuberger of Abbotsbury MR has said,[1] excess litigation cost has for too long been an endemic and unwelcome feature of the civil justice system. Problems that had to be addressed by the Civil Litigation Costs Review were not limited to the actual costs of individual cases, but were complicated by changes to the funding system, and what Sir Rupert Jackson has called the 'costs war'. Satellite litigation over costs has burgeoned over the years. It was described by Latham LJ in *Times Newspapers Ltd v Burstein*[2] as 'a growth industry, and one that is a blot on the civil justice system'. Satellite litigation was identified by Lord Neuberger[3] as one of three main causes for the failure of the Woolf reforms to reduce litigation costs. The other two were failing to implement the full package of reforms, and the lack of success, following the introduction of the CPR, in effecting a full culture change in the approach to case management.

10.02　Sir Rupert Jackson has emphasized that the 109 recommendations in the *Final Report* are designed to bring down litigation costs and promote access to justice

---

[1] 14th Implementation Lecture, para 5.
[2] [2002] EWCA Civ 1739, [2003] 1 Costs LR 111 at [29].
[3] 9th Implementation Lecture, para 4.

for all participants.[4] He summarized the main components of the reforms, so far as they apply to personal injuries claims, as:

(a) ending the recoverability of additional liabilities under conditional fee agreements (CFAs), and reverting to the form of CFAs which existed before April 2000;[5]

(b) including a cap on the success fee at 25 per cent of damages excluding damages in respect of future loss;[6]

(c) increasing general damages by 10 per cent;[7]

(d) enhancing damages by a further 10 per cent as a reward for effective claimant's Part 36 offers;[8]

(e) banning referral fees;[9] and

(f) introducing costs protection for claimants in the form of qualified one-way costs shifting (QOCS).[10]

For these measures to work, it is also necessary to keep the costs of litigation down to proportionate levels. This is in the public interest not only in personal injuries claims, but across the whole of the civil justice system. Justice that cannot be afforded is a denial of justice. Proportionality is also considered in this chapter, together with the reform of the costs rules set out in CPR, Parts 44 to 48, as in force from 1 April 2013, and related practice directions. **10.03**

The way it was put by the Ministry of Justice[11] was that: **10.04**

These civil justice reforms will restore a much needed sense of proportion and fairness to the existing regime, not by denying access to justice, but by returning fair balance to the system. The reforms will also help businesses and other defendants who have to spend too much time and money dealing with avoidable litigation, actual or threatened. Substantial unnecessary costs will be removed from the system, leading to significant savings to defendants.

B. *FINAL REPORT* RECOMMENDATIONS ON COSTS

In a sense, all 109 recommendations in the *Final Report* relate to costs. A substantial number of the recommendations are about funding, case management, and generally keeping the costs of litigation under control. These are considered **10.05**

---

4 1st Implementation Lecture.
5 See 4.22.
6 See 4.27.
7 See chapter 14.
8 See 11.29.
9 See 4.59 to 4.61.
10 See 10.07.
11 Full Package of Reforms (Ministry of Justice, 20 November 2012).

elsewhere in this book. The recommendations specifically about costs orders and the assessment of costs include:

(a) 'Proportionate costs' should be defined in the Civil Procedure Rules (CPR) by reference to sums in issue, value of non-monetary relief, complexity of litigation, conduct, and any wider factors, such as reputation or public importance; and the test of proportionality should be applied on a global basis.[12]

(b) When striking the balance between the need for predictability and the need for simplicity, the Rule Committee, the Ministry of Justice drafting team, and the authors of practice directions, protocols, and court guides should accord higher priority in future to the goal of simplicity.[13]

(c) There should be no further increases in civil court fees, save for increases which are in line with the Retail Price Index rate of inflation. All receipts from civil court fees should be ploughed back into the civil justice system.[14]

(d) The common law indemnity principle should be abrogated.[15]

(e) The Advisory Committee on Civil Costs should be disbanded and a Costs Council should be established.[16]

(f) The recoverable costs of cases in the fast track should be fixed.[17]

(g) A regime of QOCS should be introduced for personal injury cases.[18]

(h) Various recommendations on costs management.[19]

(i) If any judge at the end of a hearing within PD 43–48, para 13.2,[20] considers that he or she lacks the time or the expertise to assess costs summarily (either at that hearing or on paper afterwards), then the judge should order a substantial payment on account of costs and direct detailed assessment.[21]

(j) A new format of bills of costs should be devised, which will be more informative and capable of yielding information at different levels of generality.[22]

(k) A package of measures to improve detailed assessment proceedings should be adopted.[23]

---

[12] *Final Report*, recommendation 1.
[13] *Final Report*, recommendation 2.
[14] *Final Report*, recommendation 3.
[15] *Final Report*, recommendation 4.
[16] *Final Report*, recommendation 5.
[17] *Final Report*, recommendation 18.
[18] *Final Report*, recommendation 19.
[19] *Final Report*, recommendations 89 to 92 considered in chapter 6.
[20] Now PD 44, para 9.2.
[21] *Final Report*, recommendation 104.
[22] *Final Report*, recommendation 106.
[23] *Final Report*, recommendation 108.

Some key recommendations are not being adopted. The most prominent are the **10.06** abolition of the indemnity principle;[24] the formation of a Costs Council;[25] and introducing fixed litigation costs (not just fixed trial costs) in fast track claims.[26] The extent to which omitting these measures from the package of reforms has the effect of undermining the overall success of the Jackson reforms is a matter of concern.

C. QUALIFIED ONE-WAY COSTS SHIFTING (QOCS)

Unless the client has before-the-event (BTE) insurance (such as in a motor **10.07** insurance policy or household insurance), the abolition of the recoverability of after-the-event (ATE) insurance premiums will mean there is little incentive for litigants to insure their risk of having to pay the other side's costs if the claim is unsuccessful. There will be nothing to stop a litigant from taking out ATE cover, but experience has found that ATE premiums are often prohibitively expensive. Under the existing system, a litigant reasonably confident of winning, but aware there is a risk of losing, is often prepared to pay a substantial ATE premium because, when the claim succeeds, the premium is repaid under the costs order by the losing party.

Sir Rupert Jackson recognized that removing CFA success fees, and abolish- **10.08** ing the recoverability of ATE insurance premiums, brought the balance too far against claimants, and particularly individual claimants. Hence his recommendation for the introduction of QOCS, together with his recommendation for an uplift of 10 per cent in damages in personal injuries claims.[27]

Nature of QOCS

'Costs shifting' is a formal expression describing the usual rule that costs follow the **10.09** event or that costs are otherwise paid by one side to the other. The costs incurred by the successful party are 'shifted' to the losing party under the usual costs order. QOCS adjusts this traditional position by saying that the usual costs order should only be made in favour of one party, typically the claimant. This means that if the claimant wins, the defendant should be ordered to pay the claimant's costs in the usual way. However, if the claimant loses, QOCS means that while the claimant remains liable to pay its own lawyers' costs, the claimant will not also have to pay the successful defendant's costs under the usual order for costs to follow the event.

Under QOCS, a claimant therefore has a valuable protection against paying **10.10** the defendant's costs. As a result, there should be no need for claimants who will

---

[24] *Final Report*, recommendation 4.
[25] *Final Report*, recommendation 5.
[26] *Final Report*, recommendation 18.
[27] See chapter 14.

have the benefit of QOCS to take out ATE insurance, because normally they will not be required to pay the defendant's costs even if they lose.

10.11 QOCS is 'qualified' one-way costs shifting, because this protection to the claimant is not absolute. It is recognized that if it was an invariable rule, it would be open to abuse, with some claimants indulging in costs-inflating practices secure in the knowledge they would never be brought to account. Accordingly, under the QOCS scheme that is being introduced there are exceptions for different types of misbehaviour, and no protection against the enforcement of adverse costs orders against damages and interest recovered in the proceedings.

Government response on QOCS

10.12 Following the publication of the *Final Report* there was a public consultation exercise on implementing the proposed reforms. This was followed by the publication of the *Government Response*.

10.13 The *Government Response* endorsed the introduction of QOCS in personal injuries and clinical negligence claims,[28] not least because defendants in these cases are often well-resourced, so there is an inequality of arms. However, there would be two exceptions:

(a) Misbehaviour. In cases where the claimant has acted fraudulently, frivolously or unreasonably in pursuing proceedings, it was felt that costs protection should be lost.

(b) Financial eligibility. The government's view was that very wealthy claimants should not have the benefit of costs protection under QOCS.

Categories of case to be covered

10.14 As from 1 April 2013, QOCS will apply to personal injury and clinical negligence cases. Sir Rupert Jackson primarily recommended QOCS for personal injuries claims, but also said that it should be considered for other categories of claim, particularly those where traditionally there is an inequality of arms between claimants and defendants,[29] and proposed that QOCS should be applied to defamation claims.[30]

10.15 The *Government Response* stated[31] that QOCS will not be extended beyond personal injury and clinical negligence cases at this stage, so the normal costs shifting rules will continue to apply in other cases.[32]

---

[28] *Government Response*, para 11.

[29] *Final Report*, Executive Summary, para 2.7.

[30] *Final Report*, recommendation 65.

[31] *Government Response*, para 11.

[32] Subject to the transitional provisions described in chapter 2. These include continuing with the recoverability regime for CFA success fees and other additional liabilities in defamation and breach of privacy claims, see 2.19.

Misbehaviour

The rationale for the proposal in the *Government Response* that QOCS would **10.16** not apply in the case of misbehaviour is that in such cases the claimant has forfeited the right to costs protection. Drawing the categories of cases where QOCS would be lost fairly tightly should ensure that a reasonable claimant will not be at risk of paying the other side's costs on behaviour grounds.[33]

This was expanded by the Ministerial Statement of 17 July 2012.[34] This stated **10.17** that QOCS protection would be lost if:

(a) the claim is found to be fraudulent on the balance of probabilities;

(b) the claimant has failed to beat a defendant's Part 36 offer to settle; or

(c) the case has been struck out where the claim discloses no reasonable cause of action or where it is otherwise an abuse of the court's process (or is otherwise likely to obstruct the just disposal of the proceedings).

The misbehaviour exceptions as enacted are discussed at 10.34 to 10.49. **10.18**

No financial eligibility requirement

It has been pointed out that not all claimants need QOCS protection. Expensive **10.19** libel claims by wealthy individuals with 100 per cent CFA uplifts were one of the obvious abuses of the pre-Jackson system. At one stage it was proposed that QOCS would not be available to the very wealthy.[35] An obvious problem with that proposal was when and how the claimant's financial resources would be assessed for that purpose. As the financial means exception was only intended to apply to a very small number of 'very wealthy' claimants, the costs of making that assessment in all cases far outweighed its value. The Ministerial Statement of 17 July 2012 included a decision that QOCS will apply to all claimants whatever their means, so there is no financial test to determine eligibility.

No minimum payment towards the defendant's costs

It was also suggested that unsuccessful claimants who are protected by QOCS **10.20** should nevertheless be required to make a small payment towards a successful defendant's costs. The purpose of the suggestion was to prevent speculative claims. The *Government Response* stated the government would continue to discuss with stakeholders whether any such minimum payment should be payable

---

[33] *Government Response*, para 11.

[34] Ministerial Statement by the Parliamentary Under-Secretary of State, Ministry of Justice (Jonathan Djanogly) on 17 July 2012 on the Implementation of Part 2 of the Legal Aid, Sentencing and Punishment of Offenders Act 2012: Civil Litigation Funding and Costs. In this book referred to as 'the Ministerial Statement of 17 July 2012'.

[35] *Government Response*, para 11.

by a losing claimant.[36] However, this suggestion was rejected in the Ministerial Statement of 17 July 2012, which confirmed that, subject to the costs recovery provisions,[37] there is to be no minimum payment by a losing claimant, so there will be no contribution towards defendants' costs.

D. QOCS FROM 1 APRIL 2013

10.21 No primary legislation was required for the implementation of QOCS, which was within existing rule-making powers.[38]

Cases covered by QOCS

10.22 QOCS will not apply to proceedings in which the claimant has entered into a pre-commencement funding arrangement.[39] This means that if the claimant, for example, entered into a CFA before 1 April 2013, QOCS will not apply.

10.23 The provisions on QOCS[40] apply to proceedings which include a claim for damages:

(a) for personal injuries;

(b) under the Fatal Accidents Act 1976; or

(c) which arises out of death or personal injury and survives for the benefit of an estate by virtue of the Law Reform (Miscellaneous Provisions) Act 1934, s 1(1).[41]

10.24 Applications for disclosure before proceedings start[42] are excluded from the scope of QOCS.[43]

10.25 There is an extended definition of 'claimant' for the purposes of the rules on QOCS,[44] namely:

In this Section, 'claimant' means a person bringing a claim to which this Section applies or an estate on behalf of which such a claim is brought, and includes a person making a counterclaim or an additional claim.

---

[36] *Government Response,* para 11.

[37] See 10.21 to 10.50.

[38] In Civil Procedure Act 1997, s 2, and by virtue of the court's jurisdiction on costs under Senior Courts Act 1981, s 51.

[39] As defined by CPR, r 48.2 (see r 44.17). Pre-commencement funding arrangements are discussed at 2.07 to 2.14.

[40] Which can be found in CPR, rr 44.14 to 44.16.

[41] CPR, r 44.13(1)

[42] Pursuant to Senior Courts Act 1981, s 33, or County Courts Act 1984, s 52, and see also CPR, r 31.16.

[43] CPR, r 44.13(1), proviso.

[44] In CPR, r 44.13(2).

This is intended to mean that it does not matter whether the personal injuries **10.26** claim is brought by an original claimant or in a defence and counterclaim or in an additional claim, such as a third-party claim, under Part 20. It probably achieves that aim by the use of the phrase 'person bringing a claim to which this Section applies',[45] being an implicit reference back to the personal injuries claims spelt out in r 44.13(1). The wording of r 44.13(2) is perhaps not as clear as it could be, and it could be taken as meaning that a defendant to a claim for personal injuries (say the claimant's employer) who brings a third-party claim against another tortfeasor (say the occupier of the premises) is a 'claimant' for the purposes of QOCS because it has made an additional claim in proceedings in which a personal injuries claim has been brought. No doubt the courts will ensure such a strained interpretation of the provision is avoided.

Effect of QOCS

One-way costs shifting is achieved by CPR, r 44.14(1), in a somewhat obscure **10.27** fashion. This provides:

Subject to rr 44.15 and 44.16, orders for costs made against a claimant may be enforced without the permission of the court but only to the extent that the aggregate amount in money terms of such orders does not exceed the aggregate amount in money terms of any orders for damages and interest made in favour of the claimant.

Claimant loses the case

If the claimant loses the case with no award of damages, the effect is that no **10.28** costs will be payable by the claimant, because the aggregate amount referred to in r 44.14(1) is nil. The rule does not prevent an adverse costs order being made against the unsuccessful claimant, but instead provides that any costs order that is made is not enforceable against the claimant. It is therefore rather like the costs protection granted to legally aided parties, and the familiar 'football pools' orders that have been made for many years (which provide that costs being ordered against an assisted party are not to be enforced without the court's permission). Although r 44.14(1) is similar to a football pools order in effect, it is not the same. Under r 44.14(1), all the court has to do is to make a normal adverse costs order against the unsuccessful claimant. The order may but need not say that it may not be enforced without the court's permission. Rule 44.14(1) then applies with the effect that (as nothing has been recovered in the litigation) nothing is payable by the claimant towards the defendant's costs. Procedures that apply in legal aid cases for seeking permission to enforce the costs order on the basis that the claimant's financial circumstances have improved do not apply, because under r 44.14(1) the financial exposure of the claimant is limited to the money award in the actual proceedings.

---

[45] CPR, r 44.13(2).

Claimant partially successful

10.29 In cases where the claimant is partially successful, CPR, r 44.14(1), operates in a slightly different way. First, the court will have to decide what costs order to make given the respective degrees of success of the parties and the other factors set out in what is now r 44.2. If the court makes a full or partial costs award in favour of the claimant, r 44.14 has no application. However, if the court makes an adverse costs order against the claimant (whether a full costs order in favour of the defendant, or a percentage costs order in favour of the defendant), r 44.14(1) applies to restrict the amount of costs that the defendant can recover from the claimant to the aggregate amount in money terms of any orders for damages and interest made in favour of the claimant. In such a case QOCS does not provide full costs protection for the claimant, because the money award may be eaten up by the costs order in favour of the defendant, but the claimant is protected in the sense that taking into account such sums as it was awarded in the case, the claimant will not have to pay anything beyond the total award to the defendant under the defendant's costs order.

Claimant fails to obtain judgment that is more advantageous
than Part 36 offer

10.30 The real reason for the byzantine wording of CPR, r 44.14(1), is to deal with split costs orders under r 36.14(2) where the defendant has made a Part 36 offer and the claimant has failed to achieve a judgment more advantageous than that offer. Assuming the claimant with the benefit of QOCS has succeeded on liability and obtained a money award, r 36.14(2) says that unless the court considers it unjust to do so, it will award costs to the claimant up to the end of the relevant period[46] and award the defendant its costs thereafter.

10.31 The two costs orders can be set off against each other.[47] The net effect, especially if the Part 36 offer was made in the early stages of the claim, is that there is often a net costs liability due from the claimant to the defendant under an order made under r 36.14(2). By virtue of r 44.14(1), that net costs liability can be enforced without permission against the awards in favour of the claimant for damages and interest, up to the extent of reducing those figures to zero.

Time for enforcing costs orders against claimants

10.32 An order for costs made against a claimant may be enforced only after the proceedings have been concluded and the costs have been assessed or agreed.[48]

---

[46] As defined by CPR, r 36.3(1)(c).
[47] CPR, r 44.12.
[48] CPR, r 44.14(2).

Credit scoring

An order for costs which is enforced only to the extent permitted by CPR, **10.33**
r 44.14(1), shall not be treated as an unsatisfied or outstanding judgment for the
purposes of any court record.[49]

Misbehaviour under CPR, Part 44, Section II

CPR, r 44.15, provides: **10.34**

Orders for costs made against the claimant may be enforced to the full extent of such
orders without the permission of the court where the proceedings have been struck out
on the grounds that—

(a) the claimant has disclosed no reasonable grounds for bringing the proceedings;

(b) the proceedings are an abuse of the court's process; or

(c) the conduct of—

    (i)   the claimant; or

    (ii) a person acting on the claimant's behalf and with the claimant's knowledge of
      such conduct,

is likely to obstruct the just disposal of the proceedings.

With respect to the Civil Procedure Rule Committee, this comes nowhere near **10.35**
implementing the idea in the *Final Report*. Claimants who lose the protection
granted by QOCS should be those who have forfeited the right to costs protection through either:

(a) advancing a fraudulent claim; or

(b) abusing the court system.

The expression used in point (b) above is deliberately not the same as the term **10.36**
'abuse of process', which is used in CPR, r 3.4(2)(b). This is because claims are
struck out regularly under r 3.4(2) for all sorts of reasons that are not blameworthy, and do not amount to abusing the civil justice system. The genesis of
the problem is no doubt the use of r 3.4(2) phraseology in the Ministerial Statement of 17 July 2012. What seems to have happened is that r 44.15 has faithfully
reproduced the wording used in that statement, but has not necessarily enacted
the intention behind it.

---

[49] CPR, r 44.14(3).

Claims that have been struck out

10.37 What CPR, r 44.15, has done is largely to replicate the wording of r 3.4(2). Adopting the same words as are used in r 3.4(2) means that the courts will inevitably apply the same principles in interpreting r 44.15 as they have done for many years in interpreting r 3.4(2).[50] It means that costs protection will be lost under r 44.15 in, among others, the following situations:

(a) Where a claim is struck out due to drafting errors by the claimant's legal representatives or the claimant if acting in person. Striking out in such cases is on the ground that the claim discloses no reasonable cause of action. It does not necessarily mean it is not a genuine claim.

(b) Where a claim is struck out on the basis that it is seeking to extend the situations where there is a duty of care, perhaps because the law is not yet ready to make the necessary extension. It would mean that many of the cases that have formulated the boundaries of the law of negligence are ones where costs protection under QOCS would not apply.

(c) Where a claim is time-barred. Time-barred claims are struck out on the basis that they are an abuse of process, because limitation is only a procedural defence, which does not determine whether there were reasonable grounds for bringing the claim. Many strike-out applications engaging the Limitation Act 1980, ss 14 and 33, are very difficult to call, and it seems bizarre that if they are successful then costs protection is lost. What is also strange is that costs protection under QOCS will not be lost under r 44.15 if, instead of the limitation point being taken on a striking-out application, it is taken as a preliminary issue, because r 44.15 only applies if the claim is struck out.

(d) A claim may be struck out as an abuse of process even if the strict rules of *res judicata* do not apply, but on the basis that the claim could and should have been brought in earlier proceedings.[51] This may be a little more blameworthy than the other examples, but the cases in this area show that often incredibly tight distinctions are made in these applications.[52]

10.38 In all these cases costs protection will be lost. However, costs protection will not be lost if instead of taking a point on a striking-out application, judgment is obtained against the claimant, either on an application for summary judgment or on the trial of a preliminary issue. Where a claim has been struck out on any of the stated grounds, an order for costs against the claimant may be enforced to the full extent of the order without the permission of the court.[53] It seems from

---

[50] And its predecessors under the Rules of the Supreme Court.
[51] *Henderson v Henderson* (1843) 3 Hare 100; *Johnson v Gore Wood & Co* [2002] 2 AC 1.
[52] For example, *Jameson v Central Electricity Generating Board* [2000] 1 AC 455.
[53] CPR, r 44.15.

the wording that there is no discretion to reimpose QOCS costs protection in these cases.

Of course there are plenty of other situations where claims are struck out[54] **10.39** where the claimant fully deserves to lose its costs protection under QOCS. Claims which are totally without merit, claims deliberately aimed at abusing the court's process, and fraudulent claims will fall into this category. A practical solution would be to adopt the first of these as being the test for automatic loss of QOCS protection under r 44.15: that costs protection is lost if a claim is struck out[55] with the court recording in the order that it considers that the claim was totally without merit.[56]

Loss of QOCS costs protection: fraudulent claims

The second problem with CPR, r 44.15, is that it only applies if the claim has **10.40** actually been struck out. Many fraudulent claims will not come within r 44.15 because it is extremely difficult to strike out a claim on the basis that it is fraudulent. The nature of such an allegation means it is rarely going to be a suitable issue to decide on an interim application, and so it will usually be left to be determined at trial. If the case proceeds through to trial, there are various reasons why it will not then be struck out even if fraud is found. In these cases the defendant may make an application for permission to remove the claimant's QOCS costs protection under r 44.16(1). For r 44.16(1) to apply the court needs to find on the balance of probabilities that the claim was fundamentally dishonest.

A common manifestation of the problem of fraudulent claims is the staged **10.41** road traffic accident, often taking place at a roundabout or road junction at relatively low speed.

Tampering with the evidence in a genuine claim has also been a problem for **10.42** a very long time. This happened in *Arrow Nominees Inc v Blackledge*,[57] where it was held that a litigant who was guilty of conduct that put the fairness of the trial in jeopardy and prevented the court from doing justice could be penalized by striking out the claim as an abuse of process. In *Arrow Nominees Inc v Blackledge*, it was persistent and flagrant fraud intended to frustrate a fair trial that made striking out appropriate.

In *Ul-Haq v Shah*,[58] the problem was that two of the claimants had genuine **10.43** claims arising out of a road traffic accident, but the third claimant was found not

---

[54] Under CPR, r 3.4(2).

[55] Under CPR, r 3.4(2).

[56] Under CPR, r 3.4(6). This could be extended to equivalent situations, such as refusing permission to appeal, striking out an appellant's notice, or dismissing an appeal that is totally without merit under r 52.10(5), (6).

[57] [2000] 2 BCLC 167.

[58] [2009] EWCA Civ 542, [2010] 1 WLR 616.

to have been in the car at all. The judge found that the first two claimants had conspired to support the fraudulent claim of the third claimant, and ordered them to pay two thirds of the defendant's costs. In *Masood v Zahoor*[59] the trial judge found that both sides attempted to deceive the court by widespread forging of documents.

10.44   In *Summers v Fairclough Homes Ltd*[60] the claimant had been injured at work. At a split trial the claimant won on liability, leaving damages to be assessed. His schedule of past and future loss and expense was formulated on the basis that he had a serious continuing injury which prevented him from returning to work, and the claim was valued at more than £800,000. Undercover surveillance evidence was then obtained which the defendant alleged showed the claimant was grossly and dishonestly exaggerating his claim. At the trial on quantum the judge found that the claimant suffered genuine, serious injuries, but that he had recovered sufficiently to be regarded as fully fit for work at about the date of the first of the surveillance tapes. The judge found that the claimant had deliberately lied to the medical experts and to the Department of Work and Pensions, had signed false statements of truth on his schedules, and had lied on oath at the hearing. A number of adverse findings were made by the judge, who also refused to draw any inferences from the evidence that would have been favourable to the claimant. Nevertheless, quantum for the injuries and losses that were genuine was assessed at £80,000.

10.45   In *Summers v Fairclough Homes Ltd* it was held that in theory a striking-out order could be made, even at the end of the trial in such a case. However, this power is likely to be used only rarely for two reasons. First, it will be more appropriate at that stage of the proceedings for the judge to make the necessary findings (probably with wide adverse inferences being drawn against the dishonest party), and for judgment to follow in the usual way.[61] Secondly, the judgment on the genuine part of the claim is a possession,[62] so should only be lost if striking out performs a legitimate aim and is a proportionate means of achieving that aim.[63]

10.46   It was held that while this was a serious case of abuse of process, it would have been wrong in principle to strike it out. Even though the claimant was guilty of persistently pursuing his case on a basis he knew to be false, he had suffered significant injuries, his award in damages reflected multiple adverse findings of fact, and he had been penalized in interest and costs. Depriving him of the award in damages would have been neither proportionate nor just.

10.47   While there are examples of actual striking-out orders being made in fraudulent claims (in which event costs protection under QOCS is lost automatically[64]),

---

[59] [2009] EWCA Civ 650, [2010] 1 WLR 746.
[60] [2012] UKSC 26, [2012] 1 WLR 2004.
[61] Lord Clarke of Stone-cum-Ebony at [43].
[62] Within the meaning of the European Convention on Human Rights, Protocol 1, art 1.
[63] Lord Clarke of Stone-cum-Ebony at [46] and [47].
[64] Under CPR, r 44.15.

this is therefore going to be unusual. In most cases of alleged fraud the court will need to conduct a hearing to decide whether the required level of dishonesty can be established to the civil standard of proof. Usually this should be done at trial,[65] but it follows from *Summers v Fairclough Homes Ltd* that it will only rarely be appropriate to strike out the claim at that stage.

Allegations of fundamental dishonesty in settled and discontinued claims

Unless there are exceptional circumstances, the court will not inquire into whether the claim was fundamentally dishonest if the proceedings have been settled.[66] **10.48**

Where a personal injuries claim has been discontinued, the effect of CPR, r 44.14(1), is that generally the claimant has costs protection under QOCS which overrides the usual costs position after a claim is discontinued.[67] However, the court may in such a case inquire into whether the claim was fundamentally dishonest under r 44.16(1), and can do so even if the notice of discontinuance has not been set aside.[68] **10.49**

Proceedings for the financial benefit of another

The court may grant permission to enforce a costs order against a claimant who would otherwise have costs protection under QOCS if the proceedings include a claim which is made for the financial benefit of another person.[69] Examples are subrogated claims and claims for credit hire,[70] but do not include the provision of personal services rendered gratuitously for things like personal care, domestic assistance etc.[71] In such a case the court may also make a non-party costs order[72] against that other person,[73] and in fact usually will do so.[74] **10.50**

E. INDEMNITY PRINCIPLE

The 'indemnity principle' is that a party cannot be liable to pay more to the other side in costs than the winner is liable to pay its own lawyers. Once it is established **10.51**

---

[65] PD 44, para 12.4(a).

[66] PD 44, para 12.4(b).

[67] CPR, r 38.6(1), provides that unless the court orders otherwise, a claimant who discontinues is liable for the costs of the defendant.

[68] PD 44, para 12.4(c).

[69] CPR, r 44.16(2).

[70] PD 44, para 12.2.

[71] PD 44, para 12.3.

[72] Senior Courts Act 1981, s 51, and CPR, r 46.2.

[73] CPR, r 44.16(3).

[74] PD 44, para 12.5.

that solicitors acted for a receiving party there is a presumption that the client is liable to pay the solicitors, and the onus is on the paying party to rebut that presumption. In order to do that it has to be shown there are no circumstances in which the solicitor would look to the client for payment.[75] Thus, if the lawyers representing the successful party have intimated that their client need 'not worry' about paying their fees, there is a prospect that the court will hold the loser has no liability in costs.[76] The importance of entering into a formal retainer with the client was emphasized by *Times Newspapers Ltd v Burstein*,[77] where the receiving party's lawyers produced evidence of a valid retainer to pay their fees. In reply the paying party produced evidence to show that the receiving party was impecunious and did not have the ability to pay his solicitors. The receiving party thus argued that the retainer was, in truth, an illegal CFA, that there was no valid retainer, and that there was no liability on the paying party to pay his lawyers. The Court of Appeal relied on the fact that there was a retainer in rejecting the receiving party's argument.

10.52   For a short time it was thought that the indemnity principle had passed into history after the decision in *Thai Trading Co v Taylor*.[78] However, subsequent developments have made it clear that the indemnity principle is still adhered to.[79]

10.53   A CFA in the prescribed form 'shall not be unenforceable'[80] as being champertous. This means that CFAs that do not comply with the requirements of Courts and Legal Services Act (CLSA) 1990, s 58,[81] are unenforceable.[82] Where a solicitor acts for an impecunious client without a CFA, if it is alleged there has been an infringement of the indemnity principle, it is necessary for the court to determine the true nature of the retainer. A similar formula is used for damages-based agreements (DBAs) in the CLSA 1990, s 58AA.[83]

Abolition of the indemnity principle

10.54   Recommendation 4 in the *Final Report* was to the effect that the common law indemnity principle should be abrogated. A great deal of the satellite litigation

---

[75] *Meretz Investments NV v ACP Ltd* [2007] EWHC 2635 (Ch), [2008] 1 Costs LR 42.
[76] *British Waterways Board v Norman* (1993) 26 HLR 232.
[77] [2002] EWCA Civ 1739, [2003] 1 Costs LR 111.
[78] [1998] QB 781.
[79] *Hughes v Kingston upon Hull City Council* [1999] QB 1193; *Awwad v Geraghty & Co* [2001] QB 570; amendments made to Solicitors' Practice Rules 1990, r 8(1), and Solicitors Act 1974, s 60(3), which provides that a client of a solicitor is not entitled to recover from any other person under an order for the payment of any costs to which a contentious business agreement relates more than the amount payable to the solicitor in respect of those costs under the agreement.
[80] CLSA1990, s 58.
[81] See 4.24.
[82] *Times Newspapers Ltd v Burstein* [2002] EWCA Civ 1739, [2003] 1 Costs LR 111.
[83] See 4.69.

on costs is based on arguments founded on the indemnity principle.[84] By finding some technical defect, a paying party may be able to persuade the court that the funding arrangement is unenforceable between the client and the legal representative. If so, applying the indemnity principle, the paying party escapes all liability for the receiving party's costs because nothing is payable to the legal representative by the client.[85] Escaping liability for costs on a technicality is very attractive for paying parties, and in almost all cases is wholly without merit.

Is legislation required to abolish the indemnity principle?

A note of doubt over whether primary legislation would be required to abolish 10.55 the indemnity principle can be seen at page 472 of the *Final Report* in the list of primary legislation required, which refers to such legislation 'as is necessary' for this purpose. Access to Justice Act 1999, s 31, amended Senior Courts Act 1981, s 51(2), by adding that rules of court may provide that the amount awarded to a party in respect of costs need not be limited to the amount that would have been payable by the party if costs had not been awarded. As amended, s 51(2) says:

Without prejudice to any general power to make rules of court, such rules may make provision for regulating matters relating to the costs of those proceedings including, in particular, prescribing scales of costs to be paid to legal or other representatives or for securing that the amount awarded to a party in respect of the costs to be paid by him to such representatives is not limited to what would have been payable by him to them if he had not been awarded costs.

The amendment made by Access to Justice Act 1999, s 31, was primarily aimed 10.56 at enabling the CPR to provide for a losing party to pay all the costs of the successful party (including any success fee) where the successful party had entered into a CFA.[86] However, its wording is sufficiently wide to permit the removal of part or even the entire operation of the indemnity principle.

While primary legislation is not required to abolish the indemnity principle 10.57 as a general principle, legislation is needed to deal specifically with CFAs and DBAs. This is because, as noted above, the primary legislation dealing with CFAs[87] and DBAs[88] adverts to the indemnity principle when it says that CFAs and DBAs that comply with the statutory criteria shall not be unenforceable.

Current position on the indemnity principle

It seems there has been next to no debate about this since the *Final Report*. For 10.58 example, abolition of the indemnity principle was not mentioned in the *Govern-*

---

[84] As mentioned in the *Final Report*, ch 4, para 3.8.
[85] For further details see the *Final Report*, ch 5.
[86] See the former CPR, r 44.3A, as in force before 1 April 2013.
[87] CLSA 1990, s 58(1).
[88] CLSA 1990, s 58AA(1).

ment Response. Primary legislation has not been passed abolishing the indemnity principle, and the power to remove it by rules of court under Senior Courts Act 1981, s 51(2), has not been exercised. It therefore remains.

10.59   In addition to CLSA 1990, ss 58 and 58AA, on CFAs and DBAs, there are occasional references in the new version of the costs rules in the CPR and practice directions to the indemnity principle. Perhaps the most prominent example is in the statement of truth required on costs budgets,[89] which commences by saying: 'The costs stated to have been incurred do not exceed the costs which my client is liable to pay in respect of such work'.

10.60   Unfortunately, it is inevitable that as the indemnity principle remains part of costs law, satellite litigation over costs will also remain.

CFA satellite litigation

10.61   As discussed at 4.22 and 4.27, amendments made by LASPO 2012, s 44, have imposed an increased number of requirements that must be complied with if a CFA in a personal injuries claim which includes a success fee is to be enforceable. This is a cause for great concern. CFAs had to comply with multiple requirements in the period up to 1 November 2005,[90] which spawned a large body of case law over whether various failures to follow the requirements rendered the funding arrangement unenforceable.

10.62   Given an increasing number of technical disputes over compliance with the secondary legislation, the only sane solution was to sweep away all the technicalities by revoking all the statutory instruments imposing additional requirements on CFAs[91] with effect from 1 November 2005. The result was that for CFAs entered into from 1 November 2005 the only requirements were the bare minimum statutory requirements set out in CLSA 1990, s 58.[92]

10.63   While this drastically reduced the number of technical points taken by paying parties seeking to avoid their liabilities under costs orders, there continued to be a stream of technical decisions reaching the Court of Appeal. An example is *Sibthorpe v Southwark London Borough Council*.[93] The claimant (the receiving party) was funded under a CFA which included an indemnity to the effect that if the claimant lost and was not covered by insurance, the solicitors would indemnify her against payment of the other side's costs. This meant the solicitors had

---

[89] PD 22, para 2.2A.

[90] Conditional Fee Agreements Regulations 2000 (SI 2000/692); Collective Conditional Fee Agreements Regulations 2000 (SI 2000/2988); Conditional Fee Agreements (Miscellaneous Amendments) Regulations 2003 (SI 2003/1240); Conditional Fee Agreements (Miscellaneous Amendments) (No 2) Regulations 2003 (SI 2003/3344).

[91] As set out in the preceding footnote. This was effected by the commendably short Conditional Fee Agreements (Revocation) Regulations 2005 (SI 2005/2305).

[92] See 4.25.

[93] [2011] EWCA Civ 25, [2011] 1 WLR 2111.

a financial interest in the litigation, and on that basis the paying party said the arrangement was champertous. It has never previously been held to be champertous to run the risk of a loss if a claim fails without any corresponding gain if the claim succeeds. Given the way in which law reform is developing in relation to funding of litigation, with a widening of the permissible methods of paying for legal services, the Court of Appeal felt that it was the wrong time to be moving in the opposite direction by increasing the reach of champerty. It was therefore held that the indemnity was not champertous, and the paying party remained liable for the claimant's costs.

Increasing the number of requirements for personal injuries CFAs with success fees substantially increases the risks of satellite litigation in this area. It is hardly meritorious. The underlying purpose of such disputes is simply to evade the normal consequences of an adverse costs order. Relying on a perceived defect in the agreement between the receiving party and its legal representative is a windfall for the paying party, and rarely if ever affects the paying party during the litigation. It distorts the balance built into the overall scheme for funding litigation, racks up further unnecessary costs, ties up judicial resources, and is a blot on the English civil justice system. **10.64**

Third-party funding satellite litigation

As discussed at 4.75, *Arkin v Borchard Lines Ltd (Nos 2 and 3)*[94] is widely regarded as having established that a properly structured litigation funding agreement (LFA) does not infringe the rules against maintenance and champerty. LFAs were regarded as supporting the public policy of ensuring access to justice, and will be effective provided suitable safeguards are included in the LFA. **10.65**

The problem in the future may be that, in the continued absence of primary legislation regulating third-party funding, the position may not be nearly as secure as a cursory look at *Arkin v Borchard Lines Ltd (Nos 2 and 3)* might suggest. The primary argument in the case was over the basis, if any, on which the third-party funder should be required to meet the costs of the other side if the case was unsuccessful. Although reference is made to whether the third-party funding agreement was valid or champertous, really neither side had any interest in saying that it was unenforceable. The funder obviously did not want a ruling striking down its entire third-party funding business. The successful party, in practical terms, wanted its costs met by the third-party funder rather than the litigant. A head-on challenge may not meet with such a favourable result for third-party funders. **10.66**

The actual point in the case also shows the scope for satellite litigation in claims with third-party funding. As adverse costs orders against third-party funders are a variety of non-party costs order under Senior Courts Act 1981, **10.67**

---

[94] [2005] EWCA Civ 655, [2005] 1 WLR 3055.

s 51, they necessarily involve balancing a range of factors, which in turn depend on investigating the actual arrangement with the third-party funder. There is plenty of potential future satellite litigation in this area.

F. PROPORTIONALITY

10.68 Proportionality was intended to be a central concept of the CPR. It was included as a component of the overriding objective[95] and was the only component within that rule to be broken down into its constituent parts. The profession has therefore known since 1998 that dealing with cases justly includes ensuring, so far as practicable, that they are dealt with in ways that are proportionate:

(a) to the amount of money involved;

(b) to the importance of the case;

(c) to the complexity of the issues; and

(d) to the financial position of each party.

10.69 Proportionality should have been an important consideration throughout the life of a case, particularly when case management directions were being made, and costs being incurred. Whether the successful party had in fact conducted the case in a proportionate manner should have been called into scrutiny on any assessment of costs, which, if they were payable on the standard basis, would only be allowed if they were reasonably incurred, reasonable in amount, and proportionate to the matters in issue.[96]

10.70 So much for theory. Practice was quite another matter.

Old test

10.71 In *Lownds v Home Office*,[97] it was held that on a standard-basis assessment where proportionality is in issue, a preliminary judgment on the proportionality of the costs as a whole should be made at the outset. If the judge concluded that the overall costs were not disproportionate, the assessment took place applying the reasonableness tests in the old CPR, r 44.4(2). If the judge concluded the overall costs may be disproportionate, each item would be scrutinized applying two tests (reasonableness and necessity), which might lead to some further costs being disallowed.

10.72 The key to proportionality under the old CPR provisions[98] was to be found in the former PD 43–48, para 11.2, which stated that: 'In any proceedings there will

---

[95] CPR, r 1.1(2)(c).

[96] Former CPR, r 44.4(1) and (2)(a), as in force before 1 April 2013.

[97] [2002] EWCA Civ 365, [2002] 1 WLR 2450.

[98] *Lownds v Home Office* [2002] EWCA Civ 365, [2002] 1 WLR 2450 at [26] to [28].

be costs which will inevitably be incurred and which are *necessary* for the successful conduct of the case' (emphasis added). If the appropriate conduct of the proceedings made costs necessary then the requirement of proportionality did not prevent recovery of those costs. The threshold required to meet necessity was higher than that of reasonableness, but it was still a standard which a competent solicitor should be able to achieve without undue difficulty,[99] with the courts being careful not to impose too high a standard with the benefit of hindsight. Solicitors were not obliged to conduct litigation at uneconomic rates, which meant that in modest claims the proportion of costs was likely to be higher than in larger claims.[100] The time spent on an issue at trial may not be an accurate guide to the amount of time properly spent in preparing that issue for trial.[101] The court would have regard to whether the appropriate level of fee earner and counsel were employed, whether offers to settle had been made, whether unnecessary experts had been instructed, and various other matters. Regard also had to be given to the amount which it was reasonable for the receiving party to believe might be recovered.

Ineffectiveness of *Lownds* in controlling costs

Willis v Nicholson[102] was a road traffic accident case in which the claimant was knocked off his motorcycle suffering serious injuries, resulting in a claim said to have a value of £5 million. A costs capping order was sought. Costs estimates produced by the claimant at a point a few months before trial showed past costs of about £500,000, with future costs estimated at £459,000. Buxton LJ[103] explained how ineffective the principles developed under the CPR had been in controlling civil costs: **10.73**

The very high costs of civil litigation in England and Wales is a matter of concern not merely to the parties in a particular case, but for the litigation system as a whole. While disputants should be given every encouragement to settle their differences without going to court, that encouragement should not include the making of litigation prohibitively costly so that litigants are deterred irrespective of the merits of their case. One element in the present high cost of litigation is undoubtedly the expectations as to annual income of the professionals who conduct it. The costs system as it at present operates cannot do anything about that, because it assesses the proper charge for work on the basis of the market rates charged by the professions, rather than attempting the no doubt difficult task of placing an objective value on the work. When the CPR replaced the RSC, and encouraged active intervention by the court and the application of public values and not merely those values with which the parties were comfortable, it was hoped that that practice might change; and that hope was reinforced when this court said, in para [2] of its judgment in *Lownds v Home Office*:[104]

---

[99] *Lownds v Home Office* per Lord Woolf CJ at [37].
[100] Former PD 43–48, para 11.2.
[101] Former PD 43–48, para 11.3.
[102] [2007] EWCA Civ 199, [2007] PIQR P22.
[103] At [18] to [19].

Proportionality played no part in the taxation of costs under the RSC. The only test was that of reasonableness. The problem with that test, standing on its own, was that it institutionalised, as reasonable, the level of costs which were generally charged by the profession at the time when professional services were rendered. If a rate of charges was commonly adopted it was taken to be reasonable and so allowed on taxation even though the result was far from reasonable.

However, in the event nothing seems to have changed. That is because, as explained in para [29] of the same judgment, 'proportionality' is achieved by determining whether it was necessary to incur any particular item of costs. And then, '[w]hen an item of costs is necessarily incurred then a reasonable amount for the item should normally be allowed': and the reasonable amount per hour of the professional's time continues to be determined by the market. How that occurred, and further observations on the present position in respect of the assessment of rates, is to be found helpfully set out in more detail in Zuckerman, *Civil Procedure* (2nd edition), at paras 26.74 to 26.87.

Final Report

10.74 In the *Final Report*[105] Sir Rupert Jackson said proportionality of costs is not simply a matter of comparing the sum in issue with the amount of costs incurred, important though that comparison is. It is also necessary to evaluate any non-monetary remedies sought and any rights which are in issue, in order to compare the overall value of what is at stake in the claim with the costs of resolution. Proportionality has to be considered by reference to:[106]

(a) the sums at stake;

(b) the value of any non-monetary remedies claimed and any rights in issue;

(c) the complexity of the litigation;

(d) the conduct of the parties; and

(e) any wider factors, such as reputational issues or public importance.

10.75 In particular, the *Final Report* said:

(a) disproportionate costs do not become proportionate just because they were necessary;[107] and

(b) disproportionate costs should be disallowed in standard-basis assessments.[108]

10.76 On the latter point, it means that costs should be reduced if the total figure for costs is disproportionate, and also if the costs of individual items are

---

[104] [2002] 1 WLR 2450.
[105] *Final Report*, ch 3, para 5.5.
[106] *Final Report*, ch 3, para 5.6.
[107] *Final Report*, ch 3, para 5.10.
[108] *Final Report*, ch 3, para 5.12.

disproportionate. Further, on a standard-basis assessment proportionality prevails over reasonableness.[109] What the court should be doing on a standard-basis assessment is first to make an assessment of reasonable costs based on the individual items in the bill of costs. Then, the court should stand back and consider whether the total figure is disproportionate or the figures for various items are disproportionate. Finally it should reduce any disproportionate figure to come within the bounds of proportionality.

New proportionality test

A draft definition of proportionality was proposed in the *Final Report*[110] which **10.77** has been adopted, with very minor changes, into the new costs rules as CPR, r 44.3(5). This provides:

Costs incurred are proportionate if they bear a reasonable relationship to—

(a)   the sums in issue in the proceedings;

(b)   the value of any non-monetary relief in issue in the proceedings;

(c)   the complexity of the litigation;

(d)   any additional work generated by the conduct of the paying party; and

(e)   any wider factors involved in the proceedings, such as reputation or public importance.

Standard-basis assessment

Where the court is to assess the amount of costs on the standard basis the court **10.78** will not allow costs which have been unreasonably incurred or are unreasonable in amount.[111] On a standard basis assessment the court will:[112]

(a)   only allow costs which are proportionate to the matters in issue. Costs which are disproportionate in amount may be disallowed or reduced even if they were reasonably or necessarily incurred; and

(b)   resolve any doubt which it may have as to whether costs were reasonably and proportionately incurred or were reasonable and proportionate in amount in favour of the paying party.

The second sentence in sub-para (a) is new, as is the reference to proportionality **10.79** in resolving doubts in sub-para (b). 'Proportionality' under the new r 44.3(2) is intended to come into play when an assessment of 'reasonable' costs will result

---

[109] *Final Report*, ch 3, para 5.13.
[110] *Final Report*, ch 3, para 5.15.
[111] CPR, r 44.3(1), which replicates the old r 44.4.
[112] CPR, r 44.3(2).

in an excessive figure. As stated by Sir Rupert Jackson in the *Final Report*,[113] in essence proportionality trumps reasonableness.

10.80   The new proportionality test applies only to cases commenced on or after 1 April 2013.[114]

Guidance on the new test

10.81   A deliberate decision has been made not to elaborate on the new proportionality test by including detailed guidance in the relevant practice direction. Sir Rupert Jackson's view is that the rule as drafted is sufficiently clear.[115] Simplicity is felt to promote certainty and the avoidance of technical satellite litigation.[116]

Operation of the new proportionality test

10.82   What Sir Rupert Jackson envisaged was that the new proportionality test should be applied in different ways in different situations.[117] They may be categorized as follows:

(a) Cases where it is obvious at the outset that the costs claimed are proportionate. In these cases the only issue to consider is the reasonableness of the individual items on the bill of costs.[118]

(b) Cases where it is obvious from the outset that the costs claimed are disproportionate. In these cases the costs judge will have to consider the reasonableness of each item on the bill. The judge will also have to consider how to reduce the bill to a proportionate level. This may be achieved by reducing particular items, or by reducing the overall total to reach a proportionate figure.

(c) Borderline cases where it is unclear whether the bill is disproportionate until after the costs judge has dealt with the reasonableness of the individual items in the bill. In these cases the costs judge should not be constrained, whether by a practice direction or anything else, on how to approach the task of ensuring the costs allowed are both reasonable and proportionate.

Indemnity-basis assessment

10.83   Assessment of costs on the indemnity basis remains unchanged.[119]

---

[113] *Final Report*, ch 40, para 7.22.

[114] CPR, r 44.3(7).

[115] 3rd Implementation Lecture, para 2.1.

[116] 3rd Implementation Lecture, para 2.3, and which is part of the purpose behind recommendation 2 of the *Final Report*.

[117] 3rd Implementation Lecture, para 2.2.

[118] CPR, r 44.3.

[119] The relevant rules can be found in CPR, r 44.3, and PD 44, para 6.1.

G. REVISION OF COSTS PROVISIONS IN THE CPR

Origins and destinations

As mentioned above, recommendation 2 of the *Final Report* is to the effect that **10.84** when considering the balance between predictability and simplicity, greater emphasis should be given to simplicity when it comes to the rules and practice directions on costs. Removal of recoverability of additional liabilities has allowed a substantial number of rules to be removed. The result is that the new costs provisions are considerably shorter than before. They have also been reorganized, so that there are now five practice directions dealing with costs, rather than the monolithic PD 43–48, which always proved very difficult to navigate.

Table 10.1 is a table of origins of the provisions in the new CPR, Parts 44 to **10.85** 48. There is no Part 43 in the new version of the rules. Table 10.2 is a table of destinations for the old provisions in CPR, Parts 43 to 48. Where there is no entry in the right hand column it means the old provision has been deleted and not replaced. Table 10.3 is a table of origins of the provisions in the new PD 44 to PD 48. Table 10.4 is a table of destinations for the old provisions in PD 43–48. Where there is no entry in the right hand column it means the old provision has been deleted and not replaced.

TABLE 10.1 Table of origins of the costs provisions in the CPR in force from 1 April 2013

CPR as in force from 1 April 2013	Origin in the CPR as in force immediately before 1 April 2013
Section I	
General	
44.1	43.2
44.2	44.3
44.3	44.4
44.4	44.5
44.5	48.3
44.6	44.7 and 44.6
44.7	44.8
44.8	44.2
44.9	44.12
44.10	44.13
44.11	44.14
44.12	44.3(9)
44.13 to 44.17	NEW

Continued

TABLE 10.1 (*Continued*)

CPR as in force from 1 April 2013	Origin in the CPR as in force immediately before 1 April 2013
Section III	
Damages-Based Agreements	
44.18	NEW
Part 45	
Fixed Costs	
Section I	
Fixed Costs	
45.1	45.1
45.2	45.2
45.3	45.3
45.4	45.4
45.5	45.2A
45.6	45.4A
45.7	45.5
45.8	45.6
Section II	
RTAs Fixed Recoverable Costs	
45.9	45.7
45.10	45.8
45.11	45.9
45.12	45.10
45.13	45.12
45.14	45.13
45.15	45.14
Section III	
Pre-action Protocol for Low Value Personal Injury Claims in RTAs	
45.16	45.27
45.17	45.28
45.18	45.29
45.19	45.30
45.20	45.32
45.21	45.33
45.22	45.34
45.23	45.35
45.24	45.36
45.25	45.37
45.26	45.38
45.27	45.39
45.28	45.40
45.29	NEW
Section IV	
Scale Costs for Claims in a Patents County Court	
45.30	45.41
45.31	45.42
45.32	45.43

TABLE 10.1 (*Continued*)

CPR as in force from 1 April 2013	Origin in the CPR as in force immediately before 1 April 2013
Section V	
Fixed Costs: HM Revenue and Customs	
45.33	45.44
45.34	45.45
45.35	45.46
45.35	45.47
Section VI	
Fast Track Trial Costs	
45.37	46.1
45.38	46.2
45.39	46.3
45.40	46.4
Section VII	
Costs Limits in Aarhus Convention Claims	
45.41 to 45.44	NEW
Part 46	
Costs Special Cases	
Section I	
Costs Payable by or to Particular Persons	
46.1	48.1
46.2	48.2
46.3	48.4
46.4	48.5
46.5	48.6
46.6	48.6A
46.7	44.3C
Section II	
Costs Relating to Legal Representatives	
46.8	48.7
46.9	48.8
46.10	48.10
Section III	
Costs on Allocation and Reallocation	
46.11	44.9
46.12	44.10
46.13	44.11
Section IV	
Costs-only Proceedings	
46.14	44.12A
Part 47	
Procedure for Detailed Assessment of Costs and Default Provisions	
Section I	
General Rules about Detailed Assessment	
47.1	47.1
47.2	47.2

Continued

149

TABLE 10.1 (*Continued*)

CPR as in force from 1 April 2013	Origin in the CPR as in force immediately before 1 April 2013
47.3	47.3
47.4	47.4

Section II
Costs Payable by One Party to Another—Commencement of Detailed Assessment Proceedings

47.5	47.5
47.6	47.6
47.7	47.7
47.8	47.8
47.9	47.9
47.10	47.10

Section III
Costs Payable by One Party to Another—Default Provisions

47.11	47.11
47.12	47.12

Section IV
Costs Payable by One Party to Another—Procedure Where Points of Dispute are Served

47.13	47.13
47.14	47.14
47.15	NEW

Section V
Interim Costs Certificate and Final Costs Certificate

47.16	47.15
47.17	47.16

Section VI
Detailed Assessment Procedure for Costs of a LSC Funded Client or an Assisted Person where Costs are Payable out of the Community Legal Service Fund

47.18	47.17
47.19	47.17A

Section VII
Costs of Detailed Assessment Proceedings

47.20	47.18

Section VIII
Appeals from Authorised Court Officers in Detailed Assessment Proceedings

47.21	47.20(1)
47.22	47.21
47.23	47.22
47.24	47.23

Part 48
Part 2 of Legal Aid, Sentencing and Punishment of Offenders Act 2012 relating to Civil Litigation Funding and Costs: Transitional Provision in Relation to Pre-commencement Funding Arrangements

48.1 to 48.2	NEW

TABLE 10.2 Table of destinations of the costs provisions in the CPR in force immediately before 1 April 2013

CPR as in force immediately before 1 April 2013	Destination in CPR as in force from 1 April 2013
Part 43	
Scope of Cost Rules and Definitions	
43.1	
43.2	44.1
43.3	44.1(1)(f)
43.4	44.1(1)(g)
Part 44	
General Rules about Costs	
44.1	
44.2	44.8
44.3	44.12
44.3A	
44.3B	
44.3C	46.7
44.4	44.3
44.5	44.4
44.6	44.6
44.7	44.6
44.8	44.7
44.9	46.11
44.10	46.12
44.11	46.13
44.12	44.9
44.12A	46.14
44.12B	
44.12C	
44.13	44.10
44.14	44.11
44.15	
44.16	
44.17	
44.18	3.19
44.19	3.20
44.20	3.21
Part 45	
Fixed Costs	
Section I	
Fixed Costs	
45.1	45.1
45.2	45.2
45.2A	45.5
45.3	45.3
45.4	45.4
45.4A	45.6
45.5	45.7
45.6	45.8

Continued

151

TABLE 10.2 (*Continued*)

CPR as in force immediately before 1 April 2013	Destination in CPR as in force from 1 April 2013
Section II	
Road Traffic Accidents—Fixed Recoverable Costs	
45.7	45.9
45.8	45.10
45.9	45.11
45.10	45.12
45.11	
45.12	45.13
45.13	45.14
45.14	45.15
Section III	
Fixed Percentage Increase in Road Traffic Accident Claims	
45.15	
45.16	
45.17	
45.18	
45.19	
Section IV	
Fixed Percentage Increase in Employers' Liability Claims	
45.20	
45.21	
45.22	
Section V	
Fixed Recoverable Success Fees in Employer's Liability Disease Claims	
45.23	
45.24	
45.25	
45.26	
Section VI	
Pre-action Protocol for Low Value Personal Injury Claims in Road Traffic Accidents	
45.27	45.16
45.28	45.28
45.29	45.18
45.30	45.19
45.31	
45.32	45.20
45.33	45.21
45.34	45.22
45.35	45.23
45.36	45.24
45.37	45.25
45.38	45.26
45.39	45.27
45.40	45.28
Section VII	
Scale Costs for Claims in a Patents County Court	
45.41	45.30
45.42	45.31
45.43	45.32

TABLE 10.2 (*Continued*)

CPR as in force immediately before 1 April 2013	Destination in CPR as in force from 1 April 2013
Section VIII	
Fixed Costs: HM Revenue and Customs	
45.44	45.33
45.45	45.34
45.46	45.35
45.47	45.35
Part 46	
Fast Track Trial Costs	
46.1	45.37
46.2	45.38
46.3	45.39
46.4	45.40
Part 47	
Procedure for Detailed Assessment of Costs and Default Provisions	
Section I	
General Rules about Detailed Assessment	
47.1	47.1
47.2	47.2
47.3	47.3
47.4	47.4
Section II	
Costs Payable by One Party to Another—Commencement of Detailed Assessment Proceedings	
47.5	47.5
47.6	47.6
47.7	47.7
47.8	47.8
47.9	47.9
47.10	47.10
Section III	
Costs Payable by One Party to Another—Default Provisions	
47.11	47.11
47.12	47.12
Section IV	
Costs Payable by One Party to Another—Procedure where Points of Dispute are Served	
47.13	47.13
47.14	47.14
Section V	
Interim Costs Certificate and Final Costs Certificate	
47.15	47.16
47.16	47.17
Section VI	
Detailed Assessment Procedure for Costs of an Assisted Person where Costs are Payable Out of the Legal Aid Fund	
47.17	47.18
47.17A	47.19

Continued

TABLE 10.2 (*Continued*)

CPR as in force immediately before 1 April 2013	Destination in CPR as in force from 1 April 2013
Section VII	
Costs of Detailed Assessment Proceedings	
47.18	47.20
47.19	
Section VIII	
Appeals from Authorised Court Officers in Detailed Assessment Proceedings	
47.20	47.21
47.21	47.22
47.22	47.23
47.23	47.24
Part 48	
Costs — Special Cases	
48.1	46.1
48.2	46.2
48.3	46.3
48.4	
48.5	46.4
48.6	46.5
48.6A	46.6
48.7	46.8
48.8	46.9
48.9	Revoked by SI 2001/256
48.10	46.10

TABLE 10.3 Table of origins of the provisions in the new PD 44 to PD 48 in force from 1 April 2013

Practice directions as in force from 1 April 2013	Origin in PD 43–48 as in force immediately before 1 April 2013
Practice Direction 44	
General Rules about Costs	
Section I	
General	
PD 44, para 1.1 Documents and Forms	NEW
PD 44, para 1.2	NEW
PD 44, para 2.1 VAT	5.1
PD 44, para 2.2	5.2
PD 44, para 2.3	5.3
PD 44, para 2.4	5.4
PD 44, para 2.5	5.5
PD 44, para 2.6	5.6
PD 44, para 2.7	5.7
PD 44, para 2.8	5.8
PD 44, para 2.9	5.9
PD 44, para 2.10	5.10

TABLE 10.3 (*Continued*)

Practice directions as in force from 1 April 2013	Origin in PD 43–48 as in force immediately before 1 April 2013
PD 44, para 2.11	5.11
PD 44, para 2.12	5.18 and 5.19
PD 44, para 2.13	5.20
PD 44, para 2.14	5.21
PD 44, para 3.1 Costs Budgets	NEW
PD 44, para 3.2	NEW, but see 6.5A(1)
PD 44, para 3.3	NEW, but see 6.5A(2)
PD 44, para 3.4	NEW, but see 6.6(1)
PD 44, para 3.5	NEW, but see 6.6(2)
PD 44, para 3.6	NEW, but see 6.6(2)(b)(ii)
PD 44, para 3.7	NEW, but see 6.6(2)(b)(i)
PD 44, para 4.1 Discretion as to Costs	NEW
PD 44, para 4.2	8.5
PD 44, para 5.1 Fees of Counsel	8.7(2), (3)
PD 44, para 5.2	8.8
PD 44, para 6.1 Basis of Assessment	NEW
PD 44, para 6.2	NEW
PD 44, para 7.1 Costs Pursuant to Contract	50.2
PD 44, para 7.2	50.3
PD 44, para 7.3	50.4
PD 44, para 8.1 Procedure for Assessing Costs	12.1
PD 44, para 8.2	12.2
PD 44, para 8.3	NEW
PD 44, para 9.1 Summary Assessment	13.1
PD 44, para 9.2	13.2
PD 44, para 9.3	13.3
PD 44, para 9.4	13.4
PD 44, para 9.5	13.5
PD 44, para 9.6	13.6
PD 44, para 9.7	13.8
PD 44, para 9.8	13.9
PD 44, para 9.9	13.11
PD 44, para 9.10	13.13
PD 44, para 10.1 Duty to Notify Client	7.1
PD 44, para 10.2	7.2
PD 44, para 10.3	7.3
PD 44, para 11.1 Misconduct	18.1
PD 44, para 11.2	18.2
PD 44, para 11.3	18.3
Section II Qualified One-way Costs Shifting PD 44, para 12.1 to 12.7	NEW
Practice Direction 45 Fixed Costs	
Section I Fixed Costs PD 45, para 1.1	24.1
PD 45, para 1.2	24.2
PD 45, para 1.3	24.3

Continued

TABLE 10.3 (*Continued*)

Practice directions as in force from 1 April 2013	Origin in PD 43–48 as in force immediately before 1 April 2013
Section II	
RTAs: Fixed Recoverable Costs	
PD 45, para 2.1	25A.1
PD 45, para 2.2	25A.2
PD 45, para 2.3	25A.3
PD 45, para 2.4	25A.4
PD 45, para 2.5	25A.5
PD 45, para 2.6	25A.6
PD 45, para 2.7	25A.7
PD 45, para 2.8	25A.8
PD 45, para 2.9	25A.9
PD 45, para 2.10	25A.10
Section IV	
Scale Costs in Patent County Courts	
PD 45, para 3.1	25C.1
PD 45, para 3.2	25C.2
PD 45, para 3.3	25C.3
Section VI	
Fast Track Trial Costs	
PD 45, para 4.1	26.1
PD 45, para 4.2	26.2
PD 45, para 4.3	26.3(b)
Section VII	
Costs Limits in Aarhus Convention Claims	
PD 45, para 5.1	NEW
PD 45, para 5.2	NEW
Practice Direction 46	
Costs Special Cases	
PD 46, para 1.1 Trustees and Personal Representatives	50A.1 and 50A.2
PD 46, para 1.2	50A.3
PD 46, para 2.1 Child or Protected Party	51.1
PD 46, para 3.1 Litigants in Person	52.1
PD 46, para 3.2	52.2
PD 46, para 3.3	52.3
PD 46, para 3.4	52.4
PD 46, para 4.1 Pro Bono Representation	10A.2
PD 46, para 5.1 Wasted Costs Orders	53.9
PD 46, para 5.2	53.1
PD 46, para 5.3	53.2
PD 46, para 5.4	53.5
PD 46, para 5.5	53.4
PD 46, para 5.6	53.5
PD 46, para 5.7	53.6
PD 46, para 5.8	53.7
PD 46, para 5.9	53.8
PD 46, para 6.1 Solicitor and Client	54.1
PD 46, para 6.2	54.2
PD 46, para 6.3	54.4

TABLE 10.3 *(Continued)*

Practice directions as in force from 1 April 2013	Origin in PD 43–48 as in force immediately before 1 April 2013
PD 46, para 6.4	56.2
PD 46, para 6.5	56.3
PD 46, para 6.6	56.5
PD 46, para 6.7	56.6
PD 46, para 6.8	56.7
PD 46, para 6.9	56.9
PD 46, para 6.10	56.10
PD 46, para 6.11	56.11
PD 46, para 6.12	56.12
PD 46, para 6.13	56.13(1)
PD 46, para 6.14	56.13(3)
PD 46, para 6.15	56.14
PD 46, para 6.16	56.15
PD 46, para 6.17	56.16
PD 46, para 6.18	56.17(2)
PD 46, para 6.19	56.18(2)
PD 46, para 7.1 Small Claims and Fast Track	15.1
PD 46, para 8.1 Costs Following Allocation etc	16.2 and 16.3
PD 46, para 8.2	NEW
PD 46, para 9.1 Costs-only Proceedings	17.1
PD 46, para 9.2	17.2
PD 46, para 9.3	17.3
PD 46, para 9.4	NEW but see 17.3(5)
PD 46, para 9.5	17.4
PD 46, para 9.6	17.5
PD 46, para 9.7	17.6
PD 46, para 9.8	17.7
PD 46, para 9.9	NEW, but see 17.8
PD 46, para 9.10	NEW, but see 17.9
PD 46, para 9.11	17.10(1)
PD 46, para 9.12	NEW, but see 17.11
Practice Direction 47 **Detailed Assessment**	
PD 47, para 1.1 Time for Assessment	28.1(1), (2)
PD 47, para 1.2	28.1(3)
PD 47, para 1.3	28.1(4)
PD 47, para 1.4	28.1(5)
PD 47, para 2.1 No Stay Pending Appeal	29.1(2)
PD 47, para 3.1 Authorised Court Officer	30.1(1)
PD 47, para 3.2	30.1(3)
PD 47, para 3.3	30.1(4)
PD 47, para 4.1 Venue for Detailed Assessment	31.1
PD 47, para 4.2	31.1A
PD 47, para 4.3	31.2
PD 47, para 5.1 Detailed Assessment Proceedings	32.1
PD 47, para 5.2	32.3
PD 47, para 5.3	32.8(2)
PD 47, para 5.4	32.9

Continued

TABLE 10.3 (*Continued*)

Practice directions as in force from 1 April 2013	Origin in PD 43–48 as in force immediately before 1 April 2013
PD 47, para 5.5	32.10
PD 47, para 5.6	32.11
PD 47, para 5.7	4.1
PD 47, para 5.8	4.2
PD 47, para 5.9	4.3
PD 47, para 5.10	4.4
PD 47, para 5.11	4.5
PD 47, para 5.12	4.6
PD 47, para 5.13	4.7
PD 47, para 5.14	4.8
PD 47, para 5.15	4.9
PD 47, para 5.16	4.10
PD 47, para 5.17	4.11
PD 47, para 5.18	4.12
PD 47, para 5.19	4.13
PD 47, para 5.20	4.14
PD 47, para 5.21	4.15
PD 47, para 5.22	4.16
PD 47, para 6.1 Period for Commencing	33.1 and 33.2
PD 47, para 6.2	33.3 and 33.4
PD 47, para 7.1 Sanction for Delay	34.1
PD 47, para 8.1 Points of Dispute	35.1
PD 47, para 8.2	35.2 and 35.3
PD 47, para 8.3	NEW
PD 47, para 9.1 Where Costs Are Agreed	36.1
PD 47, para 9.2	36.2
PD 47, para 9.3	36.4
PD 47, para 9.4	36.5
PD 47, para 10.1 Default Costs Certificate	37.1
PD 47, para 10.2	37.3
PD 47, para 10.3	37.4
PD 47, para 10.4	37.5
PD 47, para 10.5	37.6
PD 47, para 10.6	37.7
PD 47, para 10.7	37.8
PD 47, para 10.8	NEW
PD 47, para 11.1 Setting Aside Default Costs Certificate	38.1
PD 47, para 11.2	38.2
PD 47, para 11.3	38.3
PD 47, para 12.1 Optional Reply	NEW, but see 39.1 and 39.2
PD 47, para 12.2	NEW
PD 47, para 13.1 Detailed Assessment Hearing	40.1
PD 47, para 13.2	40.2
PD 47, para 13.3	40.4
PD 47, para 13.4	40.5
PD 47, para 13.5	NEW
PD 47, para 13.6	40.6(1)
PD 47, para 13.7	40.8
PD 47, para 13.8	40.9

TABLE 10.3 (*Continued*)

Practice directions as in force from 1 April 2013	Origin in PD 43–48 as in force immediately before 1 April 2013
PD 47, para 13.9	not used
PD 47, para 13.10	40.10
PD 47, para 13.11	40.11
PD 47, para 13.12	40.12
PD 47, para 13.13	40.14
PD 47, para 13.14	40.16
PD 47, para 14.1 Provisional Assessment	NEW
PD 47, para 14.2 to 14.6	NEW
PD 47, para 15.1 Interim Certificate	41.1(1)
PD 47, para 16.1 Final Costs Certificate	42.1
PD 47, para 16.2	42.2
PD 47, para 16.3	42.3
PD 47, para 16.4	42.4
PD 47, para 16.5	42.5
PD 47, para 16.6	42.6
PD 47, para 16.7	42.7
PD 47, para 16.8	42.8
PD 47, para 16.9	42.9
PD 47, para 16.10	42.10
PD 47, para 16.11	42.11
PD 47, para 16.12	42.12
PD 47, para 17.1 Community Legal Service Fund	43.2
PD 47, para 17.2	43.3
PD 47, para 17.3	43.5
PD 47, para 17.4	43.8
PD 47, para 17.5	43.9
PD 47, para 17.6	49.1 and 49.2
PD 47, para 17.7	49.3
PD 47, para 17.8	49.4
PD 47, para 17.9	49.5
PD 47, para 17.10	49.6 and 49.7
PD 47, para 17.11	49.8
PD 47, para 18.1 Costs Payable out of a Fund	44.1
PD 47, para 18.2	44.2
PD 47, para 18.3	44.3
PD 47, para 18.4	44.4
PD 47, para 18.5	44.5
PD 47, para 18.6	44.6
PD 47, para 18.7	44.8
PD 47, para 18.8	44.9
PD 47, para 18.9	44.10
PD 47, para 19 Offers to Settle under Part 36	46.2
PD 47, para 20.1 Appeals from Authorised Officer	47.1
PD 47, para 20.2	47.2
PD 47, para 20.3	48.1
PD 47, para 20.4	48.2
PD 47, para 20.5	48.3
PD 47, para 20.6	48.4

Continued

Table 10.3 (*Continued*)

Practice directions as in force from 1 April 2013	Origin in PD 43–48 as in force immediately before 1 April 2013
Practice Direction 48	
Transitional Provision Legal Aid, Sentencing and Punishment of Offenders Act 2012 Part 2	
PD 48, para 1.1 Transitional Provisions General	NEW
PD 48, para 1.2	NEW
PD 48, para 1.3	NEW
PD 48, para 1.4	NEW
PD 48, para 2.1 Mesothelioma Claims	NEW
PD 48, para 2.2	NEW
PD 48, para 3.1 Insolvency, Publication, Privacy	NEW
PD 48, para 3.2	NEW
PD 48, para 4.1 Clinical Negligence Claims	NEW
PD 48, para 4.2	NEW

Table 10.4 Table of destinations of the provisions in PD 43–48 (the Costs Practice Direction) in force immediately before 1 April 2013

PD 43–48	Destination in practice directions in force from 1 April 2013
Section 1 Introduction	
1.1	
1.2	
1.3	
1.4	
1.5	
Section 2 Scope of Costs Rules and Definitions	
2.1	
2.2	
2.3	
2.4	
2.5	
Section 3 Model Forms for Claims for Costs	
3.1	
3.2	
3.3	
3.4	
3.5	
3.6	
3.7	
3.8	
Section 4 Form and Contents of Bills of Costs	
4.1	PD 47, para 5.7
4.2	PD 47, para 5.8
4.3	PD 47, para 5.9
4.4	PD 47, para 5.10
4.5	PD 47, para 5.11

TABLE 10.4 (*Continued*)

PD 43–48	Destination in practice directions in force from 1 April 2013
4.6	PD 47, para 5.12
4.7	PD 47, para 5.13
4.8	PD 47, para 5.14
4.9	PD 47, para 5.15
4.10	PD 47, para 5.16
4.11	PD 47, para 5.17
4.12	PD 47, para 5.18
4.13	PD 47, para 5.19
4.14	PD 47, para 5.20
4.15	PD 47, para 5.21
4.16	PD 47, para 5.22
4.17	
4.18	
Section 5 Special Provisions Relating to VAT	
5.1	PD 44, para 2.1 VAT
5.2	PD 44, para 2.2
5.3	PD 44, para 2.3
5.4	PD 44, para 2.4
5.5	PD 44, para 2.5
5.6	PD 44, para 2.6
5.7	PD 44, para 2.7
5.8	PD 44, para 2.8
5.9	PD 44, para 2.9
5.10	PD 44, para 2.10
5.11	PD 44, para 2.11
5.12	
5.13	
5.14	
5.15	
5.16	
5.17	
5.18	PD 44, para 2.12
5.19	PD 44, para 2.12
5.20	PD 44, para 2.13
5.21	PD 44, para 2.14
Section 6 Estimates of Costs	
6.1	
6.2	
6.3	
6.4	
6.5	
6.5A(1)	Refer to PD 44, para 3.2
6.5A(2)	Refer to PD 44, para 3.3
6.6(1)	Refer to PD 44, para 3.4
6.6(2)	Refer to PD 44, para 3.5
6.6(2)(b)(i)	Refer to PD 44, para 3.7
6.6(2)(b)(ii)	Refer to PD 44, para 3.6

Continued

TABLE 10.4 (*Continued*)

PD 43–48	Destination in practice directions in force from 1 April 2013
Section 7 Solicitor's Duty to Notify Client: Rule 44.2	
7.1	PD 44, para 10.1 Duty to Notify Client
7.2	PD 44, para 10.2
7.3	PD 44, para 10.3
Section 8 Court's Discretion and Circumstances to Be Taken into Account When Exercising Its Discretion as to Costs: Rule 44.3	
8.1	
8.2	
8.3	
8.4	
8.5	PD 44, para 4.2
8.6	
8.7	PD 44, para 5.1 Fees of Counsel
8.8	PD 44, para 5.2
Section 9 Costs Orders Relating to Funding Arrangements: Rule 44.3A	
9.1	
9.2	
Section 10 Limits on Recovery under Funding Arrangements: Rule 4.3B	
10.1	
10.2	
Section 10A Orders in Respect of Pro Bono Representation: Rule 44.3C	
10A.1	
10A.2	PD 46, para 4.1 Pro Bono Representation
Section 11 Factors to Be Taken into Account in Deciding the Amount of Costs: Rule 44.5	
11.1	
11.2	
11.3	
11.4	
11.5	
11.6	
11.7	
11.8	
11.9	
11.10	
11.11	
Section 12 Procedure for Assessing Costs: Rule 44.7	
12.1	PD 44, para 8.1 Procedure for Assessing Costs
12.2	PD 44, para 8.2
12.3	
Section 13 Summary Assessment: General Provisions	
13.1	PD 44, para 9.1 Summary Assessment
13.2	PD 44, para 9.2
13.3	PD 44, para 9.3
13.4	PD 44, para 9.4
13.5	PD 44, para 9.5
13.6	PD 44, para 9.6

TABLE 10.4 (*Continued*)

PD 43–48	Destination in practice directions in force from 1 April 2013
13.7	
13.8	PD 44, para 9.7
13.9	PD 44, para 9.8
13.10	
13.11	PD 44, para 9.9
13.12	
13.13	PD 44, para 9.10

Section 14 Summary Assessment Where Costs Claimed Include an Additional Liability

14.1	
14.2	
14.3	
14.4	
14.5	
14.6	
14.7	
14.8	
14.9	

Section 15 Costs on the Small Claims Track and Fast Track: Rule 44.9

15.1	PD 46, para 7.1 Small Claims and Fast Track

Section 16 Costs Following Allocation and Reallocation: Rule 44.11

16.1	
16.2	PD 46, para 8.1 Costs Following Allocation etc
16.3	PD 46, para 8.1 Costs Following Allocation etc

Section 17 Costs-only Proceedings: Rule 44.12A

17.1	PD 46, para 9.1 Costs-only Proceedings
17.2	PD 46, para 9.2
17.3	PD 46, para 9.3
17.3(5)	Refer to PD 46, para 9.4
17.4	17.4
17.5	17.5
17.6	17.6
17.7	17.7
17.8	Refer to PD 46, para 9.9
17.9	Refer to PD 46, para 9.10
17.10	PD 46, para 9.11
17.11	PD 46, para 9.12

Section 18 Court's Powers in Relation to Misconduct: Rule 44.14

18.1	PD 44, para 11.1 Misconduct
18.2	PD 44, para 11.2
18.3	PD 44, para 11.3

Section 19 Providing Information about Funding Arrangements: Rule 44.15

19.1	
19.2	
19.3	
19.4	
19.5	
19.6	

Continued

TABLE 10.4 (*Continued*)

PD 43–48	Destination in practice directions in force from 1 April 2013

Section 20 Procedure Where Legal Representative Wishes to Recover from His Client an Agreed Percentage Increase Which Has Been Disallowed or Reduced on Assessment: Rule 44.16

20.1
20.2
20.3
20.4
20.5
20.6
20.7
20.8

Section 21 Application of Costs Rules: Rule 44.17

21.1
21.2
21.3
21.4
21.5
21.6
21.7
21.8
21.9
21.10
21.11
21.12
21.13
21.14
21.15
21.16
21.17
21.18
21.19
21.19A
21.20

Section 22 Orders for Costs to Which Section 11 of the Access to Justice Act 1999 Applies

22.1
22.2
22.3
22.4
22.5
22.6
22.7
22.8
22.9

Section 23 Determination Proceedings and Similar Proceedings under the Community Legal Service (Costs) Regulations 2000

23.1
23.2
23.3
23.4
23.5

TABLE 10.4 (*Continued*)

PD 43–48	Destination in practice directions in force from 1 April 2013
23.6	
23.7	
23.8	
23.9	
23.10	
23.11	
23.12	
23.13	
23.14	
23.15	
23.16	
23.17	
23.18	
Section 23A Costs Capping Orders	
23A.1	PD 3F, para 1.1
23A.2	PD 3F, para 1.2
23A.3	PD 3F, para 2
23A.4	PD 3F, para 3
23A.5	PD 3F, para 4.1
Section 23B Costs Capping Orders in Relation to Trust Funds	
23B.1	PD 3F, para 5.1
23B.2	PD 3F, paras 5.2, 5.3
23B.3	PD 3F, para 5.4
23B.4	PD 3F, para 5.5
23B.5	PD 3F, para 5.6
Section 24 Fixed Costs in Small Claims	
24.1	PD 45, para 1.1
24.2	PD 45, para 1.2
Section 24A Claims to Which Part 45 Does Not Apply	
24A	
Section 25 Fixed Costs on the Issue of a Default Costs Certificate	
25.1	
25.2	
Section 25A Road Traffic Accidents: Fixed Recoverable Costs in Costs-only Proceedings	
25A.1	PD 45, para 2.1
25A.2	PD 45, para 2.2
25A.3	PD 45, para 2.3
25A.4	PD 45, para 2.4
25A.5	PD 45, para 2.5
25A.6	PD 45, para 2.6
25A.7	PD 45, para 2.7
25A.8	PD 45, para 2.8
25A.9	PD 45, para 2.9
25A.10	PD 45, para 2.10
Section 25B Fixed Recoverable Success Fees in Employer's Liability Disease Claims	
25B.1	

Continued

TABLE 10.4 *(Continued)*

PD 43–48	Destination in practice directions in force from 1 April 2013
Section 25C Scale Costs for Proceedings in a Patents County Court	
25C.1	PD 45, para 3.1
25C.2	PD 45, para 3.2
25C.3	PD 45, para 3.3
Section 26 Scope of Part 46: Rule 46.1	
26.1	PD 45, para 4.1
26.2	PD 45, para 4.2
26.3	PD 45, para 4.3
26.4	
Section 27 Power to Award More or Less Than the Amount of Fast Track Trial Costs: Rule 46.3	
27.1	
27.2	
27.3	
Section 28 Time When Assessment May Be Carried Out: Rule 47.1	
28.1(1), (2)	PD 47, para 1.1 Time for Assessment
28.1(3)	PD 47, para 1.2
28.1(4)	PD 47, para 1.3
28.1(5)	PD 47, para 1.4
28.2	
Section 29 No Stay of Detailed Assessment Where There Is an Appeal: Rule 47.2	
29.1(1)	
29.1(2)	PD 47, para 2.1 No Stay Pending Appeal
Section 30 Powers of an Authorised Court Officer: Rule 47.3	
30.1(1)	PD 47, para 3.1 Authorised Court Officer
30.1(2)	
30.1(3)	PD 47, para 3.2
30.1(4)	PD 47, para 3.3
Section 31 Venue for Detailed Assessment Proceedings: Rule 47.4	
31.1	PD 47, para 4.1 Venue for Detailed Assessment
31.1A	PD 47, para 4.2
31.2	PD 47, para 4.3
Section 32 Commencement of Detailed Assessment Proceedings: Rule 47.6	
32.1	PD 47, para 5.1 Detailed Assessment Proceedings
32.2	
32.3	PD 47, para 5.2
32.4	
32.5	
32.6	
32.7	
32.8(1)	
32.8(2)	PD 47, para 5.3
32.9	PD 47, para 5.4
32.10	PD 47, para 5.5
32.11	PD 47, para 5.6

TABLE 10.4 (*Continued*)

PD 43–48	Destination in practice directions in force from 1 April 2013

Section 33 Period for Commencing Detailed Assessment Proceedings: Rule 47.7

33.1	PD 47, para 6.1 Period for Commencing
33.2	PD 47, para 6.1 Period for Commencing
33.3	PD 47, para 6.2
33.4	PD 47, para 6.2

Section 34 Sanction for Delay in Commencing Detailed Assessment Proceedings: Rule 47.8

34.1	PD 47, para 7.1 Sanction for Delay

Section 35 Points of Dispute and Consequences of Not Serving: Rule 47.9

35.1	PD 47, para 8.1 Points of Dispute
35.2	PD 47, para 8.2
35.3	PD 47, para 8.2
35.4	
35.5	
35.6	
35.7	

Section 36 Procedure Where Costs Are Agreed: Rule 47.10

36.1	PD 47, para 9.1 Where Costs Are Agreed
36.2	PD 47, para 9.2
36.3	
36.4	PD 47, para 9.3
36.5	PD 47, para 9.4

Section 37 Default Costs Certificate: Rule 47.11

37.1	PD 47, para 10.1 Default Costs Certificate
37.2	
37.3	PD 47, para 10.2
37.4	PD 47, para 10.3
37.5	PD 47, para 10.4
37.6	PD 47, para 10.5
37.7	PD 47, para 10.6
37.8	PD 47, para 10.7

Section 38 Setting Aside Default Costs Certificate: Rule 47.12

38.1	PD 47, para 11.1 Setting Aside Default Costs Certificate
38.2	PD 47, para 11.2
38.3	PD 47, para 11.3
38.4	

Section 39 Optional Reply: Rule 47.13

39.1	Refer to PD 47, para 12.1 Optional Reply
39.2	Refer to PD 47, para 12.1 Optional Reply

Section 40 Detailed Assessment Hearing: Rule 47.14

40.1	PD 47, para 13.1 Detailed Assessment Hearing
40.2	PD 47, para 13.2
40.3	
40.4	PD 47, para 13.3
40.5	PD 47, para 13.4

Continued

Table 10.4 (*Continued*)

PD 43–48	Destination in practice directions in force from 1 April 2013
40.6(1)	PD 47, para 13.6
40.6(2), (3)	
40.7	
40.8	PD 47, para 13.7
40.9	PD 47, para 13.8
40.10	PD 47, para 13.10
40.11	PD 47, para 13.11
40.12	PD 47, para 13.12
40.13	
40.14	PD 47, para 13.13
40.15	
40.16	PD 47, para 13.14
Section 41 Power to Issue an Interim Certificate: Rule 47.15	
41.1(1)	PD 47, para 15.1 Interim Certificate
41.1(2)	
Section 42 Final Costs Certificate: Rule 47.16	
42.1	PD 47, para 16.1 Final Costs Certificate
42.2	PD 47, para 16.2
42.3	PD 47, para 16.3
42.4	PD 47, para 16.4
42.5	PD 47, para 16.5
42.6	PD 47, para 16.6
42.7	PD 47, para 16.7
42.8	PD 47, para 16.8
42.9	PD 47, para 16.9
42.10	PD 47, para 16.10
42.11	PD 47, para 16.11
42.12	PD 47, para 16.12
Section 43 Detailed Assessment Procedure Where Costs Are Payable Out of the Community Legal Service Fund: Rule 47.17	
43.1	
43.2	PD 47, para 17.1 Community Legal Service Fund
43.3	PD 47, para 17.2
43.4	
43.5	PD 47, para 17.3
43.6	
43.7	
43.8	PD 47, para 17.4
43.9	PD 47, para 17.5
Section 44 Costs of Detailed Assessment Proceedings Where Costs are Payable Out of a Fund Other than the Community Legal Service Fund: Rule 47.14A	
44.1	PD 47, para 18.1 Costs Payable Out of a Fund
44.2	PD 47, para 18.2
44.3	PD 47, para 18.3
44.4	PD 47, para 18.4
44.5	PD 47, para 18.5
44.6	PD 47, para 18.6

TABLE 10.4 (*Continued*)

PD 43–48	Destination in practice directions in force from 1 April 2013
44.7	
44.8	PD 47, para 18.7
44.9	PD 47, para 18.8
44.10	PD 47, para 18.9
Section 45 Liability for Costs of Detailed Assessment Proceedings: Rule 47.18	
45.1	
45.2	
45.3	
45.4	
45.5	
Section 46 Offers to Settle without Prejudice Save as to the Costs of the Detailed Assessment Proceedings: Rule 47.19	
46.1	
46.2	PD 47, para 19 Offers to Settle under Part 36
46.3	
46.4	
Section 47 Appeals from Authorised Court Officers in Detailed Assessment Proceedings: Right of Appeal: Rule 47.20	
47.1	PD 47, para 20.1 Appeals from Authorised Officer
47.2	PD 47, para 20.2
Section 48 Procedure on Appeal from Authorised Court Officers: Rule 47.22	
48.1	PD 47, para 20.3
48.2	PD 47, para 20.4
48.3	PD 47, para 20.5
48.4	PD 47, para 20.6
Section 49 Costs Payable by the LSC at Prescribed Rates	
49.1	PD 47, para 17.6
49.2	PD 47, para 17.6
49.3	PD 47, para 17.7
49.4	PD 47, para 17.8
49.5	PD 47, para 17.9
49.6	PD 47, para 17.10
49.7	PD 47, para 17.10
49.8	PD 47, para 17.11
Section 49A Costs Payable by the Trustee for Civil Recovery under a Recovery Order	
49A.1	
49A.2	
49A.3	
49A.4	
49A.5	
49A.6	
49A.7	
49A.8	
49A.9	

Continued

TABLE 10.4 (*Continued*)

PD 43–48	Destination in practice directions in force from 1 April 2013

Section 50 Amount of Costs Where Costs Are Payable Pursuant to Contract: Rule 48.3

50.1	
50.2	PD 44, para 7.1 Costs Pursuant to Contract
50.3	PD 44, para 7.2
50.4	PD 44, para 7.3

Section 50A Limitation on Court's Power to Award Costs in Favour of Trustee or Personal Representative: Rule 48.4

50A.1	PD 46, para 1.1 Trustees and Personal Representatives
50A.2	PD 46, para 1.1
50A.3	PD 46, para 1.2

Section 51 Costs Where Money Is Payable by or to a Child or Protected Party: Rule 48.5

51.1	PD 46, para 2.1 Child or Protected Party

Section 52 Litigants in Person: Rule 48.6

52.1	PD 46, para 3.1 Litigants in Person
52.2	PD 46, para 3.2
52.3	PD 46, para 3.3
52.4	PD 46, para 3.4
52.5	

Section 53 Personal Liability of Legal Representative for Costs — Wasted Costs Orders: Rule 48.7

53.1	PD 46, para 5.2
53.2	PD 46, para 5.3
53.3	
53.4	PD 46, para 5.5
53.5	PD 46, para 5.4
53.6	PD 46, para 5.7
53.7	PD 46, para 5.8
53.8	PD 46, para 5.9
53.9	PD 46, para 5.1 Wasted Costs Orders
53.10	

Section 54 Basis of Detailed Assessment of Solicitor and Client Costs: Rule 48.8

54.1	PD 46, para 6.1 Solicitor and Client
54.2	PD 46, para 6.2
54.3	
54.4	PD 46, para 6.3
54.5	
54.6	
54.7	
54.8	

Section 55 deleted

Section 56 Procedure on Assessment of Solicitor and Client Costs: Rule 48.10

56.1	
56.2	PD 46, para 6.4
56.3	PD 46, para 6.5
56.4	

TABLE 10.4 (*Continued*)

PD 43–48	Destination in practice directions in force from 1 April 2013
56.5	PD 46, para 6.6
56.6	PD 46, para 6.7
56.7	PD 46, para 6.8
56.8	
56.9	PD 46, para 6.9
56.10	PD 46, para 6.10
56.11	PD 46, para 6.11
56.12	PD 46, para 6.12
53.13(1)	PD 46, para 6.13
56.13(2)	PD 46, para 6.14
56.13(3)	
56.14	PD 46, para 6.15
56.15	PD 46, para 6.16
56.16	PD 46, para 6.17
56.17(1)	
56.17(2)	PD 46, para 6.18
56.18(1)	
56.18(2)	PD 46, para 6.19
56.19	
Section 57 Transitional Arrangements	
57.1	
57.2	
57.3	
57.4	
57.5	
57.6	
57.7	
57.8	
57.9	

Fixed costs

Several Sections of the old CPR, Part 45, have been omitted, because they dealt **10.86** with success fees and other additional liabilities. Fixed trial costs in fast track claims have been moved from the old CPR, Part 46, to Section VI of the new Part 45.

Costs: special cases

Special rules dealing with various situations used to be located in the old CPR, **10.87** Part 48. These provisions have mainly been moved to the new Part 46.

H. ASSESSMENT AND CHANGE OF TRACK

10.88 The main differences in assessing costs of claims on different tracks, other than the application of the reasonableness and proportionality principles, remain unchanged. They are:

(a) that normal party and party costs are not in general recoverable in small claims cases;[120] and

(b) there are fixed trial costs in fast track claims.[121]

Change of track

10.89 Any orders for costs made before a claim is allocated will not be affected by allocation.[122] Where a claim is allocated to a track and the court subsequently reallocates that claim to a different track, then unless the court orders otherwise:[123]

(a) any special rules about costs applying to the first track, will apply to the claim up to the date of reallocation; and

(b) any special rules about costs applying to the second track, will apply from the date of reallocation.

Cases not allocated to a track

10.90 A costs judge is not permitted to reopen the costs order made by the trial judge or recorded in an interim or consent order.[124] If the costs order provides for assessment on the standard basis, it is therefore not open to the costs judge to conduct the assessment of costs on the small claims track basis,[125] or on the fast track basis (with fixed fast track trial costs) if the claim has been allocated to the multi-track.[126]

10.91 While the costs judge is not permitted to rewrite the costs order in the manner described in the previous paragraph, the costs judge is entitled to take into account all the circumstances of the case,[127] which may include the fact that the

---

[120] CPR, r 27.14.

[121] Now in CPR, rr 45.37 to 45.40.

[122] CPR, r 46.13(1).

[123] CPR, r 46.13(2).

[124] *O'Beirne v Hudson* [2010] EWCA Civ 52, [2010] 1 WLR 1717 at [16]; *Drew v Whitbread plc* [2010] EWCA Civ 53, [2010] 1 WLR 1725.

[125] *O'Beirne v Hudson.*

[126] *Drew v Whitbread plc.*

[127] New CPR, r 44.4(1), as in force from 1 April 2013.

claim 'would almost certainly have been allocated to the small claims track if it had been allocated'.[128] This has been adopted into the new costs provisions by CPR, r 46.13(3), which provides:

Where the court is assessing costs on the standard basis of a claim which concluded without being allocated to a track, it may restrict those costs to costs that would have been allowed on the track to which the claim would have been allocated if allocation had taken place.

At that stage the costs judge may consider whether it was reasonable for the paying party to pay the costs of a lawyer. The costs judge would not be bound to disallow the costs of retaining a lawyer, but the fact that the claim would have been allocated to the small claims track is a highly material circumstance in deciding what to allow on the assessment.[129] In making that decision the costs judge should give the items on the bill very anxious scrutiny to see whether the costs of each item were necessarily or reasonably incurred, and thus whether it is reasonable for the paying party to pay more than would be recoverable in a case that was allocated to the small claims track.[130] **10.92**

O'Beirne v Hudson was applied in *Dockerill v Tullett*[131] to applications to approve child settlements in low-value claims. The costs judge must take a realistic view on the underlying claim for damages, and ensure the costs are proportionate. If it is likely the claim would have been allocated to the small claims track, costs need to be assessed by reference to the small claims track. This may well mean, for example, that the costs of briefing counsel for the approval hearing will not be recoverable, unless there is some complexity in the case justifying the presence of counsel. **10.93**

I. LITIGANTS IN PERSON

Recommendation 17 of the *Final Report* was to the effect that the hourly rate for litigants in person should be increased to £20. The *Government Response*[132] accepted that an increase was warranted because the prescribed rates for successful litigants in person had not been increased since the mid-1990s. Business representatives in particular had supported this change, for those cases in which business people represent themselves in court. It was recognized[133] that effecting this change could be taken forward more swiftly and independently than the main Jackson reforms. Accordingly, the hourly rate for litigants in person was **10.94**

---

[128] *O'Beirne v Hudson* per Waller LJ at [16].
[129] *O'Beirne v Hudson* per Waller LJ at [17].
[130] *O'Beirne v Hudson* per Waller LJ at [19] and [22].
[131] [2012] EWCA Civ 184, [2012] 1 WLR 2092.
[132] At para 15.
[133] At para 35.

increased from £9.25 per hour to £18 per hour with effect from 1 October 2011 by amending what used to be PD 43–48, para 52.4.[134]

J. COSTS-ONLY PROCEEDINGS

10.95 There have been some changes to the provisions on costs-only proceedings, which are now in CPR, r 46.14. They are still commenced by Part 8 claim form.[135] Under the new version of the rule the court may make an order for the assessment of the relevant costs, rather than restricting the court to making an order for a detailed assessment.[136] While detailed assessment is the general rule, the court may alternatively make a summary assessment.[137] The court is also given a power to order the claim to continue as a Part 7 claim,[138] rather than being forced to dismiss the proceedings if they were disputed.

K. DETAILED ASSESSMENT

10.96 Provisions dealing with the detailed assessment of costs remain in CPR, Part 47. For the most part the provisions have been adopted unchanged from the former provisions, but there are some innovations.

Powers of authorized court officers

10.97 The jurisdiction of authorized court officers has been increased to £35,000 for senior executive officers, and to £110,000 for principal officers.[139]

Bill of costs

10.98 There is a simplified bill of costs. Further, if the only dispute between the parties is as to disbursements,[140] the bill of costs needs only:

(a) a title page;

(b) background information;

(c) a list of disbursements; and

(d) brief written submissions in respect of those disbursements.

---

[134] This provision is now in PD 46, para 3.4.
[135] CPR, r 46.14(3).
[136] CPR, r 46.14(5).
[137] PD 46, para 9.9.
[138] PD 46, para 9.10.
[139] PD 47, para 3.1.
[140] PD 47, para 5.7.

Points of dispute

Under the new rules points of dispute must be short and to the point.[141] They must follow Precedent G in the Schedule of Costs Precedents annexed to PD 47 so far as practicable. They must: **10.99**

(a) identify any general points or matters of principle which require decision before the individual items in the bill are addressed; and

(b) identify specific points, stating concisely the nature and grounds of dispute.

Once a point has been made it should not be repeated but the item numbers where the point arises should be inserted in the left-hand box as shown in Precedent G. **10.100**

Open offer

The paying party must state in an open letter accompanying the points of dispute what sum, if any, that party offers to pay in settlement of the total costs claimed.[142] The paying party may also make an offer under Part 36. **10.101**

Reply

This remains optional.[143] When used it must be limited to points of principle and concessions only. It must not contain general denials, specific denials or standard-form responses.[144] **10.102**

Provisional assessment

Provisional assessment applies to any detailed assessment proceedings commenced in the High Court or a county court on or after 1 April 2013 in which the costs claimed do not exceed £75,000.[145] CPR, Part 47, is modified as set out in PD 47, para 14.2. In these cases, when the receiving party files its request for a detailed assessment in form N258 it must also file the necessary documents,[146] an additional copy of the bill, including a statement of the costs claimed in respect of the detailed assessment drawn on the assumption there will not be a hearing (which is not to exceed £1,500[147]), and the offers made in the assessment. Part **10.103**

---

[141] PD 47, para 8.2.
[142] PD 47, para 8.3.
[143] CPR, r 47.13.
[144] PD 47, para 12.1.
[145] CPR, r 47.15(1), and PD 47, para 14.1.
[146] As listed at PD 47, paras 8.3 and 13.2.
[147] CPR, r 47.15(5).

36 offers and without-prejudice offers must be in a sealed envelope marked 'Part 36 offers'.

10.104   On receipt of these papers the court will undertake a provisional assessment of the bill,[148] normally within six weeks. No party is permitted to attend the provisional assessment.[149] Once the provisional assessment has been carried out the court will return Precedent G (the points of dispute and any reply) with the court's decisions noted on it,[150] together with a notice stating that any party who wishes to challenge any aspect of the provisional assessment must, within 21 days of the receipt of the notice, file and serve on all other parties a written request for an oral hearing. If no such request is filed and served within that period, the provisional assessment shall be binding upon the parties, save in exceptional circumstances.[151]

10.105   Within 14 days of receipt of Precedent G the parties must agree the total sum due to the receiving party on the basis of the court's decisions. If the parties are unable to agree the arithmetic, they must refer the dispute back to the court for a decision on the basis of written submissions.[152] If a party requests an oral hearing,[153] its written request must identify the items it wishes to be reviewed, and it must provide a time estimate for the hearing.[154] A party who requests an oral hearing will pay the costs of and incidental to the hearing unless either the costs are adjusted by at least 20 per cent in its favour or the court otherwise orders.[155]

Part 36 offers in assessment

10.106   The rules on this have been recast, and can be found in CPR, r 47.20(4) and (7).

L. INTEREST ON COSTS

10.107   Rather shockingly, it transpires from *Simcoe v Jacuzzi UK Group plc*[156] that CPR, r 40.8(1), is ineffective in county court proceedings because it was made without the concurrence of the Treasury, which was required by County Courts Act 1984, s 74. CPR, r 40.8(1), provides that interest payable on a judgment pursuant to Judgments Act 1838, s 17, or County Courts Act 1984, s 74, shall begin

---

[148] CPR, r 47.15(3).
[149] PD 47, para 14.4(1).
[150] PD 47, para 14.4(2).
[151] CPR, r 47.15(7).
[152] PD 47, para 14.4(2).
[153] Under CPR, r 45.15(7).
[154] CPR, r 47.15(8).
[155] CPR, r 47.15(10).
[156] [2012] EWCA Civ 137, [2012] 1 WLR 2393.

to run from the date of the judgment unless another rule or the court provides otherwise. In the event it made no real difference in *Simcoe v Jacuzzi UK Group plc*, because the fallback provisions[157] produced the same answer.

New CPR, r 44.9(4) (which re-enacts old r 44.12(2)), and new r 47.20(6) (which is completely new) deal with interest on costs. It is likely to be necessary to obtain Treasury approval for them for the same reason as in *Simcoe v Jacuzzi UK Group plc*. **10.108**

Perhaps the more important part of the decision in *Simcoe v Jacuzzi UK Group plc* is that it holds that in both the High Court and county courts interest on orders for costs to be assessed runs from the date of the costs order (the 'incipitur date') rather than the date on which the costs are assessed or agreed (the 'allocatur date'). This is the normal rule,[158] and, as CPR, r 40.8(1), expressly says, can be departed from if the court otherwise orders. The fact that the successful party is funded under a CFA is not a reason for departing from the normal rule. **10.109**

M. PRO BONO COSTS

Pro bono costs orders

Most of the provisions dealing with pro bono costs orders have been re-enacted in the new provisions in the CPR and practice directions by the Jackson reforms. The court may order any person to make a payment to the prescribed charity in respect of pro bono representation of a party.[159] The prescribed charity is the Access to Justice Foundation.[160] In considering whether to order a payment to the prescribed charity, and the terms of such an order, the court must have regard to whether it would, apart from Legal Services Act 2007, s 194, have made an order in favour of the party with the pro bono representation and the terms of the order it would have made.[161] Such an order cannot be made in respect of representation before 1 October 2008.[162] Nor can it be made against another person with pro bono representation, or a person with public funding.[163] **10.110**

An order under s 194(3) must be for fixed costs where CPR, Part 45, would otherwise apply.[164] Where Part 45 does not apply, the court may determine the **10.111**

---

[157] County Courts (Interest on Judgment Debts) Order 1991 (SI 1991/1184), art 2.
[158] *Simcoe v Jacuzzi UK Group plc* [2012] EWCA Civ 137, [2012] 1 WLR 2393 at [35].
[159] Legal Services Act 2007, s 194(3).
[160] Legal Services Act 2007, s 194(8); Legal Services Act 2007 (Prescribed Charity) Order 2008 (SI 2008/2680).
[161] Legal Services Act 2007, s 194(4).
[162] Legal Services Act 2007, s 194(11).
[163] Legal Services Act 2007, s 194(6).
[164] CPR, r 46.7(1)(a).

amount of the payment (other than a sum equivalent to fixed costs) to be made by the paying party to the prescribed charity by:

(a) making a summary assessment; or

(b) making an order for detailed assessment,

of a sum equivalent to all or part of the costs the paying party would have been ordered to pay to the party with pro bono representation in respect of that representation had it not been provided free of charge.[165] An order under Legal Services Act 2007, s 194(3), must specify that the payment by the paying party must be made to the prescribed charity.[166]

Assessment of pro bono costs

10.112 To assist the court in making a summary assessment of the amount payable to the prescribed charity, the party who has pro bono representation must prepare, file, and serve a written statement of the sum equivalent to the costs that party would have claimed for that legal representation had it not been provided free of charge.[167] Where there is an order for detailed assessment and the receiving party had pro bono representation for part only of the proceedings, the bill of costs must be divided into different parts to differentiate between the different periods of funding.[168] The bill of costs must not include a claim for VAT in respect of the pro bono costs.[169]

10.113 The receiving party is required to keep the prescribed charity informed by sending it copies of the order under Legal Services Act 2007, s 194(3),[170] any default costs certificate,[171] any order setting aside or varying a default costs certificate,[172] any interim certificate,[173] and the final costs certificate.[174]

Pro bono costs in the Supreme Court

10.114 Legal Services Act 2007, s 194, has been amended by LASPO 2012, s 61, to enable the Supreme Court to make pro bono costs orders in the same way as previously applied in the lower courts. LASPO 2012, s 61, was brought into force with effect from 1 October 2012.[175]

---

[165] CPR, r 46.7(1)(b).
[166] CPR, r 46.7(2).
[167] PD 44, para 9.5(2).
[168] PD 47, para 5.8(2).
[169] PD 44, para 2.14.
[170] CPR, r 46.7(3).
[171] CPR, r 47.11(4).
[172] CPR, r 47.12(3).
[173] CPR, r 47.16(4).
[174] CPR, r 47.17(6).
[175] Legal Aid, Sentencing and Punishment of Offenders Act 2012 (Commencement No 2 and Specification of Commencement Date) Order 2012 (SI 2012/2412).

11

PART 36 OFFERS

A. INTRODUCTION

One of the aims of the Woolf reforms was to encourage parties to settle their **11.01** disputes rather than take them all the way through to trial. In order to achieve this it was seen to be essential that the parties had sufficient information about each other's case so that informed decisions could be made about making offers and about whether to accept proposals received from the other side. Although one of the criticisms of the Woolf reforms was the emphasis on front loading preparation, this has meant that in most cases the parties to civil litigation have had the information they have needed for the purpose of making and accepting offers to settle.

11.02　This has provided the foundation for the success of Part 36 offers under the Woolf reforms. Success in this context[1] is in promoting the settlement of civil disputes, often at an early stage. Formulating clear and accessible rules on Part 36 offers has proved far more challenging.

11.03　One of the great innovations brought in by the Civil Procedure Rules (CPR) was the ability of claimants to make formal offers to settle having costs and other consequences which were set out in CPR, Part 36. The original CPR, Part 36, was replaced with effect from 6 April 2007. Until 2007, Part 36 retained the distinction previously found in Rules of the Supreme Court, ord 22, between payments in for money claims and offers made without prejudice save as to costs for other situations. That distinction was breached by *Crouch v King's Healthcare NHS Trust*,[2] which held that it was permissible for NHS Trusts in clinical dispute claims to make formal offers without making Part 36 payments despite the fact these were pure money claims. *Trustees of Stokes Pension Fund v Western Power Distribution (South West) plc*[3] went further. This held that the court could give full effect to a Part 36 offer in a money claim if the offer was clear, expressed to be open for 21 days, was genuine, and if the defendant was good for the money. This struck at the roots of the distinction between Part 36 payments and Part 36 offers, and was the main reason for the complete replacement of Part 36 with effect from 6 April 2007.

B. *FINAL REPORT* AND PART 36 OFFERS

11.04　Three issues were canvassed in the *Final Report* about Part 36 offers:

(a) reversal of *Carver v BAA plc*;[4]

(b) improving the benefits to claimants who make successful claimants' Part 36 offers; and

(c) the interplay between Part 36 offers and qualified one-way costs shifting (QOCS).

---

[1] *Final Report*, ch 41, para 1.2.
[2] [2004] EWCA Civ 1332, [2005] 1 WLR 2015.
[3] [2005] EWCA Civ 854, [2005] 1 WLR 3595.
[4] [2008] EWCA Civ 412, [2009] 1 WLR 113.

C. *FINAL REPORT* RECOMMENDATIONS ON PART 36 OFFERS

The *Final Report* made two recommendations on Part 36 offers: **11.05**

(a) One was the abolition of the decision in *Carver v BAA plc*,[5] which has already been implemented.

(b) The other was that where a defendant rejects a claimant's Part 36 offer, but fails to do better at trial than that offer, the claimant's damages should be enhanced by 10 per cent.[6]

D. IMPLEMENTATION

Government response to Part 36 recommendations

Following the consultation on the Jackson reforms, the *Government Response* of   **11.06**
March 2011 was that CPR, Part 36, would be amended to equalize the incentives between claimants and defendants to make and accept reasonable offers. The proposed amendments would apply to all civil cases, but there would be further discussion on the details.

Both main recommendations on Part 36 were accepted. Recommendation 93   **11.07**
was felt to be capable of implementation almost immediately to make it clear that where a money offer is beaten at trial, by however small a margin, the costs sanctions applicable under Part 36 will apply. While the principle of a 10 per cent increase in damages for a claimant making a successful Part 36 offer was accepted, the *Government Response* indicated an intention to explore other mechanisms for rewarding claimants in non-monetary claims, linked to costs rather than damages, to avoid satellite litigation around the court's valuation of such claims.

Ministerial Statement 17 July 2012 and Part 36

The eventual position of the government on the unresolved issues was sum-   **11.08**
marized in the Ministerial Statement of 17 July 2012. This announced that the sanctions under Part 36 would be reformed on the following basis in order to encourage early settlement:

i.   There is to be an additional amount to be paid by a defendant who does not accept a claimant's offer to settle where the court gives judgment for the claimant that is at

---

[5] *Final Report*, recommendation 93.
[6] *Final Report*, recommendation 94.

least as advantageous as an offer the claimant made to settle the claim. This additional sanction is to be calculated as 10 per cent of damages where damages are in issue, and 10 per cent of costs for non-damages claims;

ii. In mixed (damages and non-damages) claims, the sanction will be calculated as 10 per cent of the damages element of the claim;

iii. However, the sanction under these provisions is to be subject to a tapering system for claims over £500,000 so that the maximum sanction is likely to be £75,000; and

iv. There would only be one sanction applicable for split trials.

11.09 It will be seen that the position on non-monetary claims under sub-para (i) does not adopt the proposal made in the *Final Report*, and bases the 10 per cent payment on the amount of costs. This perpetuates an aspect of the perverse incentive of rewarding inefficient or expensive litigation that the Jackson reforms aimed to remove.

E. LASPO 2012 AND PART 36

11.10 LASPO 2012, s 55, was brought into force on 1 October 2012.[7] This provides for rules of court to be made to enable a court to order a defendant to pay an additional amount to a claimant following a successful claimant's Part 36 offer. The purpose of s 55 is to provide an additional incentive for a defendant to accept a reasonable Part 36 offer from a claimant.

11.11 Section 55 had to be brought into force in advance of 1 April 2013 to ensure the rule-making power was in force before the substantive rules were made. The Offers to Settle in Civil Proceedings Order 2013[8] came into force on 12 February 2013. It sets out the limits on the additional amounts that are to be paid in cases where claimants have made successful Part 36 offers.

F. REVERSAL OF *CARVER v BAA*

Decision in *Carver v BAA*

11.12 As mentioned at 11.05, one of the issues discussed in the *Final Report* was the effect of *Carver v BAA plc*,[9] which had been decided in the year before the Civil Litigation Costs Review. This case had attracted a great deal of criticism. The 2007 version of CPR, r 36.14(1), had changed the wording used by the rules in

---

[7] Legal Aid, Sentencing and Punishment of Offenders Act 2012 (Commencement No 2 and Specification of Commencement Date) Order 2012 (SI 2012/2412).

[8] SI 2013/93, see appendix 4.

[9] [2008] EWCA Civ 412, [2009] 1 WLR 113.

describing the cut-off point between successful and unsuccessful Part 36 offers to settle to whether the claimant had failed to 'obtain a judgment more advantageous' than the defendant's Part 36 offer. Before *Carver v BAA plc* it had always been held that exceeding a payment in, taking into account post-offer interest, by any margin no matter how small, was enough from the claimant's point of view to avoid incurring adverse costs consequences. Beating a payment in by a penny would technically be enough.

Carver v BAA plc held that obtaining a more advantageous judgment as **11.13** required by the post-6 April 2007 version of r 36.14(1) was a more open-textured concept than the pre-6 April 2007 phrase, which was 'fails to better'. *Carver v BAA plc* appeared to hold that the court is entitled to decide that a judgment that exceeds a Part 36 offer by a small margin might not be more advantageous to a claimant given factors such as the costs of litigating a claim through to trial and the emotional stress of taking a case to trial. On the facts the court upheld a decision that obtaining a judgment only £51 higher than the defendant's Part 36 offer was not more advantageous than the offer, being more than counterbalanced by the irrecoverable cost incurred by the claimant in continuing to contest the case. After the *Final Report*, it was held in *Gibbon v Manchester City Council*[10] that *Carver v BAA plc* was binding on all courts up to the Court of Appeal.

Carver and the *Final Report*

Almost all the comments received in the Civil Litigation Costs Review about **11.14** *Carver v BAA* asked for its reversal. The dominant reason was the uncertainty it introduced. While the judiciary might welcome the flexibility it gave in deciding questions of costs, for litigators it was almost impossible to give accurate advice. Not only did they have to advise on the likely level of damages if the case went to trial, but also predict how much leeway would be needed above that level to ensure, given the history of the case, that the likely award would be more advantageous than the offer in the *Carver* sense. The *Final Report* concluded[11] that *Carver v BAA plc* should be reversed because of the uncertainty it introduced into the process of advising upon Part 36 offers.

Reversal of *Carver* by r 36.14(1A)

For money claims, and for the money element of a claim, where the Part 36 offer **11.15** is made on or after 1 October 2011, a judgment is 'more advantageous' where it is better than the Part 36 offer in money terms by any amount, however small.[12]

[10] [2010] EWCA Civ 726, [2010] 1 WLR 2081.
[11] *Final Report*, ch 41, para 2.9.
[12] CPR, r 36.14(1A).

Rule 36.14(1A) is intended to provide a clear-cut dividing line.[13] If the judgment is even by the smallest margin better than a Part 36 offer then, subject to the discretion in what is now r 44.2, the claimant should be awarded its costs. This is so, particularly in personal injuries claims, even where the judgment is substantially lower than the amount claimed. In these cases the defendant should have protected itself by making a realistic, albeit modest, Part 36 offer.[14] In this context there is a distinction between:[15]

(a) cases where the reduction is as a result of surveillance or medical evidence, even if that shows the claimant's injuries have been exaggerated, where r 36.14(1A) applies and the claimant should be awarded standard-basis costs in the usual way; and

(b) cases where the claimant has been dishonest, where consideration should be given to depriving the claimant of the protection given by QOCS under r 44.16(1) (see 10.40).

11.16 While r 36.14(1A) overrules the decision in *Carver v BAA plc*,[16] it only does so with effect from 1 October 2011. This means that *Carver v BAA plc* is binding on all courts up to the Court of Appeal in relation to Part 36 offers made from 6 April 2007 until 30 September 2011.

Taking interest into account

11.17 Like must be compared with like. Where a Part 36 offer includes interest, the court must recalculate its award of interest to the end of the relevant period[17] in order to determine whether the judgment exceeds the terms of the offer.[18] A gloss on this was applied in *Gibbon v Manchester City Council*,[19] where the trial judge had awarded interest at 8 per cent per annum, but the Court of Appeal recalculated the award applying an interest rate of 4 per cent per annum. The stated reason was that no more than 4 per cent per annum 'could have been expected' when the Part 36 offer was made. An award of interest is just as much a part of a judgment as the principal sum, and it is with respect very difficult to understand why this additional element of uncertainty should be grafted on to the calculations that have to be made under Part 36.

---

[13] *Fox v Foundation Piling Ltd* [2011] EWCA Civ 790, [2011] 6 Costs LR 961.
[14] *Morgan v UPS* [2008] EWCA Civ 1476, [2009] 3 Costs LR 384.
[15] As recognized by *Fox v Foundation Piling Ltd*.
[16] [2008] EWCA Civ 412, [2009] 1 WLR 113.
[17] For which, see CPR, r 36.3(3).
[18] *Blackham v Entrepose UK* [2004] EWCA Civ 1109, *The Times*, 28 September 2004.
[19] [2010] EWCA Civ 726, [2010] 1 WLR 2081 at [36].

Defendant's offers in non-monetary claims

In a non-monetary claim with a Part 36 offer made by the defendant, deciding **11.18** whether the judgment is more advantageous than the offer has always had the potential for involving a difficult balancing exercise between the terms of the offer and the terms of the award at trial. In a defamation claim, comparing the terms of an offer with the eventual judgment may, depending on the terms of the offer and the events at trial, involve considering the terms and value of any apology and any damage to the reputation of the claimant arising from the evidence given at the trial.[20]

For non-money claims on and after 1 October 2011, it is submitted the **11.19** approach suggested by Bingham MR in *Roache v News Group Newspapers Ltd*[21] has a continuing validity in deciding whether a judgment is more advantageous than a Part 36 offer:

The judge must look closely at the facts of the particular case before him and ask: who, as a matter of substance and reality, has won? Has the [claimant] won anything of value which he could not have won without fighting the action through to the finish? Has the defendant substantially denied the [claimant] the prize which the [claimant] fought the action to win?

Failing to beat own Part 36 offer

It is a fundamental error to make a costs order that penalizes a party for failing **11.20** to achieve a better result at trial than the terms of its own Part 36 offer.[22]

G. CLAIMANTS' PART 36 OFFERS

The *Final Report* also considered the arguments for increasing the rewards for **11.21** a claimant who makes a successful Part 36 offer. There was a marked imbalance in the existing system. Under r 36.14(2) (which remains unchanged by the Jackson reforms), a defendant making a successful Part 36 offer would generally be awarded its costs from the end of the relevant period.[23] This often has a dramatic effect, and can potentially wipe out the entirety of the damages awarded.[24]

While the pre-Jackson rules in Part 36 sought to provide real benefits for a **11.22** claimant making a successful Part 36 offer, the *Final Report*[25] concluded that

---

[20] *Jones v Associated Newspapers Ltd* [2007] EWHC 1489 (QB), [2008] 1 All ER 240.

[21] [1998] EMLR 161 at pp 168–9, which is cited with approval in *Carver v BAA plc*.

[22] *Rolf v De Guerin* [2011] EWCA Civ 78, [2011] BLR 221.

[23] Which is usually 21 days after serving the Part 36 offer, r 36.3(1)(c).

[24] As recognized by the *Final Report*, ch 41, para 3.4.

[25] In ch 41 at paras 3.5 and 3.9.

such a claimant is insufficiently rewarded, with the result that claimants' Part 36 offers have not always been treated seriously by defendants.

Pre-Jackson consequences of failing to beat a claimant's Part 36 offer

11.23 Under the version of CPR, r 36.14(3), in force before 1 April 2013, unless the court considered it unjust to do so, where judgment was entered against a defendant which was at least as advantageous to the claimant as the proposals set out in a claimant's Part 36 offer, the court would order that the claimant was entitled to:

(a) interest on the whole or part of any sum of money (excluding interest) awarded at a rate not exceeding 10 per cent above base rate for some or all of the period starting with the date on which the relevant period expired;

(b) costs on the indemnity basis from the date on which the relevant period expired; and

(c) interest on those costs at a rate not exceeding 10 per cent above base rate.

Guidelines on ordering otherwise

11.24 Guidance on situations where it would be unjust to impose the orders authorized by CPR, r 36.14(3), is given by r 36.14(4) (which remains unchanged). This provides that in considering whether it would be unjust to make the orders referred to in para (3) (or para (2) in relation to defendants' Part 36 offers), the court will take into account all the circumstances of the case including:

(a) the terms of any Part 36 offer;

(b) the stage in the proceedings when any Part 36 offer was made, including in particular how long before the trial started the offer was made;

(c) the information available to the parties at the time when the Part 36 offer was made; and

(d) the conduct of the parties with regard to the giving or refusing to give information for the purposes of enabling the offer to be made or evaluated.

11.25 Where the court awarded interest under r 36.14(3)(a), and interest was also awarded on the same sum for the same period under any other power,[26] the total rate of interest was not permitted to exceed 10 per cent above base rate.[27]

11.26 Even this power was eroded by decisions of the courts. It was held that the court should not start with the assumption that it should award the maximum enhanced interest, but must stand back and ensure that the enhanced interest

---

[26] Such as County Courts Act 1984, s 69, or Senior Courts Act 1981, s 35A.
[27] CPR, r 36.14(5).

did not provide a disproportionate benefit.[28] Although full 10 per cent above base rate interest was awarded on occasions, such as *Blue Sphere Global Ltd v Commissioners of HM Revenue and Customs*,[29] it was more common for some lower rate to be applied. For example, in *Pankhurst v White*[30] enhanced interest on damages in a personal injuries claim was awarded at 10 per cent per annum on past losses (instead of the then current 6 per cent special account rate), and at 4 per cent per annum (instead of 2 per cent) on damages for pain, suffering, and loss of amenity. While higher than the interest rates normally applied in personal injuries claims, these rates were below 10 per cent above base rate.

While there was more appetite for making orders for indemnity basis costs **11.27** under r 36.14(3)(b), that was not as favourable to a claimant as reversing the costs incidence as occurred in favour of defendants who made successful Part 36 offers. The effectiveness of r 36.14(3)(c) was seriously diminished by decisions applying a compensatory approach to the rule.[31] For example, it was held that the purpose of an order for interest on indemnity costs is to compensate for the cost of money, or loss of the use of money, borne before trial in relation to payments made on account of costs.[32]

Final Report and claimants' Part 36 offers

To ensure there are adequate benefits for a claimant who makes a successful Part **11.28** 36 offer, the *Final Report*[33] proposed that there should be an uplift of 10 per cent on the damages awarded to claimants in such cases. It was recognized that this might produce a disproportionate benefit in high-value cases, and so it was suggested that further consultation should be undertaken over whether a taper in the additional damages would be appropriate for claims of over £500,000. It was also recognized that non-monetary claims needed a similar incentive. The suggestion made in the *Final Report*[34] was that in these cases there should be a rough and ready summary assessment of value in money terms of the monetary relief granted, so that an award of 10 per cent of that assessed value could be awarded to a claimant making a successful Part 36 offer in such a case.

---

[28] *Earl v Cantor Fitzgerald International (No 2)* (2001) LTL 3/5/2001.

[29] [2010] EWCA Civ 1448, LTL 16/12/2010.

[30] [2010] EWHC 311 (QB), [2010] 3 Costs LR 402.

[31] Examples are *KR v Bryn Alyn Community (Holdings) Ltd* [2003] EWCA Civ 383, [2003] CP Rep 49 and *Chantrey Vellacott v Convergence Group plc* (2007) LTL 3/10/2007.

[32] *Chantrey Vellacott v Convergence Group plc*.

[33] *Final Report*, ch 41, para 3.10.

[34] *Final Report*, ch 41, para 3.12.

Additional amounts to be awarded in claimants' Part 36 offers

11.29 CPR, r 36.14(3), has been amended with effect from 1 April 2013 to say:

Subject to paragraph (6), where rule 36.14(1)(b) applies, the court will, unless it considers it unjust to do so, order that the claimant is entitled to—

(a) interest on the whole or part of any sum of money (excluding interest) awarded at a rate not exceeding 10 per cent above base rate for some or all of the period starting with the date on which the relevant period expired;

(b) costs on the indemnity basis from the date on which the relevant period expired;

(c) interest on those costs at a rate not exceeding 10 per cent above base rate; and

(d) an additional amount, which shall not exceed £75,000, calculated [as set out below].

11.30 Deciding the appropriate basis on which to calculate the additional amount payable under r 36.14(3)(d) has proved controversial. The solution that has emerged makes separate provision for money and non-money claims.[35] For money claims, rules of court may provide for an 'additional amount' to be payable to a claimant making a successful Part 36 offer.[36] The Lord Chancellor must prescribe a limit to the additional amount that the rules can provide for.[37] Working within that limit, CPR, r 36.14(3)(d), requires the additional amount, which cannot exceed £75,000, to be calculated as a percentage of the sum awarded to the claimant by the court (excluding any award for costs) as follows:

Amount awarded by the court	Prescribed percentage
up to £500,000	10 per cent of the amount awarded;
above £500,000, up to £1,000,000	10 per cent of the first £500,000 and 5 per cent of any amount above that figure.

11.31 For non-money claims, a preliminary question is whether the Part 36 offer is more advantageous than the terms of the judgment.[38] This can be a difficult question for the court, as it often involves comparing detailed terms in a Part 36 offer with the terms of the judgment. Rules on making such an assessment may be made under the Offers to Settle in Civil Proceedings Order 2013.[39] Once a decision has been made that a judgment is at least as advantageous as a claimant's Part 36 offer in a non-money claim, an additional amount may be ordered

---

[35] LASPO 2012, s 55.
[36] LASPO 2012, s 55(1).
[37] LASPO 2012, s 55(3). The limit is prescribed in SI 2013/93, art 2.
[38] Offers to Settle in Civil Proceedings Order 2013, art 3(1).
[39] Art 3(3).

under r 36.14(3)(d). In non-money claims this cannot exceed £75,000.[40] LASPO 2012, s 55(5), gave some latitude on how the additional amount would actually be calculated in an individual case.[41] The Offers to Settle in Civil Proceedings Order 2013[42] in fact splits non-monetary claims into mixed claims and pure non-money claims.

In claims which include both a claim for an amount of money and a non-monetary claim, the additional amount under r 36.14(3)(d) is calculated in accordance with the following percentage of the amount awarded by the court on the money part of the claim (excluding any award for costs):[43]   **11.32**

Amount awarded by the court	Amount to be paid by the defendant
up to £500,000	10 per cent of the amount awarded;
above £500,000, up to £1,000,000	10 per cent of the first £500,000 and 5 per cent of any amount above that figure;
above £1,000,000	£75,000.[44]

In non-monetary claims with no money claim, an additional award under r 36.14(3)(d) is based on a percentage of the costs ordered to be paid by the defendant to the claimant, as follows:[45]   **11.33**

Costs ordered to be paid to the claimant	Amount to be paid by the defendant
up to £500,000	10 per cent of the amount awarded;
above £500,000, up to £1,000,000	10 per cent of the first £500,000 and 5 per cent of any amount above that figure;
above £1,000,000	£75,000.[46]

---

[40] Offers to Settle in Civil Proceedings Order 2013, art 3(5).

[41] This could have been by reference to the costs incurred, the value of any monetary relief in a mixed claim, and/or the value of any non-monetary relief.

[42] Art 3(4).

[43] Offers to Settle in Civil Proceedings Order 2013, art 3(4)(a).

[44] The third entry in this table, dealing with awards over £1,000,000, has been added editorially to make clear what appears to be the intended effect of art 3(4)(a) and CPR, r 36.14(3)(d). The wording of these provisions is open to the unintended interpretation that the court cannot order an additional amount under r 36.14(3)(d) if the money part of the judgment exceeds £1,000,000, because the second entry in the table has a ceiling of £1,000,000. However, it was probably considered that the provision that an additional amount cannot exceed £75,000 made an entry for judgments over £1,000,000 unnecessary.

[45] Offers to Settle in Civil Proceedings Order 2013, art 3(4)(b).

[46] See n 44.

Unless the court considers it unjust

11.34 The opening words of the revised CPR, r 36.14(3), remain unchanged. They allow the court to depart from the usual consequences as set out in sub-paras (a) to (d) where the court considers them unjust. As seen at 11.23 to 11.27, before the Jackson reforms were brought into effect the courts regularly found reasons why it would be unjust to make full use of the powers available under what used to be r 36.14(3)(a) to (c). The underlying problem was that the courts tended to regard the consequences in r 36.14(3) as primarily compensatory in nature. They are not. They are intended to be rewards for claimants who have made successful Part 36 offers, and they are intended to provide benefits equivalent to the costs orders available under r 36.14(2) to defendants making successful Part 36 offers.

11.35 The additional amount in r 36.14(3)(d) was seen by Sir Rupert Jackson as being an integral part of the reforms that included abolishing the recoverability of conditional fee agreement success fees and other additional liabilities. As stated in the 10th Implementation Lecture, abolition of success fees, increasing damages by 10 per cent, and the ability of claimants to augment their damages by a further 10 per cent by making an effective Part 36 offer, are parts of a balanced package. The balance in the package of reforms will only be maintained if the courts are ready to impose awards of the additional amount where the claimant has made a successful claimant's Part 36 offer.

H. QOCS AND PART 36 OFFERS

11.36 The interrelation between QOCS[47] and Part 36 offers was considered in the *Final Report*.[48] This is a difficult situation. The conclusion reached in the *Final Report* was that if a defendant makes a successful Part 36 offer in a case where the claimant has the benefit of QOCS, the claimant should forfeit, or, depending on the circumstances, substantially forfeit, the benefits of QOCS. As discussed at 10.30, the effect of CPR, r 44.14(1), is that where the court makes a split costs order under r 36.14(2), the defendant can recoup the costs ordered in its favour under r 36.14(2)(a) from the award of damages and interest made in favour of the claimant. As r 44.14(1) also says, such recoupment may not exceed the aggregate amount in money terms of the judgment for damages and interest made in favour of the claimant, other than with the permission of the court.[49]

---

[47] See 10.07 to 10.50.

[48] *Final Report*, ch 41, paras 4.1 to 4.3.

[49] Subject to the loss of the protection provided by QOCS under rr 44.15 and 44.16, see 10.34 to 10.50.

12

ALTERNATIVE DISPUTE RESOLUTION

A. INTRODUCTION

Sir Rupert Jackson has said that alternative dispute resolution (ADR), particu- **12.01** larly mediation, has a vital role to play in reducing the costs of civil disputes by fomenting the early settlement of cases.[1] Having considered the feedback and evidence received in the Civil Litigation Costs Review he concluded[2] that:

(a) mediation and joint settlement meetings are highly efficacious means of achieving a satisfactory resolution of many disputes;

(b) the benefits of mediation are not appreciated by many small and medium-sized enterprises or the general public; and

(c) although many judges and practitioners are well aware of the benefits of mediation and other forms of ADR, many are not.

---

[1] 11th Implementation Lecture, para 2.2.
[2] 11th Implementation Lecture, para 5.1.

B. *FINAL REPORT* RECOMMENDATIONS ON ADR

12.02 There were two recommendations on ADR in the *Final Report*:

(a) There should be a serious campaign (i) to ensure that all litigation lawyers and judges are properly informed about the benefits which ADR can bring and (ii) to alert the public and small businesses to the benefits of ADR.[3]

(b) An authoritative handbook should be prepared, explaining clearly and concisely what ADR is and giving details of all reputable providers of mediation. This should be the standard handbook for use at all Judicial College seminars and CPD training sessions concerning mediation.[4]

C. COURT ENCOURAGEMENT OF ADR

12.03 Mediation practitioners who gave evidence to the Civil Litigation Costs Review were very keen to persuade Sir Rupert Jackson to recommend rule changes to the Civil Procedure Rules to make the use of ADR compulsory in contested cases. The position taken by the courts, particularly in *Halsey v Milton Keynes General NHS Trust*,[5] and the pre-action protocols etc, has been that the parties are required to consider ADR, but the courts stop short of ordering them to engage in ADR. The courts encourage the use of ADR by:

(a) holding parties to pre-dispute agreements to use ADR by granting stays to proceedings commenced in breach of an ADR clause;

(b) making orders declaring the rights of the parties under ADR clauses, or providing machinery for implementing ADR clauses;

(c) ensuring the parties have addressed, or will address, whether ADR might be useful as a means of resolving their dispute, typically at case management conferences;

(d) making orders, such as the Ungley order,[6] that make it plain that the court expects serious consideration to be given to the use of ADR;

(e) imposing costs sanctions on parties who act unreasonably in relation to ADR.

---

[3] *Final Report*, recommendation 75.
[4] *Final Report*, recommendation 76.
[5] [2004] EWCA Civ 576, [2004] 1 WLR 3002.
[6] See 12.04.

Ungley order

A useful model direction is the Ungley order,[7] which was designed by Master 12.04 Ungley and originated in clinical dispute claims. The object of the order is to try to reduce the number of cases settled at the door of the court, which are wasteful both of costs and judicial time. It provides:

The parties shall by [a date usually about three months before the trial window opens] consider whether the case is capable of resolution by ADR. If any party considers the case is unsuitable for resolution by ADR that party shall be prepared to justify that decision at the conclusion of the trial, should the trial judge consider that such means of resolution were appropriate, when he is considering the appropriate costs order to make. Such means of ADR as shall be adopted shall be concluded not less than 35 days prior to the trial.

The party considering the case unsuitable for ADR shall, not less than 28 days before the commencement of the trial, file with the court a witness statement, without prejudice save as to costs, giving the reasons upon which they rely for saying that the case is unsuitable. The witness statement shall not be disclosed to the trial judge until the conclusion of the case.

Approach after the Jackson reforms

In the 11th Implementation Lecture Lord Justice Jackson commented that it 12.05 is not rule changes that are needed in this area, but a culture change. There is no need for universal compulsion to use ADR, or for universal sanctions. The existing principles give the judges all the powers they need, and the approach the court ought to take in any individual case is essentially a case management decision which ought not to be constrained by tightly drawn rules.[8] However, it is recognized in the same lecture that ADR has a significantly greater role to play in the civil justice system in the future than it has taken in the past.[9]

D. ADR HANDBOOK

Steps have been taken, under the guidance of an editorial board involving 12.06 Ramsey J, to publish an ADR Handbook[10] to coincide with the introduction of the Jackson reforms to meet the need identified in recommendation 76.[11]

---

[7] *Blackstone's Civil Practice* (Oxford: OUP, 2013), para 42.27.
[8] At para 5.4.
[9] 11th Implementation Lecture, para 5.2.
[10] S Blake, J Browne, and S Sime, *The Jackson ADR Handbook* (Oxford: OUP, 2013).
[11] As mentioned in the 11th Implementation Lecture, para 5.6.

13

APPEALS

A. *FINAL REPORT* RECOMMENDATIONS ON APPEALS

There are three recommendations relevant to appeals: **13.01**

(a) There should be a separate review of the procedures and costs rules for appeals, after decisions have been reached in relation to the recommendations in this report concerning first instance litigation (recommendation 70).

(b) Pending that review, appellate courts should have a discretionary power, upon granting permission to appeal or receiving an appeal from a no-costs jurisdiction, to order (a) that each side should bear its own costs of the appeal or (b) that the recoverable costs should be capped at a specified sum (recommendation 71).

(c) The Master of the Rolls should designate two lords justices, at least one of whom will so far as possible be a member of any constitution of the civil division of the Court of Appeal, which is called upon to consider issues concerning the interpretation or application of the CPR (recommendation 87).

B. FURTHER REVIEW

Recommendation 70, while cautious, is consistent with precedent. Sir Jeffrey **13.02** Bowman conducted a separate review of the Court of Appeal (Civil Division) in 1997 to follow and build on the *Woolf Report* in 1996. It is also sensible given (what was at the time of the *Final Review* the anticipated) replacement of the old PD 52 on appeals. This has now been implemented with the introduction of the new PD 52A to PD 52E on 1 October 2012 in place of the earlier PD 52.

C. APPEAL COSTS IN APPEALS FROM NO-COSTS JURISDICTIONS

13.03 Sir Rupert Jackson[1] referred to competing cultures that sometimes collide on appeals:

(a) the no-costs culture that applies in many tribunals, where costs shifting is seen as being an impediment to access to justice; and

(b) the costs-shifting practice in the courts, where the rule is seen as promoting access to justice.

13.04 When the courts hear an appeal from a non-costs jurisdiction the two cultures come into collision. A litigant in such an appeal finds itself at the appeal stage suddenly facing the prospect of having to pay the costs of the other side, a prospect it may not have expected when it originally embarked on its application to the tribunal. The *Final Report*[2] referred to *Eweida v British Airways plc*,[3] where the appellant brought an appeal against an Employment Tribunal's decision to dismiss a religious discrimination claim. She was refused a costs protection order because her claim was not made in public law litigation. Her alternative claim for a costs capping order was refused largely on the ground that, even if there was a risk of costs being disproportionately incurred by the other side, that could be controlled by the costs judge on assessment. The unsatisfactory result in *Eweida v British Airways plc* seems to have been accepted in *Unison v Kelly*,[4] where an alternative route to providing costs protection on an appeal from a tribunal was found (by granting permission to appeal on condition that no costs were sought from the respondent).

13.05 Recommendation 71 has been implemented by adding CPR, r 52.9A, which provides:

(1) In any proceedings in which costs recovery is normally limited or excluded at first instance, an appeal court may make an order that the recoverable costs of an appeal will be limited to the extent which the court specifies.

(2) In making such an order the court will have regard to—

(a) the means of both parties;

(b) all the circumstances of the case; and

(c) the need to facilitate access to justice.

(3) If the appeal raises an issue of principle or practice upon which substantial sums may turn, it may not be appropriate to make an order under paragraph (1).

---

[1] *Final Report*, ch 34, para 3.4.
[2] At ch 34, para 3.5.
[3] [2009] EWCA Civ 1025, [2010] CP Rep 6.
[4] [2012] EWCA Civ 1148, [2012] IRLR 591.

(4) An application for such an order must be made as soon as practicable and will be determined without a hearing unless the court orders otherwise.

D. DESIGNATED COURT OF APPEAL JUDGES

Recommendation 87 has a great deal to commend it in promoting consistency **13.06** and in giving the Court of Appeal the opportunity of driving through the ethos change required for the success of the Jackson reforms.

E. SECOND APPEALS

An amendment has been made to PD 52C, dealing with second appeals. By **13.07** para 5A, an application to make a second appeal must identify in the grounds of appeal:

(a) the important point of principle or practice; or

(b) the compelling reason,

which is said to justify the grant of permission to appeal.

14

DAMAGES FOR PERSONAL INJURIES, SUFFERING, AND DISTRESS

A. INTRODUCTION

Replacing recoverable success fees and after-the-event (ATE) insurance pre- **14.01** miums under old-style conditional fee agreements (CFAs) with non-recoverable success fees under new style CFAs and damages-based agreements (DBAs) was recognized by the *Final Report* as leaving a funding shortfall. Sir Rupert Jackson disavowed the idea that claimants in personal injuries claims should be fully protected against the costs of their litigation: some liability for a party's own costs was seen as a beneficial discipline over litigation. However, removing recoverability would push the balance too far, and needed to be redressed. In particular, there was concern that provision should be made to assist claimants in personal injuries claims (and some other classes of litigation) in meeting the 25 per cent success fee they might be required to pay their own lawyers in successful cases funded by new-style CFAs.[1]

These concerns were addressed by introducing qualified one-way costs shifting[2] **14.02** and by proposing a 10 per cent increase in awards for pain, suffering, and loss

---

[1] *Final Report*, ch 10, para 5.3.
[2] See chapter 10.

199

of amenity (PSLA). As was made clear in *Simmons v Castle*,[3] the primary purpose behind introducing the 10 per cent increase in damages was to compensate claimants as a class for the loss of recoverability of success fees and other additional liabilities. Together these reforms are seen as forming part of a coherent package.[4]

B. *FINAL REPORT* RECOMMENDATIONS ON TORT DAMAGES

14.03 Balancing recommendation 9, on repealing the statutory provisions on the recoverability of CFA success fees, is recommendation 10, that the level of damages for personal injuries, nuisance, and all other civil wrongs to individuals should be increased by 10 per cent. A similar recommendation to raise awards in defamation and breach of privacy claims by 10 per cent was made by recommendation 65.

C. INCREASING NON-PECUNIARY GENERAL DAMAGES BY 10 PER CENT

14.04 Much of the debate over disproportionate costs has focused on personal injuries claims, and the *Government Response* for the most part adopted a personal injuries mindset. The *Final Report* took a far more wide-ranging approach. It recommended that consideration should be given to increasing damages in a range of types of claim, not only personal injuries claims. For example, the *Government Response* limited this part of the proposed reforms to personal injuries cases, but it adopted the *Final Report's* recommendation that damages for non-pecuniary loss should be increased by 10 per cent to provide a fund from which lawyers in these cases can take their CFA success fees. Pecuniary loss for this purpose primarily means damages for PSLA, but is much wider.[5]

D. IMPLEMENTATION

14.05 Introduction of the 10 per cent increase in personal injuries awards has been achieved by the simple expedient of issuing general guidance in a Court of Appeal judgment. The relevant case is *Simmons v Castle*.[6] The original judgment[7] left a number of unanswered questions, and the guidance was amended

---

[3] [2012] EWCA Civ 1288, [2013] 1 All ER 334 at [27].
[4] *Simmons v Castle* at [7].
[5] See 14.06 to 14.11.
[6] [2012] EWCA Civ 1039, [2012] EWCA Civ 1288, [2013] 1 All ER 334.
[7] [2012] EWCA Civ 1039.

in a supplementary judgment.[8] As stated by Lord Diplock in *Wright v British Railways Board*,[9] the Court of Appeal is, generally speaking, the tribunal best qualified to give guidelines on non-economic loss. A similar exercise in keeping guidelines for awards for PSLA up to date was undertaken by the Court of Appeal in *Heil v Rankin*.[10]

E. AWARDS COVERED BY THE 10 PER CENT UPLIFT

According to the first judgment in *Simmons v Castle*,[11] the 10 per cent increase in damages would extend not only to personal injury claims but also to other tort claims, and would apply to general damages awards for (i) PSLA in respect of personal injuries claims; (ii) nuisance; (iii) defamation; and (iv) all other torts which cause suffering, inconvenience, or distress to individuals.   **14.06**

The way in which the original judgment[12] was worded gave rise to a number of ambiguities. While it was clear that the 10 per cent increase would extend to tort claims other than personal injury actions,[13] it was unclear if it covered (for example) personal injuries claims in contract, or whether the whole of the damages award in nuisance and defamation claims was subject to the increase, or just the personal suffering elements of the award. In clearing up the ambiguities relating to personal injuries claims, in the second judgment[14] the Court of Appeal also clarified most of the other points.   **14.07**

Revised guidance on the cases covered by the 10 per cent increase was summarized as follows:[15]   **14.08**

Accordingly, we take this opportunity to declare that, with effect from 1 April 2013, the proper level of general damages in all civil claims for (i) pain and suffering, (ii) loss of amenity, (iii) physical inconvenience and discomfort, (iv) social discredit, (v) mental distress, or (vi) loss of society of relatives, will be 10 per cent higher than previously, unless the claimant falls within LASPO 2012, s 44(6). It therefore follows that, if the action now under appeal had been the subject of a judgment after 1 April 2013, then (unless the claimant had entered into a CFA before that date) the proper award of general damages would be 10 per cent higher than that agreed in this case, namely £22,000 rather than £20,000.

---

[8] [2012] EWCA Civ 1288. Both judgments are reported at [2013] 1 All ER 334.
[9] [1983] 2 AC 773 at p 785.
[10] [2001] QB 272.
[11] [2012] EWCA Civ 1039, [2013] 1 All ER 334 at [6], [14], and [20].
[12] At [20].
[13] At [14].
[14] *Simmons v Castle* [2012] EWCA Civ 1288, [2013] 1 All ER 334.
[15] *Simmons v Castle* [2012] EWCA Civ 1288, [2013] 1 All ER 334 at [50].

14.09 The guidance on the heads of damage covered by the 10 per cent increase as set out in sub-paras (i) to (vi) above was based on the categories of damages set out in *McGregor on Damages*.[16]

14.10   The 10 per cent increase is not limited to awards for PSLA in claims based on negligence or even in tort, but also extends to a range of heads of damage, and where these heads of damage are available, the 10 per cent increase applies regardless of the nature of the cause of action.[17] The increase extends to other torts, which will include claims in breach of statutory duty, nuisance, defamation,[18] assault, battery, harassment, malicious prosecution, false imprisonment, and any other tort which causes suffering, inconvenience, or distress to individuals. The increase also applies to many breach of contract claims,[19] many professional negligence claims, holiday claims, discrimination claims, landlord and tenant claims, and others with a personal injury element. As Lord Judge CJ said,[20] 'we can see no good reason why the 10 per cent increase should be limited so as to exclude any type of claim'. If there are any doubtful cases, they will have to be dealt with on a case-by-case basis.[21]

14.11   A number of points should be kept in mind:

(a) The increase is limited to the award for PSLA and other heads of damage broadly relating to personal suffering as defined in para [50] of the second judgment,[22] and does not cover damages for economic loss.

(b) The increase only applies to claims involving personal suffering to an individual.

(c) The 10 per cent increase applies to all claimants, and is not restricted to claimants funded by CFAs.[23]

F. EFFECT OF THE 10 PER CENT UPLIFT

14.12 The 10 per cent increase in general damages is closely connected with the proposal that successful lawyers in personal injuries CFA-funded cases will have their CFA success fees limited to 25 per cent of the damages awarded (other than

---

[16] 18th edn (London: Sweet & Maxwell, 2009), ch 3.

[17] *Simmons v Castle* [2012] EWCA Civ 1288, [2013] 1 All ER 334 at [50]: the increase is not restricted to particular categories of civil claims.

[18] There is an inconsistency between the 10 per cent increase applying in defamation and breach of privacy claims, and the continuation of recoverability of additional liabilities in the transitional provisions, see 2.20.

[19] *Simmons v Castle* [2012] EWCA Civ 1288, [2013] 1 All ER 334 at [46].

[20] *Simmons v Castle* [2012] EWCA Civ 1288, [2013] 1 All ER 334 at [46].

[21] *Simmons v Castle* [2012] EWCA Civ 1288, [2013] 1 All ER 334 at [49].

[22] *Simmons v Castle* [2012] EWCA Civ 1288, [2013] 1 All ER 334 at [50].

[23] *Simmons v Castle* [2012] EWCA Civ 1288, [2013] 1 All ER 334 at [41] to [44].

those for future care and loss).[24] Whether a claimant is better off overall depends on the amount of the claimant's base costs, which in turn is affected by factors such as how early the case settles, the percentage of the agreed success fee, and the breakdown of the damages award between PSLA, other past losses, and future care and loss. Claimants under the new system whose case proceeds a long way towards trial may find that even with a costs order against the defendant, a significant part of the damages awarded will have to be used to pay their legal representatives' success fees.

Sir Rupert Jackson was advised by Professor Paul Fenn, the economist adviser **14.13** to the Civil Litigation Costs Review, that a 10 per cent increase in general damages would leave claimants no worse off in the great majority of personal injuries cases.[25] That advice actually indicated that in cases that settle early, which is the great majority of cases, claimants would be better off. Overall 61 per cent of claimants would benefit from the changes, with 29 per cent worse off. The figures also indicated that claimants in road traffic accidents tended to benefit more from the changes than claimants in employer's liability and public liability cases. The fact that the number of road traffic cases greatly exceeds the number of cases in the other two categories explains the overall outcome of the study.

While an across-the-board increase in damages for PSLA in personal injuries **14.14** could be seen as a windfall for claimants not using CFAs, it was felt in the *Final Report*[26] that this was justified because the level of general damages in personal injuries cases needed to be increased in any event.[27]

The graphs provided by Professor Fenn show that while claimants overall are **14.15** better off with these changes, the difference is not very great. The effect on other interest groups has not been analysed to the same extent. However, it seems almost inevitable that claimants' legal representatives will find it a great deal more difficult to run a litigation practice profitably under the new system, and defendants and their insurers will have substantially less financial exposure than before. It is to be hoped that these benefits to insurers will be reflected in a reduction in insurance premiums, but of course there is no direct connection between the two.

G. TRANSITIONAL ARRANGEMENTS

The increase approved by *Simmons v Castle*[28] takes effect on 1 April 2013. The **14.16** first judgment[29] said the cut-off point was whether judgment was given on or

---

[24] See 4.27.
[25] *Final Report*, ch 10, para 5.4.
[26] *Final Report*, ch 10, para 5.6.
[27] Citing the Law Commission's report on *Damages for Personal Injury: Non-pecuniary Loss* (Law Com 257, 1998).
[28] [2012] EWCA Civ 1039, [2012] EWCA Civ 1288, [2013] 1 All ER 334.
[29] [2012] EWCA Civ 1039, [2013] 1 All ER 334 at [19], [20].

after 1 April 2013. The problem with that is that there will be cases funded by CFAs in the pre-Jackson form which will reach trial after 1 April 2013. If those cases benefited from the 10 per cent increase in damages they would have the best of both worlds: recoverable success fees etc under the pre-Jackson funding regime, and the 10 per cent increase in damages which was meant to compensate claimants for losing the benefits of recoverability.

14.17   To avoid the obvious injustice of double compensation for the expense of funding, in its second judgment the Court of Appeal[30] accepted that the 10 per cent increase in damages should not apply to claimants who had entered into CFAs before 1 April 2013. The way it was actually put by Lord Judge CJ[31] was that 'we would ... exclude those claimants who fall within the ambit of LASPO 2012, s 44(6)'.[32]

14.18   There were two reasons for adopting this slightly technical language:

(a) it has the effect of guaranteeing there is identity between the successful claimants who are statutorily entitled to recover their success fees from defendants and those who are disentitled from enjoying the 10 per cent increase in general damages; and

(b) any risk of satellite litigation will be restricted to the risks of satellite litigation already inherent in s 44(6), and does not create further definitions which might provoke challenges in the courts.

---

[30] [2012] EWCA Civ 1288, [2013] 1 All ER 334 at [31] and [40].
[31] [2012] EWCA Civ 1288, [2013] 1 All ER 334 at [40].
[32] For which, see 2.07.

15

SPECIALIST PROCEEDINGS

15.01 A substantial proportion of the *Final Report* was devoted to specialist proceedings.[1] However, there are very few provisions in the Jackson reforms being implemented on 1 April 2013 that relate specifically to specialist proceedings.

A. INTELLECTUAL PROPERTY CLAIMS

15.02 There are two sets of provisions being introduced with effect from 1 April 2013 that are relevant to intellectual property claims:

(a) the reference to the small claims track limit in CPR, r 63.27(1)(b), is changed from £5,000 to £10,000; and

(b) the scale costs provisions for claims in the Patents County Court have been reorganized within CPR, Part 45, but without material change.

B. DEFAMATION, BREACH OF CONFIDENTIALITY, AND PRIVACY

15.03 The level of damages in defamation claims has been raised by 10 per cent with effect from 1 April 2013 as recommended by the *Final Report*. This will also apply to related causes of action involving personal suffering. See chapter 14, and the doubt about how this relates to the transitional provisions discussed at 2.33.

---

[1] Within CPR, Parts 57 to 64.

15.04   There are transitional provisions dealing with funding arrangements in defamation, malicious falsehood, breach of confidence, and misuse of private information claims.[2]

C. CLINICAL NEGLIGENCE

15.05   There are special rules preserving the recoverability of after-the-event insurance premiums for experts' reports in clinical negligence claims.[3]

D. MESOTHELIOMA CLAIMS

15.06   A further review is being undertaken regarding the recoverability of success fees and other additional liabilities in mesothelioma claims. As a result there are transitional provisions dealing with funding arrangements in these claims.[4]

E. INSOLVENCY PROCEEDINGS

15.07   LASPO 2012, ss 44 and 48, are not being commenced on 1 April 2013 in relation to certain proceedings relating to insolvency. The relevant transitional provisions dealing with this are considered at 2.18.

F. ENVIRONMENTAL LAW

15.08   In claims covered by the Aarhus Convention there are special rules, to be found in CPR, rr 45.41 to 45.44, limiting costs in accordance with the principles laid down by the Convention.

---

[2] See 2.19.
[3] See 4.49.
[4] See 2.15.

APPENDIX 1

Relevant provisions of the Legal Aid, Sentencing and Punishment of Offenders Act 2012

CONTENTS

PART 2
LITIGATION FUNDING AND COSTS

Payments for legal services in civil cases

Offers to settle

Referral fees

Pro bono representation

PART 4
FINAL PROVISIONS

LEGAL AID, SENTENCING AND PUNISHMENT OF
OFFENDERS ACT 2012

2012 CHAPTER 10

An Act to make provision about legal aid; to make further provision about funding legal services; to make provision about costs and other amounts awarded in civil and criminal proceedings; to make provision about referral fees in connection with the provision of legal services; to make provision about sentencing offenders, including provision about release on licence or otherwise; to make provision about the collection of fines and other sums; to make provision about bail and about remand otherwise than on bail; to make provision about the employment, payment and transfer of persons detained in prisons and other institutions; to make provision about penalty notices for disorderly behaviour and cautions; to make provision about the rehabilitation of offenders; to create new offences of threatening with a weapon in public or on school premises and of causing serious injury by dangerous driving; to create a new offence relating to squatting; to increase penalties for offences relating to scrap metal dealing and to create a new offence relating to payment for scrap metal; and to amend section 76 of the Criminal Justice and Immigration Act 2008.

[1st May 2012]

BE IT ENACTED by the Queen's most Excellent Majesty, by and with the advice and consent of the Lords Spiritual and Temporal, and Commons, in this present Parliament assembled, and by the authority of the same, as follows:—

PART 2
LITIGATION FUNDING AND COSTS

Payments for legal services in civil cases

Conditional fee agreements: success fees

44—(1) In section 58 of the Courts and Legal Services Act 1990 (conditional fee agreements), in subsection (2)—
    (a) omit 'and' after paragraph (a), and

208

    (b) after paragraph (b) insert 'and (c) references to a success fee, in relation to a conditional fee agreement, are to the amount of the increase.'

(2) After subsection (4) of that section insert—

'(4A) The additional conditions are applicable to a conditional fee agreement which—
    (a) provides for a success fee, and
    (b) relates to proceedings of a description specified by order made by the Lord Chancellor for the purposes of this subsection.

(4B) The additional conditions are that—
    (a) the agreement must provide that the success fee is subject to a maximum limit,
    (b) the maximum limit must be expressed as a percentage of the descriptions of damages awarded in the proceedings that are specified in the agreement,
    (c) that percentage must not exceed the percentage specified by order made by the Lord Chancellor in relation to the proceedings or calculated in a manner so specified, and
    (d) those descriptions of damages may only include descriptions of damages specified by order made by the Lord Chancellor in relation to the proceedings.'

(3) In section 58A of that Act (conditional fee agreements: supplementary), in subsection (5) after 'section 58(4)' insert ', (4A) or (4B)'.

(4) For subsection (6) of that section substitute—

'(6) A costs order made in proceedings may not include provision requiring the payment by one party of all or part of a success fee payable by another party under a conditional fee agreement.'

(5) In section 120(4) of that Act (regulations and orders subject to parliamentary approval) after '58(4),' insert '(4A) or (4B),'.

(6) The amendment made by subsection (4) does not prevent a costs order including provision in relation to a success fee payable by a person ('P') under a conditional fee agreement entered into before the day on which that subsection comes into force ('the commencement day') if—
    (a) the agreement was entered into specifically for the purposes of the provision to P of advocacy or litigation services in connection with the matter that is the subject of the proceedings in which the costs order is made, or
    (b) advocacy or litigation services were provided to P under the agreement in connection with that matter before the commencement day.

Damages-based agreements

45—(1) Section 58AA of the Courts and Legal Services Act 1990 (damages-based agreements) is amended as follows.

(2) In subsection (1) omit 'relates to an employment matter and'.

(3) In subsection (2)—
    (a) after 'But' insert '(subject to subsection (9))', and
    (b) omit 'relates to an employment matter and'.

(4) Omit subsection (3)(b).

(5) After subsection (4)(a) insert—

'(aa) must not relate to proceedings which by virtue of section 58A(1) and (2) cannot be the subject of an enforceable conditional fee agreement or to proceedings of a description prescribed by the Lord Chancellor;'.

(6) In subsection (4)(b), at the beginning insert 'if regulations so provide,'.

(7) In subsection (4)(d) for 'has provided prescribed information' substitute 'has complied with such requirements (if any) as may be prescribed as to the provision of information'.

(8) After subsection (6) insert—

'(6A) Rules of court may make provision with respect to the assessment of costs in proceedings where a party in whose favour a costs order is made has entered into a damages-based agreement in connection with the proceedings.'

(9) After subsection (7) insert—

'(7A) In this section (and in the definitions of "advocacy services" and "litigation services" as they apply for the purposes of this section) "proceedings" includes any sort of proceedings for resolving disputes (and not just proceedings in a court), whether commenced or contemplated.'

(10) After subsection (8) insert—

'(9) Where section 57 of the Solicitors Act 1974 (non-contentious business agreements between solicitor and client) applies to a damages-based agreement other than one relating to an employment matter, subsections (1) and (2) of this section do not make it unenforceable.

(10) For the purposes of subsection (9) a damages-based agreement relates to an employment matter if the matter in relation to which the services are provided is a matter that is, or could become, the subject of proceedings before an employment tribunal.'

(11) In the heading of that section omit 'relating to employment matters'.

(12) In section 120(4) of that Act (regulations and orders subject to parliamentary approval) for '58AA' substitute '58AA(4)'.

(13) The amendments made by subsections (1) to (11) do not apply in relation to an agreement entered into before this section comes into force.

Recovery of insurance premiums by way of costs

46—(1) In the Courts and Legal Services Act 1990, after section 58B insert—

'Recovery of insurance premiums by way of costs

58C—(1) A costs order made in favour of a party to proceedings who has taken out a costs insurance policy may not include provision requiring the payment of an amount in respect of all or part of the premium of the policy, unless such provision is permitted by regulations under subsection (2).

(2) The Lord Chancellor may by regulations provide that a costs order may include provision requiring the payment of such an amount where—

(a) the order is made in favour of a party to clinical negligence proceedings of a prescribed description,

(b) the party has taken out a costs insurance policy insuring against the risk of incurring a liability to pay for one or more expert reports in respect of clinical negligence in connection with the proceedings (or against that risk and other risks),

(c) the policy is of a prescribed description,

(d) the policy states how much of the premium relates to the liability to pay for an expert report or reports in respect of clinical negligence ("the relevant part of the premium"), and

(e) the amount is to be paid in respect of the relevant part of the premium.

(3) Regulations under subsection (2) may include provision about the amount that may be required to be paid by the costs order, including provision that the amount must not exceed a prescribed maximum amount.

(4) The regulations may prescribe a maximum amount, in particular, by specifying—

(a) a percentage of the relevant part of the premium;

(b) an amount calculated in a prescribed manner.

(5) In this section—

"clinical negligence" means breach of a duty of care or trespass to the person committed in the course of the provision of clinical or medical services (including dental or nursing services);

"clinical negligence proceedings" means proceedings which include a claim for damages in respect of clinical negligence;

"costs insurance policy", in relation to a party to proceedings, means a policy insuring against the risk of the party incurring a liability in those proceedings;

"expert report" means a report by a person qualified to give expert advice on all or most of the matters that are the subject of the report;

"proceedings" includes any sort of proceedings for resolving disputes (and not just proceedings in court), whether commenced or contemplated.'

(2) In the Access to Justice Act 1999, omit section 29 (recovery of insurance premiums by way of costs).

(3) The amendments made by this section do not apply in relation to a costs order made in favour of a party to proceedings who took out a costs insurance policy in relation to the proceedings before the day on which this section comes into force.

Recovery where body undertakes to meet costs liabilities

47—(1) In the Access to Justice Act 1999, omit section 30 (recovery where body undertakes to meet costs liabilities).

(2) The repeal made by subsection (1) does not apply in relation to a costs order made in favour of a person to whom a body gave an undertaking before the day on which this section comes into force if the undertaking was given specifically in respect of the costs of other parties to proceedings relating to the matter which is the subject of the proceedings in which the costs order is made.

Sections 44 and 46 and diffuse mesothelioma proceedings

48—(1) Sections 44 and 46 may not be brought into force in relation to proceedings relating to a claim for damages in respect of diffuse mesothelioma until the Lord Chancellor has—

(a) carried out a review of the likely effect of those sections in relation to such proceedings, and

(b) published a report of the conclusions of the review.

(2) In this section 'diffuse mesothelioma' has the same meaning as in the Pneumoconiosis etc (Workers' Compensation) Act 1979.

Offers to settle

Payment of additional amount to successful claimant

55—(1) Rules of court may make provision for a court to order a defendant in civil proceedings to pay an additional amount to a claimant in those proceedings where—

    (a) the claim is a claim for (and only for) an amount of money,

    (b) judgment is given in favour of the claimant,

    (c) the judgment in respect of the claim is at least as advantageous as an offer
to settle the claim which the claimant made in accordance with rules of
court and has not withdrawn in accordance with those rules, and

    (d) any prescribed conditions are satisfied.

(2) Rules made under subsection (1) may include provision as to the assessment of
whether a judgment is at least as advantageous as an offer to settle.

(3) In subsection (1) 'additional amount' means an amount not exceeding a prescribed percentage of the amount awarded to the claimant by the court (excluding any amount awarded in respect of the claimant's costs).

(4) The Lord Chancellor may by order provide that rules of court may make provision for a court to order a defendant in civil proceedings to pay an amount
calculated in a prescribed manner to a claimant in those proceedings where—

    (a) the claim is or includes a non-monetary claim,

    (b) judgment is given in favour of the claimant,

    (c) the judgment in respect of the claim is at least as advantageous as an offer
to settle the claim which the claimant made in accordance with rules of
court and has not withdrawn in accordance with those rules, and

    (d) any prescribed conditions are satisfied.

(5) An order under subsection (4) must provide for the amount to be calculated by
reference to one or more of the following—

    (a) any costs ordered by the court to be paid to the claimant by the defendant
in the proceedings;

    (b) any amount awarded to the claimant by the court in respect of so much of
the claim as is for an amount of money (excluding any amount awarded in
respect of the claimant's costs);

    (c) the value of any non-monetary benefit awarded to the claimant.

(6) An order under subsection (4)—

    (a) must provide that rules made under the order may include provision as to
the assessment of whether a judgment is at least as advantageous as an offer
to settle, and

    (b) may provide that such rules may make provision as to the calculation of the
value of a non-monetary benefit awarded to a claimant.

(7) Conditions prescribed under subsection (1)(d) or (4)(d) may, in particular,
include conditions relating to—

    (a) the nature of the claim;

    (b) the amount of money awarded to the claimant;

    (c) the value of the non-monetary benefit awarded to the claimant.

(8) Orders under this section are to be made by the Lord Chancellor by statutory
instrument.

(9) A statutory instrument containing an order under this section is subject to
annulment in pursuance of a resolution of either House of Parliament.

(10) Rules of court and orders made under this section may make different provision in relation to different cases.

(11) In this section—

'civil proceedings' means proceedings to which rules of court made under the Civil Procedure Act 1997 apply;

'non-monetary claim' means a claim for a benefit other than an amount of money;

'prescribed' means prescribed by order made by the Lord Chancellor.

Referral fees

Rules against referral fees

56—(1) A regulated person is in breach of this section if—

   (a) the regulated person refers prescribed legal business to another person and is paid or has been paid for the referral, or

   (b) prescribed legal business is referred to the regulated person, and the regulated person pays or has paid for the referral.

(2) A regulated person is also in breach of this section if in providing legal services in the course of prescribed legal business the regulated person—

   (a) arranges for another person to provide services to the client, and

   (b) is paid or has been paid for making the arrangement.

(3) Section 59 defines 'regulated person'.

(4) 'Prescribed legal business' means business that involves the provision of legal services to a client, where—

   (a) the legal services relate to a claim or potential claim for damages for personal injury or death,

   (b) the legal services relate to any other claim or potential claim for damages arising out of circumstances involving personal injury or death, or

   (c) the business is of a description specified in regulations made by the Lord Chancellor.

(5) There is a referral of prescribed legal business if—

   (a) a person provides information to another,

   (b) it is information that a provider of legal services would need to make an offer to the client to provide relevant services, and

   (c) the person providing the information is not the client;

and 'relevant services' means any of the legal services that the business involves.

(6) 'Legal services' means services provided by a person which consist of or include legal activities (within the meaning of the Legal Services Act 2007) carried on by or on behalf of that person; and a provider of legal services is a person authorised to carry on a reserved legal activity within the meaning of that Act.

(7) 'Client'—

   (a) where subsection (4)(a) applies, means the person who makes or would make the claim;

   (b) where subsection (4)(c) applies, has the meaning given by the regulations.

(8) Payment includes any form of consideration whether any benefit is received by the regulated person or by a third party (but does not include the provision of hospitality that is reasonable in the circumstances).

Effect of rules against referral fees

57—(1) The relevant regulator must ensure that it has appropriate arrangements for monitoring and enforcing the restrictions imposed on regulated persons by section 56.

(2) A regulator may make rules for the purposes of subsection (1).

(3) The rules may in particular provide for the relevant regulator to exercise in relation to anything done in breach of that section any powers (subject to subsections (5) and (6)) that the regulator would have in relation to anything done by the regulated person in breach of another restriction.

(4) Where the relevant regulator is the Financial Services Authority, section 58 applies instead of subsections (1) to (3) (and (7) to (9)).

(5) A breach of section 56—

(a) does not make a person guilty of an offence, and

(b) does not give rise to a right of action for breach of statutory duty.

(6) A breach of section 56 does not make anything void or unenforceable, but a contract to make or pay for a referral or arrangement in breach of that section is unenforceable.

(7) Subsection (8) applies in a case where—

(a) a referral of prescribed legal business has been made by or to a regulated person, or

(b) a regulated person has made an arrangement as mentioned in section 56(2) (a),

and it appears to the regulator that a payment made to or by the regulated person may be a payment for the referral or for making the arrangement (a 'referral fee').

(8) Rules under subsection (2) may provide for the payment to be treated as a referral fee unless the regulated person shows that the payment was made—

(a) as consideration for the provision of services, or

(b) for another reason,

and not as a referral fee.

(9) For the purposes of provision made by virtue of subsection (8) a payment that would otherwise be regarded as consideration for the provision of services of any description may be treated as a referral fee if it exceeds the amount specified in relation to services of that description in regulations made by the Lord Chancellor.

Regulation by FSA

58—(1) The Treasury may make regulations to enable the Financial Services Authority, where it is the relevant regulator, to take action for monitoring and enforcing compliance with the restrictions imposed on regulated persons by section 56.

(2) The regulations may apply, or make provision corresponding to, any of the provisions of the Financial Services and Markets Act 2000 with or without modification.

(3) Those provisions include in particular—
  (a) provisions as to investigations, including powers of entry and search and criminal offences;
  (b) provisions for the grant of an injunction in relation to a contravention or anticipated contravention;
  (c) provisions giving Ministers or the Financial Services Authority powers to make subordinate legislation;
  (d) provisions for the Financial Services Authority to charge fees.

(4) The regulations may make provision corresponding to the provision that may be made by virtue of section 57(7) to (9) (but as if the reference to the Lord Chancellor were a reference to the Treasury).

(5) The power to make regulations under this section is subject to section 57(5) and (6).

Regulators and regulated persons

59—(1) In relation to a referral of business within section 56(4)(a)—
  (a) a regulator is any person listed in column 1 below;
  (b) a regulated person is any person listed in column 2;
  (c) a regulator in column 1 is the relevant regulator in relation to the corresponding person in column 2.

1. Regulator	2. Regulated person
the Financial Services Authority	an authorised person (within the meaning of the Financial Services and Markets Act 2000) of a description specified in regulations made by the Treasury
the Claims Management Regulator	a person authorised by the Regulator under section 5(1)(a) of the Compensation Act 2006 to provide regulated claims management services
the General Council of the Bar	a person authorised by the Council to carry on a reserved legal activity within the meaning of the Legal Services Act 2007
the Law Society	a person authorised by the Society to carry on a reserved legal activity within the meaning of the Legal Services Act 2007
a regulatory body specified for the purposes of this subsection in regulations made by the Lord Chancellor	a person of a description specified in the regulations in relation to the body

(2) In relation to a referral of prescribed legal business of any other kind—
  (a) a regulator is any person listed in column 1 below and specified in relation to business of that kind in regulations made by the Lord Chancellor;
  (b) a regulated person is any person specified in accordance with column 2 in relation to business of that kind;

(c) a person specified under paragraph (a) in relation to business of that kind is the relevant regulator in relation to a person specified in accordance with the corresponding entry in column 2 in relation to business of that kind.

1. Regulator	2. Regulated person
the Financial Services Authority	an authorised person (within the meaning of the Financial Services and Markets Act 2000) of a description specified in regulations made by the Treasury
the Claims Management Regulator	a person who is authorised by the Regulator under section 5(1)(a) of the Compensation Act 2006 to provide regulated claims management services and is of a description specified in regulations made by the Lord Chancellor
an approved regulator for the purposes of Part 3 of the Legal Services Act 2007 (approved legal activities);	a person who is authorised by the regulator to carry on a reserved legal activity and is of a description specified in regulations made by the Lord Chancellor
a licensing authority for the purposes of Part 5 of that Act (alternative business structures)	a person who is licensed by the authority to carry on a reserved legal activity and is of a description specified in regulations made by the Lord Chancellor

Referral fees: regulations

60—(1) This section applies to any regulations under sections 56 to 59.

(2) The regulations are to be made by statutory instrument.

(3) The power to make the regulations includes power to make consequential, supplementary, incidental, transitional, transitory or saving provision.

(4) A statutory instrument containing the regulations may not be made unless a draft of the instrument has been laid before, and approved by a resolution of, each House of Parliament.

Pro bono representation

Payments in respect of pro bono representation before the Supreme Court

61—(1) In section 194 of the Legal Services Act 2007 (power for certain courts to order losing party to make payment to charity where other party is represented pro bono) in subsection (10) for the definition of 'civil court' substitute—

"'civil court" means—
(a) the Supreme Court when it is dealing with a relevant civil appeal,
(b) the civil division of the Court of Appeal,
(c) the High Court, or
(d) any county court;

216

"relevant civil appeal" means an appeal to the Supreme Court—
  (a) from the High Court in England and Wales under Part 2 of the Administration of Justice Act 1969,
  (b) from the Court of Appeal under section 40(2) of the Constitutional Reform Act 2005, or
  (c) under section 13 of the Administration of Justice Act 1960 (appeal in cases of contempt of court) other than an appeal from an order or decision made in the exercise of jurisdiction to punish for criminal contempt of court;'.

(2) This section applies in relation to appeals to the Supreme Court only where the decision, order or judgment that is the subject of the appeal is made or given on or after the day on which this section comes into force.

PART 4
FINAL PROVISIONS

Power to make consequential and supplementary provision etc

149—(1) The Lord Chancellor or the Secretary of State may by regulations make consequential, supplementary, incidental, transitional, transitory or saving provision in relation to any provision of this Act.
  (2) The regulations may, in particular amend, repeal, revoke or otherwise modify legislation.
  (3) Regulations under this section are to be made by statutory instrument.
  (4) A statutory instrument containing regulations under this section is subject to annulment in pursuance of a resolution of either House of Parliament, subject to subsection (5).
  (5) A statutory instrument containing regulations under this section that amend or repeal an Act (whether alone or with other provision) may not be made unless a draft of the instrument has been laid before, and approved by a resolution of, each House of Parliament.
  (6) In this section—
    'Act' includes an Act or Measure of the National Assembly for Wales; 'legislation', in relation to regulations made in relation to a provision of this Act, means—
      (a) this Act or an Act passed before or in the same Session as this Act, or
      (b) an instrument made under an Act before the provision comes into force.

Financial provision

150—There is to be paid out of money provided by Parliament—
  (a) any expenditure incurred by a Minister of the Crown by virtue of this Act, and
  (b) any increase attributable to this Act in the sums payable under any other Act out of money so provided.

Commencement

151—(1) The provisions of this Act come into force on such day as the Lord Chancellor or the Secretary of State may appoint by order, subject to subsections (2) and (3).

(2) The following provisions come into force on the day on which this Act is passed—

    (a) section 77,

    (b) section 119, and

    (c) this Part.

(3) This section does not apply to section 76 (but see section 77).

(4) An order under this section is to be made by statutory instrument.

(5) An order under this section may—

    (a) appoint different days for different purposes, and

    (b) make transitional, transitory or saving provision.

(6) An order under this section bringing into force section 133, 134, 136, 137 or 138 may appoint different days for different areas.

Extent

152— (1) Parts 1 to 3 of this Act extend to England and Wales only, subject to subsections (2) to (8).[1]

    ...

(6) An amendment, repeal or revocation made by this Act has the same extent as the relevant part of the Act or instrument amended, repealed or revoked (ignoring extent by virtue of an Order in Council), subject to subsections (2), (5), (7) and (8).

    ...

(10) Sections 149, 150, 151, this section and section 154 extend to England and Wales, Scotland and Northern Ireland.

(11) But, in so far as sections 77, 149 and 151 confer power to make provision modifying or otherwise relating to a provision of, or made under or applied by, the Armed Forces Act 2006, they have the same extent as that Act (ignoring extent by virtue of an Order in Council).

Short title

154. This Act may be cited as the Legal Aid, Sentencing and Punishment of Offenders Act 2012.

COMMENCEMENT DATES

Provision	Commencement date	Commencement provision
s 44	19 January 2013 (order-making power), 1 April 2013 (other provisions with saving, see below)	SI 2013/77
s 45(1)	1 October 2012	SI 2012/2412
s 45(8)	1 October 2012	SI 2012/2412
s 45 remainder	19 January 2013 (power to make regulations and rules), 1 April 2013 (all other provisions)	SI 2013/77

[1] Subsections (2) to (5), and (7) to (9) are not relevant to the provisions reproduced in this appendix and have been omitted.

Provision	Commencement date	Commencement provision
s 46	19 January 2013 (regulation-making power), 1 April 2013 (other provisions with saving, see below)	SI 2013/77
s 48	19 January 2013	SI 2013/77
s 55	1 October 2012	SI 2012/2412
s 61	1 October 2012	SI 2012/2412
ss 149 to 152 and 154	1 May 2012	s 151(2)

The titles of the commencement orders are:

SI 2012/2412	Legal Aid, Sentencing and Punishment of Offenders Act 2012 (Commencement No 2 and Specification of Commencement Date) Order 2012
SI 2013/77	Legal Aid, Sentencing and Punishment of Offenders Act 2012 (Commencement No 5 and Saving Provision) Order 2013

The saving provision[2] is that ss 44 and 46 do not yet apply to the proceedings listed in the commencement note at the end of Appendix 2.

---

[2] SI 2013/77, art 4.

Courts and Legal Services Act 1990, sections 58 to 58C

COURTS AND LEGAL SERVICES ACT 1990
1990 CHAPTER 41

PART II
LEGAL SERVICES

Conditional fee agreements[1]

58—(1) A conditional fee agreement which satisfies all of the conditions applicable to it by virtue of this section shall not be unenforceable by reason only of its being a conditional fee agreement; but (subject to subsection (5)) any other conditional fee agreement shall be unenforceable.

(2) For the purposes of this section and section 58A—

(a) a conditional fee agreement is an agreement with a person providing advocacy or litigation services which provides for his fees and expenses, or any part of them, to be payable only in specified circumstances; [...][2]

(b) a conditional fee agreement provides for a success fee if it provides for the amount of any fees to which it applies to be increased, in specified circumstances, above the amount which would be payable if it were not payable only in specified circumstances; [and

(c) references to a success fee, in relation to a conditional fee agreement, are to the amount of the increase.][3]

(3) The following conditions are applicable to every conditional fee agreement—

(a) it must be in writing;

(b) it must not relate to proceedings which cannot be the subject of an enforceable conditional fee agreement; and

(c) it must comply with such requirements (if any) as may be prescribed by the [Lord Chancellor].[4]

---

[1] Section 58 was substituted by the Access to Justice Act 1999, s 27(1), with effect from 1 April 2000.

[2] Word 'and' repealed by LASPO 2012, s 44(1)(a).

[3] Paragraph (c) inserted by LASPO 2012, s 44(1)(b).

[4] Words substituted by: (a) Secretary of State for Constitutional Affairs Order 2003 (SI 2003/1887), sch 2, para 8(1); (b) Transfer of Functions (Lord Chancellor and Secretary of State) Order 2005 (SI 2005/3429), sch, para 2.

(4) The following further conditions are applicable to a conditional fee agreement which provides for a success fee—

   (a) it must relate to proceedings of a description specified by order made by the [Lord Chancellor];[5]

   (b) it must state the percentage by which the amount of the fees which would be payable if it were not a conditional fee agreement is to be increased; and

   (c) that percentage must not exceed the percentage specified in relation to the description of proceedings to which the agreement relates by order made by the [Lord Chancellor].[6]

[(4A) The additional conditions are applicable to a conditional fee agreement which—

   (a) provides for a success fee, and

   (b) relates to proceedings of a description specified by order made by the Lord Chancellor for the purposes of this subsection.

(4B) The additional conditions are that—

   (a) the agreement must provide that the success fee is subject to a maximum limit,

   (b) the maximum limit must be expressed as a percentage of the descriptions of damages awarded in the proceedings that are specified in the agreement,

   (c) that percentage must not exceed the percentage specified by order made by the Lord Chancellor in relation to the proceedings or calculated in a manner so specified,[7] and

   (d) those descriptions of damages may only include descriptions of damages specified by order made by the Lord Chancellor in relation to the proceedings.[8]][9]

(5) If a conditional fee agreement is an agreement to which section 57 of the Solicitors Act 1974 (non-contentious business agreements between solicitor and client) applies, subsection (1) shall not make it unenforceable.

Conditional fee agreements: supplementary[10]

58A—(1) The proceedings which cannot be the subject of an enforceable conditional fee agreement are—

   (a) criminal proceedings, apart from proceedings under section 82 of the Environmental Protection Act 1990; and

   (b) family proceedings.

(2) In subsection (1) 'family proceedings' means proceedings under any one or more of the following—

   (a) the Matrimonial Causes Act 1973;

   [(b) the Adoption and Children Act 2002;][11]

---

[5] As note 4. The relevant order is the Conditional Fee Agreements Order 2013, art 2.

[6] As note 4. The relevant order is the Conditional Fee Agreements Order 2013, art 3.

[7] The relevant order is the Conditional Fee Agreements Order 2013, art 5(1).

[8] The relevant order is the Conditional Fee Agreements Order 2013, art 5(2).

[9] Subsections (4A) and (4B) inserted by LASPO 2012, s 44(2).

[10] Section 58A was inserted by Access to Justice Act 1999, s 27(1), with effect from 1 April 2000.

[11] Subsection (2)(b) substituted by Adoption and Children Act 2002, sch 3, para 80.

    (c) the Domestic Proceedings and Magistrates' Courts Act 1978;

    (d) Part III of the Matrimonial and Family Proceedings Act 1984;

    (e) Parts I, II and IV of the Children Act 1989;

    (f) [Parts 4 and 4A][12] of the Family Law Act 1996; [...

    (fa) Chapter 2 of Part 2 of the Civil Partnership Act 2004 (proceedings for dissolution etc. of civil partnership);

    (fb) Schedule 5 to the 2004 Act (financial relief in the High Court or a county court etc.);

    (fc) Schedule 6 to the 2004 Act (financial relief in magistrates' courts etc.);

    (fd) Schedule 7 to the 2004 Act (financial relief in England and Wales after overseas dissolution etc. of a civil partnership); and][13]

    (g) the inherent jurisdiction of the High Court in relation to children.

(3) The requirements which the [Lord Chancellor][14] may prescribe under section 58(3)(c)—

    (a) include requirements for the person providing advocacy or litigation services to have provided prescribed information before the agreement is made; and

    (b) may be different for different descriptions of conditional fee agreements (and, in particular, may be different for those which provide for a success fee and those which do not).

(4) In section 58 and this section (and in the definitions of 'advocacy services' and 'litigation services' as they apply for their purposes) 'proceedings' includes any sort of proceedings for resolving disputes (and not just proceedings in a court), whether commenced or contemplated.

(5) Before making an order under section 58(4)[, (4A) or (4B)],[15] the [Lord Chancellor][16] shall consult—

    (a) the designated judges;

    (b) the General Council of the Bar;

    (c) the Law Society; and

    (d) such other bodies as he considers appropriate.

[(6) A costs order made in proceedings may not include provision requiring the payment by one party of all or part of a success fee payable by another party under a conditional fee agreement.][17]

---

[12] Words substituted by Forced Marriage (Civil Protection) Act 2007, sch 2, para 2.

[13] Word 'and' repealed, and paragraphs (fa), (fb), (fc) and (fd) inserted, by Civil Partnership Act 2004, sch 27, para 138, and sch 30.

[14] Words substituted by: (a) Secretary of State for Constitutional Affairs Order 2003 (SI 2003/1887), sch. 2, para 8(1); (b) Transfer of Functions (Lord Chancellor and Secretary of State) Order 2005 (SI 2005/3429), sch, para 2.

[15] Words inserted by LASPO 2012, s 44(3).

[16] As note 14.

[17] Subsection (6) substituted by LASPO 2012, s 44(4). Before this substitution the subsection read: '(6) A costs order made in any proceedings may, subject in the case of court proceedings to rules of court, include provision requiring the payment of any fees payable under a conditional fee agreement which provides for a success fee.'

(7) Rules of court may make provision with respect to the assessment of any costs which include fees payable under a conditional fee agreement (including one which provides for a success fee).

The following transitional provision is made by LASPO 2012, s 44(6):

(6) The amendment made by subsection (4) [of LASPO 2012, s 44, substituting a new subsection (6) in CLSA 1990 s 58A] does not prevent a costs order including provision in relation to a success fee payable by a person ('P') under a conditional fee agreement entered into before the day on which that subsection comes into force ('the commencement day')[18] if—

    (a) the agreement was entered into specifically for the purposes of the provision to P of advocacy or litigation services in connection with the matter that is the subject of the proceedings in which the costs order is made, or

    (b) advocacy or litigation services were provided to P under the agreement in connection with that matter before the commencement day.

Damages-based agreements[19]

58AA—(1) A damages-based agreement which [...][20] satisfies the conditions in subsection (4) is not unenforceable by reason only of its being a damages-based agreement.

(2) But [(subject to subsection (9))][21] a damages-based agreement which [...][22] does not satisfy those conditions is unenforceable.

(3) For the purposes of this section—

    (a) a damages-based agreement is an agreement between a person providing advocacy services, litigation services or claims management services and the recipient of those services which provides that—

        (i) the recipient is to make a payment to the person providing the services if the recipient obtains a specified financial benefit in connection with the matter in relation to which the services are provided, and

        (ii) the amount of that payment is to be determined by reference to the amount of the financial benefit obtained;

    [...][23]

(4) The agreement—

    (a)   must be in writing;

    [(aa)   must not relate to proceedings which by virtue of section 58A(1) and (2) cannot be the subject of an enforceable conditional fee agree-

---

[18] The subsection came into force for this purpose on 1 April 2013 (Legal Aid, Sentencing and Punishment of Offenders Act 2012 (Commencement No 5 and Saving Provision) Order 2013 (SI 2013/77), art 3).

[19] Section 58AA inserted by Coroners and Justice Act 2009, s 154(1) and (2), with effect from 12 November 2009. The words 'relating to employment matters' repealed from the heading by LASPO 2012, s 45(1) and (11).

[20] The words 'relates to an employment matter and' repealed by LASPO 2012, s 45(1) and (2).

[21] Words inserted by LASPO 2012, s 45(1) and (3)(a).

[22] The words 'relates to an employment matter and' repealed by LASPO 2012, s 45(1) and (3)(b).

[23] Paragraph (b) repealed by LASPO 2012, s 45(1) and (4). Paragraph (b) read: (b) a damages-based agreement relates to an employment matter if the matter in relation to which the services are provided is a matter that is, or could become, the subject of proceedings before an employment tribunal.

ment or to proceedings of a description prescribed by the Lord Chancellor;][24]

    (b)   [if regulations so provide,][25] must not provide for a payment above a prescribed amount or for a payment above an amount calculated in a prescribed manner;[26]

    (c)   must comply with such other requirements as to its terms and conditions as are prescribed;[27] and

    (d)   must be made only after the person providing services under the agreement [has complied with such requirements (if any) as may be prescribed as to the provision of information].[28]

  (5) Regulations under subsection (4) are to be made by the Lord Chancellor and may make different provision in relation to different descriptions of agreements.

  (6) Before making regulations under subsection (4) the Lord Chancellor must consult—

    (a)   the designated judges,

    (b)   the General Council of the Bar,

    (c)   the Law Society, and

    (d)   such other bodies as the Lord Chancellor considers appropriate.

[(6A) Rules of court may make provision with respect to the assessment of costs in proceedings where a party in whose favour a costs order is made has entered into a damages-based agreement in connection with the proceedings.][29]

  (7) In this section—

'payment' includes a transfer of assets and any other transfer of money's worth (and the reference in subsection (4)(b) to a payment above a prescribed amount, or above an amount calculated in a prescribed manner, is to be construed accordingly);

'claims management services' has the same meaning as in Part 2 of the Compensation Act 2006 (see section 4(2) of that Act).

[(7A) In this section (and in the definitions of 'advocacy services' and 'litigation services' as they apply for the purposes of this section) 'proceedings' includes any sort of proceedings for resolving disputes (and not just proceedings in a court), whether commenced or contemplated.][30]

  (8) Nothing in this section applies to an agreement entered into before the coming into force of the first regulations made under subsection (4).[31]

---

[24] Paragraph (aa) inserted by LASPO 2012, s 45(1) and (5).

[25] Words inserted by LASPO 2012, s 45(1) and (6).

[26] The relevant regulations are the Damages-Based Agreements Regulations 2013, regs 4 and 7.

[27] The requirements are prescribed by the Damages-Based Agreements Regulations 2013, reg 8.

[28] Words substituted by LASPO 2012, s 45(1) and (7). The words replaced were: 'has provided prescribed information'. The requirements are prescribed by the Damages-Based Agreements Regulations 2013, reg 5.

[29] Subsection (6A) inserted by LASPO 2012, s 45(1) and (8).

[30] Subsection (7A) inserted by LASPO 2012, s 45(1) and (9).

[31] The first regulations made under that subsection were the Damages-Based Agreements Regulations 2010 (SI 2010/1206), which came into force on 8 April 2010.

[(9) Where section 57 of the Solicitors Act 1974 (non-contentious business agreements between solicitor and client) applies to a damages-based agreement other than one relating to an employment matter, subsections (1) and (2) of this section do not make it unenforceable.

(10) For the purposes of subsection (9) a damages-based agreement relates to an employment matter if the matter in relation to which the services are provided is a matter that is, or could become, the subject of proceedings before an employment tribunal.][32]

The following transitional provision is made by LASPO 2012, s 45(13):

(13) The amendments [to CLSA 1990, s 58AA] made by subsections (1) to (11) [of LASPO 2012, s 45] do not apply in relation to an agreement entered into before this section comes into force.[33]

Litigation funding agreements[34]

58B—(1) A litigation funding agreement which satisfies all of the conditions applicable to it by virtue of this section shall not be unenforceable by reason only of its being a litigation funding agreement.

(2) For the purposes of this section a litigation funding agreement is an agreement under which—

(a) a person ('the funder') agrees to fund (in whole or in part) the provision of advocacy or litigation services (by someone other than the funder) to another person ('the litigant'); and

(b) the litigant agrees to pay a sum to the funder in specified circumstances.

(3) The following conditions are applicable to a litigation funding agreement—

(a) the funder must be a person, or person of a description, prescribed by the [Lord Chancellor];[35]

(b) the agreement must be in writing;

(c) the agreement must not relate to proceedings which by virtue of section 58A(1) and (2) cannot be the subject of an enforceable conditional fee agreement or to proceedings of any such description as may be prescribed by the [Lord Chancellor];[36]

(d) the agreement must comply with such requirements (if any) as may be so prescribed;

(e) the sum to be paid by the litigant must consist of any costs payable to him in respect of the proceedings to which the agreement relates together with an amount calculated by reference to the funder's anticipated expenditure in funding the provision of the services; and

---

[32] Subsections (9) and (10) inserted by LASPO 2012, s 45(1) and (10).

[33] The section came into force for this purpose on 1 April 2013 (Legal Aid, Sentencing and Punishment of Offenders Act 2012 (Commencement No 5 and Saving Provision) Order 2013 (SI 2013/77), art 3).

[34] Section 58B will be inserted when the Access to Justice Act 1999, s 28, is brought into force.

[35] Words substituted by: (a) Secretary of State for Constitutional Affairs Order 2003 (SI 2003/1887), sch. 2, para 11(1); (b) Transfer of Functions (Lord Chancellor and Secretary of State) Order 2005 (SI 2005/3429), sch, para 4(b).

[36] As note 35.

(f) that amount must not exceed such percentage of that anticipated expenditure as may be prescribed by the [Lord Chancellor][37] in relation to proceedings of the description to which the agreement relates.

(4) Regulations under subsection (3)(a) may require a person to be approved by the [Lord Chancellor] or by a prescribed person.

(5) The requirements which the [Lord Chancellor][38] may prescribe under subsection (3)(d)—

(a) include requirements for the funder to have provided prescribed information to the litigant before the agreement is made; and

(b) may be different for different descriptions of litigation funding agreements.

(6) In this section (and in the definitions of 'advocacy services' and 'litigation services' as they apply for its purposes) 'proceedings' includes any sort of proceedings for resolving disputes (and not just proceedings in a court), whether commenced or contemplated.

(7) Before making regulations under this section, the [Lord Chancellor][39] shall consult—

(a) the designated judges;

(b) the General Council of the Bar;

(c) the Law Society; and

(d) such other bodies as he considers appropriate.

(8) A costs order made in any proceedings may, subject in the case of court proceedings to rules of court, include provision requiring the payment of any amount payable under a litigation funding agreement.

(9) Rules of court may make provision with respect to the assessment of any costs which include fees payable under a litigation funding agreement.

Recovery of insurance premiums by way of costs[40]

58C—(1) A costs order made in favour of a party to proceedings who has taken out a costs insurance policy may not include provision requiring the payment of an amount in respect of all or part of the premium of the policy, unless such provision is permitted by regulations under subsection (2).

(2) The Lord Chancellor may by regulations[41] provide that a costs order may include provision requiring the payment of such an amount where—

(a) the order is made in favour of a party to clinical negligence proceedings of a prescribed description,

(b) the party has taken out a costs insurance policy insuring against the risk of incurring a liability to pay for one or more expert reports in respect of clinical negligence in connection with the proceedings (or against that risk and other risks),

(c) the policy is of a prescribed description,

---

[37] As note 35. And in subsection 4.
[38] As note 35.
[39] As note 35.
[40] Section 58C is inserted by LASPO 2012, s 46(1).
[41] The regulations made under this provision are the Recovery of Costs Insurance Premiums in Clinical Negligence Proceedings Regulations 2013 (SI 2013/92).

      (d) the policy states how much of the premium relates to the liability to pay for an expert report or reports in respect of clinical negligence ('the relevant part of the premium'), and

      (e) the amount is to be paid in respect of the relevant part of the premium.

(3) Regulations under subsection (2) may include provision about the amount that may be required to be paid by the costs order, including provision that the amount must not exceed a prescribed maximum amount.

(4) The regulations may prescribe a maximum amount, in particular, by specifying—

      (a) a percentage of the relevant part of the premium;

      (b) an amount calculated in a prescribed manner.

(5) In this section—

'clinical negligence' means breach of a duty of care or trespass to the person committed in the course of the provision of clinical or medical services (including dental or nursing services);

'clinical negligence proceedings' means proceedings which include a claim for damages in respect of clinical negligence;

'costs insurance policy', in relation to a party to proceedings, means a policy insuring against the risk of the party incurring a liability in those proceedings;

'expert report' means a report by a person qualified to give expert advice on all or most of the matters that are the subject of the report;

'proceedings' includes any sort of proceedings for resolving disputes (and not just proceedings in court), whether commenced or contemplated.

The following transitional provision is made by LASPO 2012, s 46(3):

(3) The amendments [including the insertion of CLSA 1990, s 58C] made by this section do not apply in relation to a costs order made in favour of a party to proceedings who took out a costs insurance policy in relation to the proceedings before the day on which this section comes into force.[42]

COMMENCEMENT DATES OF AMENDMENTS MADE BY LASPO 2012

Provision	Commencement date	Commencement provision
CLSA 1990, s 58AA(6A)	1 October 2012	SI 2012/2412
All other amendments made by LASPO 2012 to CLSA 1990, s 58AA	19 January 2013 (regulation-making power), 1 April 2013 (all other provisions)	SI 2013/77
Amendments made by LASPO 2012 to CLSA 1990, ss 58 and 58A, and new s 58C	19 January 2013 (power to make regulations and orders), 1 April 2013 (other provisions with saving, see below)	SI 2013/77

---

[42] The section came into force for this purpose on 1 April 2013 (Legal Aid, Sentencing and Punishment of Offenders Act 2012 (Commencement No 5 and Saving Provision) Order 2013 (SI 2013/77), art 3).

The titles of the commencement orders are:

SI 2012/2412	Legal Aid, Sentencing and Punishment of Offenders Act 2012 (Commencement No 2 and Specification of Commencement Date) Order 2012
SI 2013/77	Legal Aid, Sentencing and Punishment of Offenders Act 2012 (Commencement No 5 and Saving Provision) Order 2013

The saving provision[43] is that the amendments made by LASPO 2012 to CLSA 1990, ss 58 and 58A, and the new s 58C, do not yet apply to the following types of proceedings (which we will call 'saved proceedings'):

(a) proceedings relating to a claim for damages in respect of diffuse mesothelioma;

(b) publication and privacy proceedings;

(c) proceedings in England and Wales brought by a person acting in the capacity of—
  (i) a liquidator of a company which is being wound up in England and Wales or Scotland under Parts IV or V of the 1986 Act; or
  (ii) a trustee of a bankrupt's estate under Part IX of the 1986 Act;

(d) proceedings brought by a person acting in the capacity of an administrator appointed pursuant to the provisions of Part II of the 1986 Act;

(e) proceedings in England and Wales brought by a company which is being wound up in England and Wales or Scotland under Parts IV or V of the 1986 Act; or

(f) proceedings brought by a company which has entered administration under Part II of the 1986 Act.

The following definitions apply:[44]

'the 1986 Act' means the Insolvency Act 1986;

'company' means a company within the meaning of section 1 of the Companies Act 2006 or a company which may be wound up under Part V of the 1986 Act;

'diffuse mesothelioma' has the same meaning as in LASPO 2012, s 48(2);

'news publisher' means a person who publishes a newspaper, magazine or website containing news or information about or comment on current affairs;

'proceedings' has the same meaning as in CLSA 1990, s 58A(4);

'publication and privacy proceedings' means proceedings for—

  (a) defamation;
  (b) malicious falsehood;
  (c) breach of confidence involving publication to the general public;
  (d) misuse of private information; or
  (e) harassment, where the defendant is a news publisher.

---

[43] SI 2013/77, art 4.
[44] SI 2013/77, art 1(2).

VERSIONS OF SECTIONS 58 AND 58A WHICH APPLY
TO SAVED PROCEEDINGS

Conditional fee agreements[45]

58—(1) A conditional fee agreement which satisfies all of the conditions applicable to it by virtue of this section shall not be unenforceable by reason only of its being a conditional fee agreement; but (subject to subsection (5)) any other conditional fee agreement shall be unenforceable.

(2) For the purposes of this section and section 58A—

(a) a conditional fee agreement is an agreement with a person providing advocacy or litigation services which provides for his fees and expenses, or any part of them, to be payable only in specified circumstances; and

(b) a conditional fee agreement provides for a success fee if it provides for the amount of any fees to which it applies to be increased, in specified circumstances, above the amount which would be payable if it were not payable only in specified circumstances.

(3) The following conditions are applicable to every conditional fee agreement—

(a) it must be in writing;

(b) it must not relate to proceedings which cannot be the subject of an enforceable conditional fee agreement; and

(c) it must comply with such requirements (if any) as may be prescribed by the [Lord Chancellor].[46]

(4) The following further conditions are applicable to a conditional fee agreement which provides for a success fee—

(a) it must relate to proceedings of a description specified by order made by the [Lord Chancellor];[47]

(b) it must state the percentage by which the amount of the fees which would be payable if it were not a conditional fee agreement is to be increased; and

(c) that percentage must not exceed the percentage specified in relation to the description of proceedings to which the agreement relates by order made by the [Lord Chancellor].[48]

(5) If a conditional fee agreement is an agreement to which section 57 of the Solicitors Act 1974 (non-contentious business agreements between solicitor and client) applies, subsection (1) shall not make it unenforceable.

---

[45] Section 58 was substituted by the Access to Justice Act 1999, s 27(1), with effect from 1 April 2000.

[46] Words substituted by: (a) Secretary of State for Constitutional Affairs Order 2003 (SI 2003/1887), sch 2, para 8(1); (b) Transfer of Functions (Lord Chancellor and Secretary of State) Order 2005 (SI 2005/3429), sch, para 2.

[47] As note 45. The relevant order is the Conditional Fee Agreements Order 2013, art 2.

[48] As note 45. The relevant order is the Conditional Fee Agreements Order 2013, art 3.

Conditional fee agreements: supplementary[49]

58A—(1) The proceedings which cannot be the subject of an enforceable conditional fee agreement are—

(a) criminal proceedings, apart from proceedings under section 82 of the Environmental Protection Act 1990; and

(b) family proceedings.

(2) In subsection (1) 'family proceedings' means proceedings under any one or more of the following—

(a) the Matrimonial Causes Act 1973;

[(b) the Adoption and Children Act 2002;][50]

(c) the Domestic Proceedings and Magistrates' Courts Act 1978;

(d) Part III of the Matrimonial and Family Proceedings Act 1984;

(e) Parts I, II and IV of the Children Act 1989;

(f) [Parts 4 and 4A][51] of the Family Law Act 1996; [...

(fa) Chapter 2 of Part 2 of the Civil Partnership Act 2004 (proceedings for dissolution etc. of civil partnership);

(fb) Schedule 5 to the 2004 Act (financial relief in the High Court or a county court etc.);

(fc) Schedule 6 to the 2004 Act (financial relief in magistrates' courts etc.);

(fd) Schedule 7 to the 2004 Act (financial relief in England and Wales after overseas dissolution etc. of a civil partnership); and][52]

(g) the inherent jurisdiction of the High Court in relation to children.

(3) The requirements which the [Lord Chancellor][53] may prescribe under section 58(3)(c)—

(a) include requirements for the person providing advocacy or litigation services to have provided prescribed information before the agreement is made; and

(b) may be different for different descriptions of conditional fee agreements (and, in particular, may be different for those which provide for a success fee and those which do not).

(4) In section 58 and this section (and in the definitions of 'advocacy services' and 'litigation services' as they apply for their purposes) 'proceedings' includes any sort of proceedings for resolving disputes (and not just proceedings in a court), whether commenced or contemplated.

(5) Before making an order under section 58(4), the [Lord Chancellor][54] shall consult—

(a) the designated judges;

(b) the General Council of the Bar;

---

[49] Section 58A was inserted by Access to Justice Act 1999, s 27(1), with effect from 1 April 2000.

[50] Subsection (2)(b) substituted by Adoption and Children Act 2002, sch 3, para 80.

[51] Words substituted by Forced Marriage (Civil Protection) Act 2007, sch 2, para 2.

[52] Word 'and' repealed, and paragraphs (fa), (fb), (fc) and (fd) inserted, by Civil Partnership Act 2004, sch 27, para 138, and sch 30.

[53] Words substituted by: (a) Secretary of State for Constitutional Affairs Order 2003 (SI 2003/1887), sch. 2, para 8(1); (b) Transfer of Functions (Lord Chancellor and Secretary of State) Order 2005 (SI 2005/3429), sch, para 2.

[54] As note 53.

    (c) the Law Society; and

    (d) such other bodies as he considers appropriate.

(6) A costs order made in any proceedings may, subject in the case of court proceedings to rules of court, include provision requiring the payment of any fees payable under a conditional fee agreement which provides for a success fee.

(7) Rules of court may make provision with respect to the assessment of any costs which include fees payable under a conditional fee agreement (including one which provides for a success fee).

Civil Procedure (Amendment) Rules 2013

(SI 2013/262)

The Civil Procedure Rule Committee, having power under section 2 of the Civil Procedure Act 1997 to make rules of court under section 1 of that Act, after consulting in accordance with section 2(6)(a) of that Act, having power under section 58AA(6A) of the Courts and Legal Services Act 1990 and having power under section 55 of the Legal Aid, Sentencing and Punishment of Offenders Act 2012 makes the following Rules:

Citation, commencement and interpretation

1. These Rules may be cited as the Civil Procedure (Amendment) Rules 2013.
2. These Rules shall come into force on 1st April 2013.
3. In these Rules—
    (a) a reference to a Part or rule by number alone means the Part or rule so numbered in the Civil Procedure Rules 1998;
    (b) a reference to an Order by number and prefixed by 'RSC' means the RSC Order so numbered in Schedule 1 to those Rules; and
    (c) a reference to an Order by number and prefixed by 'CCR' means the CCR Order so numbered in Schedule 2 to those Rules.

Amendments to the Civil Procedure Rules 1998

4. In rule 1.1—
    (a) In paragraph (1), after 'justly' insert 'and at proportionate cost'; and
    (b) In paragraph (2)—
        (i) after 'justly' insert 'and at proportionate cost';
        (ii) at the end of sub-paragraph (d), omit 'and';
        (iii) at the end of sub-paragraph (e), for '.' substitute '; and'; and
        (iv) after sub-paragraph (e) insert the following sub-paragraph—

        '(f) enforcing compliance with rules, practice directions and orders.'.

5. In Part 3—
    (a) in the heading to the Part, after 'CASE' insert 'AND COSTS';
    (b) in the Table of Contents of the Part—
        (i) before the entry for rule 3.1, insert the Section heading—

        'SECTION I—CASE MANAGEMENT'
        (ii) after the entry for rule 3.10, insert the following entry—

'Power of the court to make civil restraint orders	Rule 3.11'

        ; and

(iii) after the entry for rule 3.11, insert the following Section headings and rules—

(c) before the heading for rule 3.1, insert the Section heading—

'SECTION I

Case Management';

(d) after rule 3.1(7), insert—

'(8) The court may contact the parties from time to time in order to monitor compliance with directions. The parties must respond promptly to any such enquiries from the court.';

(e) in—
  (i)   rule 3.7(1) and the words in the first set of parentheses that follow it; and
  (ii) rule 3.7A(1)(b),
  for 'an allocation', in each place that those words occur, substitute 'a directions';
(f) in rule 3.8, in the parentheses that follow paragraph (1), for 'may' substitute 'will';
(g) for rule 3.9(1), substitute—

'(1) On an application for relief from any sanction imposed for a failure to comply with any rule, practice direction or court order, the court will consider all the circumstances of the case, so as to enable it to deal justly with the application, including the need—
  (a) for litigation to be conducted efficiently and at proportionate cost; and
  (b) to enforce compliance with rules, practice directions and orders.'; and

(h) after rule 3.11, insert—

'SECTION II

Costs Management

Application of this Section and the purpose of costs management [for amended version of r 3.12 see the note at the end of this appendix]

3.12.—(1) This Section and Practice Direction 3E apply to all multi-track cases commenced on or after 1st April 2013 in—
  (a) a county court; or

    (b) the Chancery Division or Queen's Bench Division of the High
        Court (except the Admiralty and Commercial Courts),
    unless the proceedings are the subject of fixed costs or scale costs or
    the court otherwise orders. This Section and Practice Direction 3E
    shall apply to any other proceedings (including applications) where
    the court so orders.
  (2) The purpose of costs management is that the court should manage
     both the steps to be taken and the costs to be incurred by the parties
     to any proceedings so as to further the overriding objective.

Filing and exchanging budgets

3.13. Unless the court otherwise orders, all parties except litigants in person
must file and exchange budgets as required by the rules or as the court
otherwise directs. Each party must do so by the date specified in the
notice served under rule 26.3(1) or, if no such date is specified, seven days
before the first case management conference.

Failure to file a budget

3.14. Unless the court otherwise orders, any party which fails to file a budget
despite being required to do so will be treated as having filed a budget
comprising only the applicable court fees.

Costs management orders

3.15.—(1) In addition to exercising its other powers, the court may manage the
costs to be incurred by any party in any proceedings.
  (2) The court may at any time make a 'costs management order'. By
     such order the court will—
    (a) record the extent to which the budgets are agreed between the
       parties;
    (b) in respect of budgets or parts of budgets which are not agreed,
       record the court's approval after making appropriate revisions.
  (3) If a costs management order has been made, the court will there-
     after control the parties' budgets in respect of recoverable costs.

Costs management conferences

3.16.—(1) Any hearing which is convened solely for the purpose of costs management (for example, to approve a revised budget) is referred to as
a 'costs management conference'.
  (2) Where practicable, costs management conferences should be con-
     ducted by telephone or in writing.

Court to have regard to budgets and to take account of costs

3.17.—(1) When making any case management decision, the court will have
regard to any available budgets of the parties and will take into
account the costs involved in each procedural step.
  (2) Paragraph (1) applies whether or not the court has made a costs
     management order.

Assessing costs on the standard basis where a costs management order has been made

3.18. In any case where a costs management order has been made, when assessing costs on the standard basis, the court will—

(a) have regard to the receiving party's last approved or agreed budget for each phase of the proceedings; and

(b) not depart from such approved or agreed budget unless satisfied that there is good reason to do so.

(Attention is drawn to rule 44.3(2)(a) and rule 44.3(5), which concern proportionality of costs.)

SECTION III

Costs Capping

Costs capping orders—General

3.19.—(1) A costs capping order is an order limiting the amount of future costs (including disbursements) which a party may recover pursuant to an order for costs subsequently made.

(2) In this rule, 'future costs' means costs incurred in respect of work done after the date of the costs capping order but excluding the amount of any additional liability.

(3) This rule does not apply to protective costs orders.

(4) A costs capping order may be in respect of—

(a) the whole litigation; or

(b) any issues which are ordered to be tried separately.

(5) The court may at any stage of proceedings make a costs capping order against all or any of the parties, if—

(a) it is in the interests of justice to do so;

(b) there is a substantial risk that without such an order costs will be disproportionately incurred; and

(c) it is not satisfied that the risk in subparagraph (b) can be adequately controlled by—

(i) case management directions or orders made under this Part; and

(ii) detailed assessment of costs.

(6) In considering whether to exercise its discretion under this rule, the court will consider all the circumstances of the case, including—

(a) whether there is a substantial imbalance between the financial position of the parties;

(b) whether the costs of determining the amount of the cap are likely to be proportionate to the overall costs of the litigation;

(c) the stage which the proceedings have reached; and

(d) the costs which have been incurred to date and the future costs.

(7) A costs capping order, once made, will limit the costs recoverable by the party subject to the order unless a party successfully applies to vary the order. No such variation will be made unless—

(a) there has been a material and substantial change of circumstances since the date when the order was made; or

(b) there is some other compelling reason why a variation should be made.

Application for a costs capping order

3.20.—(1) An application for a costs capping order must be made on notice in accordance with Part 23.

(2) The application notice must—

    (a) set out—

        (i) whether the costs capping order is in respect of the whole of the litigation or a particular issue which is ordered to be tried separately; and

        (ii) why a costs capping order should be made; and

    (b) be accompanied by a budget setting out—

        (i) the costs (and disbursements) incurred by the applicant to date; and

        (ii) the costs (and disbursements) which the applicant is likely to incur in the future conduct of the proceedings.

(3) The court may give directions for the determination of the application and such directions may—

    (a) direct any party to the proceedings—

        (i) to file a schedule of costs in the form set out in paragraph 3 of Practice Direction 3F—Costs capping;

        (ii) to file written submissions on all or any part of the issues arising;

    (b) fix the date and time estimate of the hearing of the application;

    (c) indicate whether the judge hearing the application will sit with an assessor at the hearing of the application; and

    (d) include any further directions as the court sees fit.

Application to vary a costs capping order

3.21. An application to vary a costs capping order must be made by application notice pursuant to Part 23.'

6. In rule 16.3, in paragraph (2)(b)(i) and (ii), for '£5,000' substitute '£10,000'.

7. In Part 21—

  (a) in rule 21.10—

    (i) in paragraph (3), for 'Section VI' substitute 'Section III'; and

    (ii) in the parentheses after paragraph (3), for '48.5' substitute '46.4';

  (b) in rule 21.12—

    (i) in paragraph (2)—

        (aa) in sub-paragraph (a), for 'an insurance policy, as defined by rule 43.2(1)(m)', substitute 'a premium in respect of a costs insurance policy (as defined by section 58C(5) of the Courts and Legal Services Act 1990)' ; and

        (bb) in sub-paragraph (b), for 'an insurance premium' substitute 'a premium in respect of a costs insurance policy'; and

    (ii) in the parentheses after paragraph (3)—

        (aa) for '43.2(1)(a)' substitute '44.1(1)(a)'; and

        (bb) for '48.5(2)' substitute '46.4(2)'; and

    (iii) in paragraph (4), for '44.5(3)' substitute '44.4(3)'.

8. In Part 26—
    (a) in the Table of Contents of the Part, in the entry for 'Allocation questionnaire', for 'Allocation' substitute 'Directions';
    (b) in rule 26.2A—
        (i) in paragraph (2)—
            (aa) omit 'before the service of a notice by the court under rule 26.3(1A)'; and
            (bb) after 'the preferred court' insert 'or the defendant's home court as appropriate';
        (ii) in paragraph (5), for 'allocation' substitute 'directions'; and
        (iii) for paragraph (6) substitute—

        '(6) The relevant time for the purposes of this rule is when—
            (a) all parties have filed their directions questionnaires;
            (b) any stay ordered by the court or period to attempt settlement through mediation has expired; or
            (c) if the claim falls within Practice Direction 7D—
                (i) the defence is filed; or
                (ii) enforcement of a default judgment other than by a warrant of execution is requested,
            whichever occurs first.';

    (c) in rule 26.3—
        (i) in the heading, for 'Allocation', substitute 'Directions';
        (ii) for paragraph (1) substitute—

        '(1) If a defendant files a defence—
            (a) a court officer will—
                (i) provisionally decide the track which appears to be most suitable for the claim; and
                (ii) serve on each party a notice of proposed allocation; and
            (b) the notice of proposed allocation will—
                (i) specify any matter to be complied with by the date specified in the notice;
                (ii) require the parties to file a completed directions questionnaire and serve copies on all other parties;
                (iii) state the address of the court or the court office to which the directions questionnaire must be returned;
                (iv) inform the parties how to obtain the directions questionnaire; and
                (v) if a case appears suitable for allocation to the fast track or multi-track, require the parties to file proposed directions by the date specified in the notice.';

        (iii) omit paragraph (1A);
        (iv) in paragraph (1B), for 'allocation' substitute 'directions';
        (v) in paragraph (2), for '(1A)' substitute '(1)';

(vi) for paragraph (3), substitute—

'(3) If proceedings are automatically transferred under rule 26.2 or rule 26.2A the court in which the proceedings have been commenced—
  (a) will serve the notice of proposed allocation before the proceedings are transferred; and
  (b) will not transfer the proceedings until all parties have complied with the notice or the time for doing so has expired.';

(vii) for paragraph (4), substitute—

'(4) If rule 15.10 or rule 14.5 applies, the court will not serve a notice under rule 26.3(1) until the claimant has filed a notice requiring the proceedings to continue.';

(viii) omit paragraph (5);
(ix) for paragraph (6), substitute—

'(6) If a notice is served under rule 26.3(1)—
  (a) each party must file at court, and serve on all other parties, the documents required by the notice by no later than the date specified in it; and
  (b) the date specified will be—
    (i) if the notice relates to the small claims track, at least 14 days; or
    (ii) if the notice relates to the fast track or multi-track, at least 28 days,
    after the date when it is deemed to be served on the party in question.';

(x) for paragraph (6A), substitute—

'(6A) The date for complying with a notice served under rule 26.3(1) may not be varied by agreement between the parties.';

(xi) in paragraph (7), for 'an allocation' substitute 'a directions';
(xii) after paragraph (7), insert—

'(7A) If a claim is a designated money claim and a party does not comply with the notice served under rule 26.3(1) by the date specified—
  (a) the court will serve a further notice on that party, requiring them to comply within 7 days; and
  (b) if that party fails to comply with the notice served under subparagraph (a), the party's statement of case will be struck out without further order of the court.';

(xiii) in paragraph (8), for 'Where a party does not file an allocation questionnaire by the date specified' substitute 'If a claim is not a designated money claim and a party does not comply with the notice served under rule 26.3(1) by the date specified';
(xiv) omit paragraph (9); and
(xv) in paragraph (10)—
  (aa) for '26.3(8)' substitute '26.3(7A)(b) or 26.3(8)'; and
  (bb) for 'any party who was not in default' substitute 'any other party';

(d) in rule 26.4—
  (i)   in paragraph (1), for 'allocation' substitute 'directions'; and
  (ii) for paragraph (2) substitute—

  '(2) If all parties request a stay the proceedings will be stayed for one month and the court will notify the parties accordingly.
    (2A) If the court otherwise considers that such a stay would be appropriate, the court will direct that the proceedings, either in whole or in part, be stayed for one month, or for such other period as it considers appropriate.';

(e) in rule 26.5—
  (i)   for paragraph (1), substitute—

  '(1) The court will allocate the claim to a track—
      (a) when all parties have filed their directions questionnaires; or
      (b) when giving directions pursuant to rule 26.3(8),
      unless it has stayed the proceedings under rule 26.4.'; and

  (ii) omit paragraph (5);
(f) in rule 26.6, in—
  (i)   paragraph (1)(a)(i); and
  (ii) paragraph (3),
  for '£5,000' substitute '£10,000';
(g) omit rule 26.7(3); and
(h) in rule 26.9—
  (i)   omit paragraph (2); and
  (ii) at the end of the rule, in the words in parentheses, for 'his' substitute 'their'.
9. In Part 27—
  (a) in rule 27.1, after paragraph (2), in the words in parentheses, for '£5,000' in each place it occurs, substitute '£10,000';
  (b) in rule 27.5, for '27.14(3)(d)', substitute '27.14(2)(f)'; and
  (c) in rule 27.14—
    (i)   in paragraph (1) omit 'unless paragraph (5) applies'; and
    (ii) omit paragraphs (5) and (6).
10. In Part 29—
  (a) after the parentheses that follow rule 29.1, insert—

  '(2) When drafting case management directions both the parties and the court should take as their starting point any relevant model directions and standard directions which can be found online at www.justice.gov.uk/courts/procedure-rules/civil and adapt them as appropriate to the circumstances of the particular case.';

  (b) at the end of rule 29.2(1)(a), after 'or' insert 'may';
  (c) for rule 29.4 substitute—

  '**29.4.** The parties must endeavour to agree appropriate directions for the management of the proceedings and submit agreed directions, or their respective proposals to the court at least seven days before any case management conference. Where the court approves agreed directions, or issues its own directions, the parties will be so notified by the court and the case management conference will be vacated.'; and

(d) for rule 29.8(c)(ii), substitute—

'(ii) confirm the date for trial or the week within which the trial is to begin; and'.

11. For rule 31.5, substitute—

'**31.5.**—(1) In all claims to which rule 31.5(2) does not apply—

(a) an order to give disclosure is an order to give standard disclosure unless the court directs otherwise;

(b) the court may dispense with or limit standard disclosure; and

(c) the parties may agree in writing to dispense with or to limit standard disclosure.

(2) Unless the court otherwise orders, paragraphs (3) to (8) apply to all multi-track claims, other than those which include a claim for personal injuries.

(3) Not less than 14 days before the first case management conference each party must file and serve a report verified by a statement of truth, which—

(a) describes briefly what documents exist or may exist that are or may be relevant to the matters in issue in the case;

(b) describes where and with whom those documents are or may be located;

(c) in the case of electronic documents, describes how those documents are stored;

(d) estimates the broad range of costs that could be involved in giving standard disclosure in the case, including the costs of searching for and disclosing any electronically stored documents; and

(e) states which of the directions under paragraphs (7) or (8) are to be sought.

(4) In cases where the Electronic Documents Questionnaire has been exchanged, the Questionnaire should be filed with the report required by paragraph (3).

(5) Not less than seven days before the first case management conference, and on any other occasion as the court may direct, the parties must, at a meeting or by telephone, discuss and seek to agree a proposal in relation to disclosure that meets the overriding objective.

(6) If—

(a) the parties agree proposals for the scope of disclosure; and

(b) the court considers that the proposals are appropriate in all the circumstances,

the court may approve them without a hearing and give directions in the terms proposed.

(7) At the first or any subsequent case management conference, the court will decide, having regard to the overriding objective and the need to

limit disclosure to that which is necessary to deal with the case justly, which of the following orders to make in relation to disclosure—

(a) an order dispensing with disclosure;

(b) an order that a party disclose the documents on which it relies, and at the same time request any specific disclosure it requires from any other party;

(c) an order that directs, where practicable, the disclosure to be given by each party on an issue by issue basis;

(d) an order that each party disclose any documents which it is reasonable to suppose may contain information which enables that party to advance its own case or to damage that of any other party, or which leads to an enquiry which has either of those consequences;

(e) an order that a party give standard disclosure;

(f) any other order in relation to disclosure that the court considers appropriate.

(8) The court may at any point give directions as to how disclosure is to be given, and in particular—

(a) what searches are to be undertaken, of where, for what, in respect of which time periods and by whom and the extent of any search for electronically stored documents;

(b) whether lists of documents are required;

(c) how and when the disclosure statement is to be given;

(d) in what format documents are to be disclosed (and whether any identification is required);

(e) what is required in relation to documents that once existed but no longer exist; and

(f) whether disclosure shall take place in stages.

(9) To the extent that the documents to be disclosed are electronic, the provisions of Practice Direction 31B—Disclosure of Electronic Documents will apply in addition to paragraphs (3) to (8).'

12. After rule 32.2(2), insert—

'(3) The court may give directions—

(a) identifying or limiting the issues to which factual evidence may be directed;

(b) identifying the witnesses who may be called or whose evidence may be read; or

(c) limiting the length or format of witness statements.'.

13. In Part 35, in rule 35.4—

(a) in paragraph (2), after 'must' insert 'provide an estimate of the costs of the proposed expert evidence and';

(b) in paragraph (2)(a), after 'required' insert 'and the issues which the expert evidence will address'; and

(c) at the end of paragraph (3), after 'paragraph (2).' insert 'The order granting permission may specify the issues which the expert evidence should address.'.

14. In Part 36, in rule 36.14(3)—

(a) in subparagraph (b)—

(i) omit 'his'; and

(ii) at the end, omit 'and';

(b) in subparagraph (c), for the full stop substitute '; and'; and
(c) after subparagraph (c), insert—

'(d) an additional amount, which shall not exceed £75,000, calculated by applying the prescribed percentage set out below to an amount which is—
   (i)   where the claim is or includes a money claim, the sum awarded to the claimant by the court; or
   (ii) where the claim is only a non-monetary claim, the sum awarded to the claimant by the court in respect of costs—

Amount awarded by the court	Prescribed percentage
up to £500,000	10% of the amount awarded;
above £500,000 up to £1,000,000	10% of the first £500,000 and 5% of any amount above that figure'

15. Part 43 is revoked.
16. For Parts 44 to 48, substitute Parts 44 to 48 as set out in the Schedule to these Rules.
17. In Part 52—
(a) in the contents of the Part, after the entry for rule 52.9, insert—

'Orders to limit the recoverable costs of an appeal	Rule 52.9A'

; and
(b) after rule 52.9, insert—

'Orders to limit the recoverable costs of an appeal
52.9A.—(1) In any proceedings in which costs recovery is normally limited or excluded at first instance, an appeal court may make an order that the recoverable costs of an appeal will be limited to the extent which the court specifies.
(2) In making such an order the court will have regard to—
   (a) the means of both parties;
   (b) all the circumstances of the case; and
   (c) the need to facilitate access to justice.
(3) If the appeal raises an issue of principle or practice upon which substantial sums may turn, it may not be appropriate to make an order under paragraph (1).
(4) An application for such an order must be made as soon as practicable and will be determined without a hearing unless the court orders otherwise.'.

18. In rule 54.6(1)—
(a) at the end of subparagraph (b), omit 'and';
(b) in subparagraph (c), for the full stop substitute '; and'; and
(c) after subparagraph (c) insert—

'(d) where appropriate, the grounds on which it is contended that the claim is an Aarhus Convention claim.
(Rules 45.41 to 45.44 make provision about costs in Aarhus Convention claims.)'.

19. In Part 63, in rule 63.27(1)(b), for '£5,000' substitute '£10,000'.

20. In CCR Order 27, omit rule 7A(3).

21. In the Glossary—

(a) after the entry for 'Base rate', insert—

'Budget	An estimate of the reasonable and proportionate costs (including disbursements) which a party intends to incur in the proceedings.'

; and

(b) after the entry for 'Exemplary damages', insert—

'Damages-based agreement	A damages-based agreement is an agreement which complies with the provisions of the Damages-Based Agreements Regulations 2013.'

Transitional provisions

22.—(1) The following amendments do not apply where a defence is received before 1 April 2013—

(a) the amendments made by rules 5(e), 8(a) to (e) and (h) of these Rules; and

(b) the amendments made by paragraphs 3 and 9(a) to (j) and (m) and (n) of the 60th Update—Practice Direction amendments, that amends the Practice Directions supplementing the Civil Procedure Rules.

(2) The amendments made by rule 5(f) and (g) of these Rules do not apply to applications made before 1 April 2013 for relief from any sanction imposed for a failure to comply with any rule, practice direction or court order.

(3) The following amendments do not apply to claims issued before 1 April 2013—

(a) the amendments made by rules 6, 8(f) and (g), 9(a) and 19 of these Rules; and

(b) the amendments made by paragraphs 9(k) and (l)(i) and 10(c) of the 60th Update—Practice Direction amendments that amends the Practice Directions supplementing the Civil Procedure Rules.

(4) The amendment made by rule 10(c) of these Rules does not apply where any case management conference takes place or is due to take place before 9 April 2013.

(5) The amendment made by rule 11 of these Rules does not apply where the first case management conference takes place or is due to take place before 16 April 2013.

(6) The amendments made by rule 13 of these Rules do not apply in relation to an application for permission made before 1 April 2013.

(7) The amendments made by rule 14 of these Rules do not apply in relation to a claimant's Part 36 offer which was made before 1 April 2013.

(8) The amendments made by rule 18 and the provision made by rules 45.41 to 45.44 in the Schedule (costs limits in Aarhus Convention claims) do not apply in relation to a claim commenced before 1 April 2013.

(9) The provision made by rule 47.14(7) in the Schedule (when time for appealing against assessment starts to run) of these Rules does not apply where the final hearing was concluded before 1 April 2013.

(10) The provision made by rule 47.20(1) to (5) and (7) in the Schedule (liability for costs of detailed assessment proceedings) does not apply to detailed assessments commenced before 1 April 2013 and in relation to such detailed assessments, rules 47.18 and 47.19 as they were in force immediately before 1 April 2013 apply instead.

(11) The amendment made by rule 47.20(6) in the Schedule to these Rules (interest on the costs of detailed assessment proceedings) does not apply where the date of the default, interim or final costs certificate (as the case may be) is before 1 April 2013.

(12) Any defamation proceedings commenced before 1 April 2013 within the scope of the Defamation Proceedings Costs Management Scheme provided for by Practice Direction 51D supporting Part 51 will proceed and be completed in accordance with that scheme.

(13) Any detailed assessment commenced before 1 April 2013 under the County Court Provisional Assessment Pilot Scheme provided for by Practice Direction 51E supporting Part 51 will proceed and be completed in accordance with that scheme.

(14) Any proceedings in the Mercantile Courts and the Construction Courts commenced before 1 April 2013 that are within the scope of the Costs Management in Mercantile Courts and Construction Courts Pilot Scheme provided for by Practice Direction 51G supporting Part 51 will proceed and be completed in accordance with that scheme.

The Right Honourable Lord Dyson, MR
Stephen Richards, LJ
Peter Coulson, J
Philip Sales, J
Master Barbara Fontaine
HHJ Stephen Stewart QC
District Judge Suzanne Burn
District Judge Christopher Lethem
Nicholas Bacon QC
William Featherby QC
Professor David Grant
Edward Pepperall
Katy Peters
Qasim Nawaz
Amanda Stevens

I allow these Rules
Signed by authority of the Lord Chancellor

Helen Grant
Parliamentary Under Secretary of State
31st January 2013
Ministry of Justice

SCHEDULE

[Schedule introduced by rule 16.]

'PART 44

GENERAL RULES ABOUT COSTS

Contents of this Part

SECTION I   GENERAL

SECTION II   QUALIFIED ONE-WAY COSTS SHIFTING

SECTION III   DAMAGES-BASED AGREEMENTS

SECTION I

General

Interpretation and application

44.1.—(1) In Parts 44 to 47, unless the context otherwise requires—

'authorised court officer' means any officer of—

 (i) a county court;

 (ii) a district registry;

 (iii) the Principal Registry of the Family Division; or

 (iv) the Costs Office,

whom the Lord Chancellor has authorised to assess costs;

'conditional fee agreement' means an agreement enforceable under section 58 of the Courts and Legal Services Act 1990;

'costs' includes fees, charges, disbursements, expenses, remuneration, reimbursement allowed to a litigant in person under rule 46.5 and any fee or reward charged by a lay representative for acting on behalf of a party in proceedings allocated to the small claims track;

'costs judge' means a taxing master of the Senior Courts;

'Costs Office' means the Senior Courts Costs Office;

'costs officer' means—

 (i) a costs judge;

 (ii) a district judge; or

 (iii) an authorised court officer;

'detailed assessment' means the procedure by which the amount of costs is decided by a costs officer in accordance with Part 47;

'the Director (legal aid)' means the person designated as the Director of Legal Aid Casework pursuant to section 4 of the Legal Aid, Sentencing and Punishment of Offenders Act 2012, or a person entitled to exercise the functions of the Director;

'fixed costs' means costs the amounts of which are fixed by these rules whether or not the court has a discretion to allow some other or no amount, and include—

 (i) the amounts which are to be allowed in respect of legal representatives' charges in the circumstances set out in Section I of Part 45;

 (ii) fixed recoverable costs calculated in accordance with rule 45.11;

 (iii) the additional costs allowed by rule 45.18;

 (iv) fixed costs determined under rule 45.21;

 (v) costs fixed by rules 45.37 and 45.38;

'free of charge' has the same meaning as in section 194(10) of the 2007 Act;

'fund' includes any estate or property held for the benefit of any person or class of person and any fund to which a trustee or personal representative is entitled in that capacity;

'HMRC' means HM Revenue and Customs;

'legal aid' means civil legal services made available under arrangements made for the purposes of Part 1of the Legal Aid, Sentencing and Punishment of Offenders Act 2012;

'paying party' means a party liable to pay costs;

'the prescribed charity' has the same meaning as in section 194(8) of the 2007 Act;

'pro bono representation' means legal representation provided free of charge;

'receiving party' means a party entitled to be paid costs;

'summary assessment' means the procedure whereby costs are assessed by the judge who has heard the case or application;

'VAT' means Value Added Tax;

'the 2007 Act' means the Legal Services Act 2007.

('Legal representative' has the meaning given in rule 2.3).

(2) The costs to which Parts 44 to 47 apply include—

    (a) the following costs where those costs may be assessed by the court—

        (i) costs of proceedings before an arbitrator or umpire;

        (ii) costs of proceedings before a tribunal or other statutory body; and

        (iii) costs payable by a client to their legal representative; and

    (b) costs which are payable by one party to another party under the terms of a contract, where the court makes an order for an assessment of those costs.

(3) Where advocacy or litigation services are provided to a client under a conditional fee agreement, costs are recoverable under Parts 44 to 47 notwithstanding that the client is liable to pay the legal representative's fees and expenses only to the extent that sums are recovered in respect of the proceedings, whether by way of costs or otherwise.

Court's discretion as to costs

44.2.—(1) The court has discretion as to—

    (a) whether costs are payable by one party to another;

    (b) the amount of those costs; and

    (c) when they are to be paid.

(2) If the court decides to make an order about costs—

    (a) the general rule is that the unsuccessful party will be ordered to pay the costs of the successful party; but

    (b) the court may make a different order.

(3) The general rule does not apply to the following proceedings—

    (a) proceedings in the Court of Appeal on an application or appeal made in connection with proceedings in the Family Division; or

    (b) proceedings in the Court of Appeal from a judgment, direction, decision or order given or made in probate proceedings or family proceedings.

(4) In deciding what order (if any) to make about costs, the court will have regard to all the circumstances, including—

    (a) the conduct of all the parties;

    (b) whether a party has succeeded on part of its case, even if that party has not been wholly successful; and

    (c) any admissible offer to settle made by a party which is drawn to the court's attention, and which is not an offer to which costs consequences under Part 36 apply.

(5) The conduct of the parties includes—

    (a) conduct before, as well as during, the proceedings and in particular the extent to which the parties followed the Practice Direction—Pre-Action Conduct or any relevant pre-action protocol;

    (b) whether it was reasonable for a party to raise, pursue or contest a particular allegation or issue;

    (c) the manner in which a party has pursued or defended its case or a particular allegation or issue; and

    (d) whether a claimant who has succeeded in the claim, in whole or in part, exaggerated its claim.

(6) The orders which the court may make under this rule include an order that a party must pay—

    (a) a proportion of another party's costs;

    (b) a stated amount in respect of another party's costs;

    (c) costs from or until a certain date only;

    (d) costs incurred before proceedings have begun;

    (e) costs relating to particular steps taken in the proceedings;

    (f) costs relating only to a distinct part of the proceedings; and

    (g) interest on costs from or until a certain date, including a date before judgment.

(7) Before the court considers making an order under paragraph (6)(f), it will consider whether it is practicable to make an order under paragraph (6)(a) or (c) instead.

(8) Where the court orders a party to pay costs subject to detailed assessment, it will order that party to pay a reasonable sum on account of costs, unless there is good reason not to do so.

Basis of assessment

44.3.—(1) Where the court is to assess the amount of costs (whether by summary or detailed assessment) it will assess those costs—

    (a) on the standard basis; or

    (b) on the indemnity basis,

but the court will not in either case allow costs which have been unreasonably incurred or are unreasonable in amount.

(Rule 44.5 sets out how the court decides the amount of costs payable under a contract.)

(2) Where the amount of costs is to be assessed on the standard basis, the court will—

    (a) only allow costs which are proportionate to the matters in issue. Costs which are disproportionate in amount may be disallowed or reduced even if they were reasonably or necessarily incurred; and

    (b) resolve any doubt which it may have as to whether costs were reasonably and proportionately incurred or were reasonable and proportionate in amount in favour of the paying party.

(Factors which the court may take into account are set out in rule 44.4.)

(3) Where the amount of costs is to be assessed on the indemnity basis, the court will resolve any doubt which it may have as to whether costs were reasonably incurred or were reasonable in amount in favour of the receiving party.

(4) Where—

    (a) the court makes an order about costs without indicating the basis on which the costs are to be assessed; or

    (b) the court makes an order for costs to be assessed on a basis other than the standard basis or the indemnity basis,

the costs will be assessed on the standard basis.

(5) Costs incurred are proportionate if they bear a reasonable relationship to—

    (a) the sums in issue in the proceedings;

    (b) the value of any non-monetary relief in issue in the proceedings;

    (c) the complexity of the litigation;

    (d) any additional work generated by the conduct of the paying party; and

    (e) any wider factors involved in the proceedings, such as reputation or public importance.

(6) Where the amount of a solicitor's remuneration in respect of non-contentious business is regulated by any general orders made under the Solicitors Act 1974, the amount of the costs to be allowed in respect of any such business which falls to be assessed by the court will be decided in accordance with those general orders rather than this rule and rule 44.4.

(7) Paragraphs (2)(a) and (5) do not apply in relation to cases commenced before 1 April 2013 and in relation to such cases, rule 44.4(2)(a) as it was in force immediately before 1 April 2013 will apply instead.

Factors to be taken into account in deciding the amount of costs

44.4.—(1) The court will have regard to all the circumstances in deciding whether costs were—

    (a) if it is assessing costs on the standard basis—

        (i)   proportionately and reasonably incurred; or

        (ii) proportionate and reasonable in amount, or

    (b) if it is assessing costs on the indemnity basis—

        (i)   unreasonably incurred; or

        (ii) unreasonable in amount.

(2) In particular, the court will give effect to any orders which have already been made.

(3) The court will also have regard to—

    (a) the conduct of all the parties, including in particular—

        (i)   conduct before, as well as during, the proceedings; and

        (ii) the efforts made, if any, before and during the proceedings in order to try to resolve the dispute;

    (b) the amount or value of any money or property involved;

    (c) the importance of the matter to all the parties;

    (d) the particular complexity of the matter or the difficulty or novelty of the questions raised;

    (e) the skill, effort, specialised knowledge and responsibility involved;

    (f) the time spent on the case;

(g) the place where and the circumstances in which work or any part of it was done; and

(h) the receiving party's last approved or agreed budget.

(Rule 35.4(4) gives the court power to limit the amount that a party may recover with regard to the fees and expenses of an expert.)

Amount of costs where costs are payable under a contract

44.5.—(1) Subject to paragraphs (2) to (4), where the court assesses (whether by summary or detailed assessment) costs which are payable by the paying party to the receiving party under the terms of a contract, the costs payable under those terms are, unless the contract expressly provides otherwise, to be presumed to be costs which—

(a) have been reasonably incurred; and

(b) are reasonable in amount,

and the court will assess them accordingly.

(2) The presumptions in paragraph (1) are rebuttable. Practice Direction 44—General rules about costs sets out circumstances where the court may order otherwise.

(3) Paragraph (1) does not apply where the contract is between a solicitor and client.

Procedure for assessing costs

44.6.—(1) Where the court orders a party to pay costs to another party (other than fixed costs) it may either—

(a) make a summary assessment of the costs; or

(b) order detailed assessment of the costs by a costs officer,

unless any rule, practice direction or other enactment provides otherwise.

(Practice Direction 44—General rules about costs sets out the factors which will affect the court's decision under paragraph (1).)

(2) A party may recover the fixed costs specified in Part 45 in accordance with that Part.

Time for complying with an order for costs

44.7.—(1) A party must comply with an order for the payment of costs within 14 days of—

(a) the date of the judgment or order if it states the amount of those costs;

(b) if the amount of those costs (or part of them) is decided later in accordance with Part 47, the date of the certificate which states the amount; or

(c) in either case, such other date as the court may specify.

(Part 47 sets out the procedure for detailed assessment of costs.)

Legal representative's duty to notify the party

44.8. Where—

(a) the court makes a costs order against a legally represented party; and

(b) the party is not present when the order is made,

the party's legal representative must notify that party in writing of the costs order no later than 7 days after the legal representative receives notice of the order.

(Paragraph 10.1 of Practice Direction 44 defines 'party' for the purposes of this rule.)

Cases where costs orders deemed to have been made

44.9.—(1) Subject to paragraph (2), where a right to costs arises under—

    (a) rule 3.7 (defendant's right to costs where claim is struck out for non-payment of fees);

    (b) rule 36.10(1) or (2) (claimant's entitlement to costs where a Part 36 offer is accepted); or

    (c) rule 38.6 (defendant's right to costs where claimant discontinues),

    a costs order will be deemed to have been made on the standard basis.

(2) Paragraph 1(b) does not apply where a Part 36 offer is accepted before the commencement of proceedings.

(3) Where such an order is deemed to be made in favour of a party with pro bono representation, that party may apply for an order under section 194(3) of the 2007 Act.

(4) Interest payable under section 17 of the Judgments Act 1838 or section 74 of the County Courts Act 1984 on the costs deemed to have been ordered under paragraph (1) will begin to run from the date on which the event which gave rise to the entitlement to costs occurred.

Where the court makes no order for costs

44.10.—(1) Where the court makes an order which does not mention costs—

    (a) subject to paragraphs (2) and (3), the general rule is that no party is entitled—

      (i) to costs; or

      (ii) to seek an order under section 194(3) of the 2007 Act,

      in relation to that order; but

    (b) this does not affect any entitlement of a party to recover costs out of a fund held by that party as trustee or personal representative, or under any lease, mortgage or other security.

(2) Where the court makes—

    (a) an order granting permission to appeal;

    (b) an order granting permission to apply for judicial review; or

    (c) any other order or direction sought by a party on an application without notice,

    and its order does not mention costs, it will be deemed to include an order for applicant's costs in the case.

(3) Any party affected by a deemed order for costs under paragraph (2) may apply at any time to vary the order.

(4) The court hearing an appeal may, unless it dismisses the appeal, make orders about the costs of the proceedings giving rise to the appeal as well as the costs of the appeal.

(5) Subject to any order made by the transferring court, where proceedings are transferred from one court to another, the court to which they are transferred may deal with all the costs, including the costs before the transfer.

Court's powers in relation to misconduct

44.11.—(1) The court may make an order under this rule where—

    (a) a party or that party's legal representative, in connection with a summary or detailed assessment, fails to comply with a rule, practice direction or court order; or

    (b) it appears to the court that the conduct of a party or that party's legal representative, before or during the proceedings or in the assessment proceedings, was unreasonable or improper.

(2) Where paragraph (1) applies, the court may—

    (a) disallow all or part of the costs which are being assessed; or

    (b) order the party at fault or that party's legal representative to pay costs which that party or legal representative has caused any other party to incur.

(3) Where—

    (a) the court makes an order under paragraph (2) against a legally represented party; and

    (b) the party is not present when the order is made,

the party's legal representative must notify that party in writing of the order no later than 7 days after the legal representative receives notice of the order.

Set Off

44.12.—(1)[1] Where a party entitled to costs is also liable to pay costs, the court may assess the costs which that party is liable to pay and either—

    (a) set off the amount assessed against the amount the party is entitled to be paid and direct that party to pay any balance; or

    (b) delay the issue of a certificate for the costs to which the party is entitled until the party has paid the amount which that party is liable to pay.

SECTION II

Qualified One-Way Costs Shifting

Qualified one-way costs shifting: scope and interpretation

44.13.—(1) This Section applies to proceedings which include a claim for damages—

    (a) for personal injuries;

    (b) under the Fatal Accidents Act 1976; or

    (c) which arises out of death or personal injury and survives for the benefit of an estate by virtue of section 1(1) of the Law Reform (Miscellaneous Provisions) Act 1934,

---

[1] There is no other paragraph in r 44.12.

but does not apply to applications pursuant to section 33 of the Senior Courts Act 1981 or section 52 of the County Courts Act 1984 (applications for pre-action disclosure), or where rule 44.17 applies.

(2) In this Section, 'claimant' means a person bringing a claim to which this Section applies or an estate on behalf of which such a claim is brought, and includes a person making a counterclaim or an additional claim.

Effect of qualified one-way costs shifting

44.14.—(1) Subject to rules 44.15 and 44.16, orders for costs made against a claimant may be enforced without the permission of the court but only to the extent that the aggregate amount in money terms of such orders does not exceed the aggregate amount in money terms of any orders for damages and interest made in favour of the claimant.

(2) Orders for costs made against a claimant may only be enforced after the proceedings have been concluded and the costs have been assessed or agreed.

(3) An order for costs which is enforced only to the extent permitted by paragraph (1) shall not be treated as an unsatisfied or outstanding judgment for the purposes of any court record.

Exceptions to qualified one-way costs shifting where permission not required

44.15. Orders for costs made against the claimant may be enforced to the full extent of such orders without the permission of the court where the proceedings have been struck out on the grounds that—

(a) the claimant has disclosed no reasonable grounds for bringing the proceedings;

(b) the proceedings are an abuse of the court's process; or

(c) the conduct of—

(i) the claimant; or

(ii) a person acting on the claimant's behalf and with the claimant's knowledge of such conduct,

is likely to obstruct the just disposal of the proceedings.

Exceptions to qualified one-way costs shifting where permission required

44.16.—(1) Orders for costs made against the claimant may be enforced to the full extent of such orders with the permission of the court where the claim is found on the balance of probabilities to be fundamentally dishonest.

(2) Orders for costs made against the claimant may be enforced up to the full extent of such orders with the permission of the court, and to the extent that it considers just, where—

(a) the proceedings include a claim which is made for the financial benefit of a person other than the claimant or a dependant within the meaning of section 1(3) of the Fatal Accidents Act 1976 (other than a claim in respect of the gratuitous provision of care, earnings paid by an employer or medical expenses); or

(b) a claim is made for the benefit of the claimant other than a claim to which this Section applies.

(3) Where paragraph (2)(a) applies, the court may, subject to rule 46.2, make an order for costs against a person, other than the claimant, for whose financial benefit the whole or part of the claim was made.

Transitional provision

44.17. This Section does not apply to proceedings where the claimant has entered into a pre-commencement funding arrangement (as defined in rule 48.2).

SECTION III

Damages-Based Agreements

Award of costs where there is a damages-based agreement

44.18.—(1) The fact that a party has entered into a damages-based agreement will not affect the making of any order for costs which otherwise would be made in favour of that party.

(2) Where costs are to be assessed in favour of a party who has entered into a damages-based agreement—

(a) the party's recoverable costs will be assessed in accordance with rule 44.3; and

(b) the party may not recover by way of costs more than the total amount payable by that party under the damages-based agreement for legal services provided under that agreement.

PART 45

FIXED COSTS

Contents of this Part

Title	Number
I FIXED COSTS	
Scope of this Section	Rule 45.1
Amount of fixed commencement costs in a claim for the recovery of money or goods	Rule 45.2
When defendant only liable for fixed commencement costs	Rule 45.3
Costs on entry of judgment in a claim for the recovery of money or goods	Rule 45.4
Amount of fixed commencement costs in a claim for the recovery of land or a demotion claim	Rule 45.5
Costs on entry of judgment in a claim for the recovery of land or a demotion claim	Rule 45.6
Miscellaneous fixed costs	Rule 45.7
Fixed enforcement costs	Rule 45.8

SECTION I

Fixed Costs

Scope of this Section

45.1.—(1) This Section sets out the amounts which, unless the court orders otherwise, are to be allowed in respect of legal representatives' charges.

    (2) This Section applies where—

        (a) the only claim is a claim for a specified sum of money where the value of the claim exceeds £25 and—

            (i) judgment in default is obtained under rule 12.4(1);

            (ii) judgment on admission is obtained under rule 14.4(3);

            (iii) judgment on admission on part of the claim is obtained under rule 14.5(6);

            (iv) summary judgment is given under Part 24;

            (v) the court has made an order to strike out a defence under rule 3.4(2)(a) as disclosing no reasonable grounds for defending the claim; or

            (vi) rule 45.4 applies;

        (b) the only claim is a claim where the court gave a fixed date for the hearing when it issued the claim and judgment is given for the delivery of goods, and the value of the claim exceeds £25;

        (c) the claim is for the recovery of land, including a possession claim under Part 55, whether or not the claim includes a claim for a sum of money and the defendant gives up possession, pays the amount claimed, if any, and the fixed commencement costs stated in the claim form;

        (d) the claim is for the recovery of land, including a possession claim under Part 55, where one of the grounds for possession is arrears of rent, for which the court gave a fixed date for the hearing when it issued the claim and judgment is given for the possession of land (whether or not the order for possession is suspended on terms) and the defendant—

            (i) has neither delivered a defence, or counterclaim, nor otherwise denied liability; or

(ii)   has delivered a defence which is limited to specifying his proposals for the payment of arrears of rent;

(e) the claim is a possession claim under Section II of Part 55 (accelerated possession claims of land let on an assured shorthold tenancy) and a possession order is made where the defendant has neither delivered a defence, or counterclaim, nor otherwise denied liability;

(f) the claim is a demotion claim under Section III of Part 65 or a demotion claim is made in the same claim form in which a claim for possession is made under Part 55 and that demotion claim is successful; or

(g) a judgment creditor has taken steps under Parts 70 to 73 to enforce a judgment or order.

(Practice Direction 7B sets out the types of case where a court will give a fixed date for a hearing when it issues a claim.)

(3) No sum in respect of legal representatives' charges will be allowed where the only claim is for a sum of money or goods not exceeding £25.

(4) Any appropriate court fee will be allowed in addition to the costs set out in this Section.

(5) The claim form may include a claim for fixed commencement costs.

Amount of fixed commencement costs in a claim for the recovery of money or goods

45.2.—(1) The amount of fixed commencement costs in a claim to which rule 45.1(2)(a) or (b) applies—

(a) will be calculated by reference to Table 1; and

(b) the amount claimed, or the value of the goods claimed if specified, in the claim form is to be used for determining the band in Table 1 that applies to the claim.

(2) The amounts shown in Table 4 are to be allowed in addition, if applicable.

TABLE 1   Fixed costs on commencement of a claim for the recovery of money or goods

Relevant band	Where the claim form is served by the court or by any method other than personal service by the claimant	Where— the claim form is served personally by the claimant; and there is only one defendant	Where there is more than one defendant, for each additional defendant personally served at separate addresses by the claimant
Where— the value of the claim exceeds £25 but does not exceed £500	£50	£60	£15
Where— the value of the claim exceeds £500 but does not exceed £1,000	£70	£80	£15

(Continued)

TABLE 1 (*Continued*)

Relevant band	Where the claim form is served by the court or by any method other than personal service by the claimant	Where— the claim form is served personally by the claimant; and there is only one defendant	Where there is more than one defendant, for each additional defendant personally served at separate addresses by the claimant
Where— the value of the claim exceeds £1,000 but does not exceed £5,000; or the only claim is for delivery of goods and no value is specified or stated on the claim form	£80	£90	£15
Where— the value of the claim exceeds £5,000	£100	£110	£15

When defendant only liable for fixed commencement costs

45.3. Where—
  (a) the only claim is for a specified sum of money; and
  (b) the defendant pays the money claimed within 14 days after being served with the particulars of claim, together with the fixed commencement costs stated in the claim form,
the defendant is not liable for any further costs unless the court orders otherwise.

Costs on entry of judgment in a claim for the recovery of money or goods

45.4. Where—
  (a) the claimant has claimed fixed commencement costs under rule 45.2; and
  (b) judgment is entered in a claim to which rule 45.1(2)(a) or (b) applies in the circumstances specified in Table 2, the amount to be included in the judgment for the claimant's legal representative's charges is the total of—
    (i) the fixed commencement costs; and
    (ii) the relevant amount shown in Table 2.

TABLE 2 Fixed Costs on Entry of Judgment in a claim for the recovery of money or goods

	Where the amount of the judgment exceeds £25 but does not exceed £5,000	Where the amount of the judgment exceeds £5,000
Where judgment in default of an acknowledgment of service is entered under rule 12.4(1) (entry of judgment by request on claim for money only)	£22	£30

(Continued)

TABLE 2 (*Continued*)

	Where the amount of the judgment exceeds £25 but does not exceed £5,000	Where the amount of the judgment exceeds £5,000
Where judgment in default of a defence is entered under rule 12.4(1) (entry of judgment by request on claim for money only)	£25	£35
Where judgment is entered under rule 14.4 (judgment on admission), or rule 14.5 (judgment on admission of part of claim) and claimant accepts the defendant's proposal as to the manner of payment	£40	£55
Where judgment is entered under rule 14.4 (judgment on admission), or rule 14.5 (judgment on admission of part of claim) and court decides the date or time of payment	£55	£70
Where summary judgment is given under Part 24 or the court strikes out a defence under rule 3.4(2)(a), in either case, on application by a party	£175	£210
Where judgment is given on a claim for delivery of goods under a regulated agreement within the meaning of the Consumer Credit Act 1974 and no other entry in this table applies	£60	£85

Amount of fixed commencement costs in a claim for the recovery of land or a demotion claim

45.5.—(1) The amount of fixed commencement costs in a claim to which rule 45.1(2)(c), (d) or (f) applies will be calculated by reference to Table 3.

(2) The amounts shown in Table 4 are to be allowed in addition, if applicable.

TABLE 3 Fixed costs on commencement of a claim for the recovery of land or a demotion claim

Where the claim form is served by the court or by any method other than personal service by the claimant	Where— the claim form is served personally by the claimant; and there is only one defendant	Where there is more than one defendant, for each additional defendant personally served at separate addresses by the claimant
£69.50	£77.00	£15.00

Costs on entry of judgment in a claim for the recovery of land or a demotion claim

45.6.—(1) Where—

(a) the claimant has claimed fixed commencement costs under rule 45.5; and

(b) judgment is entered in a claim to which rule 45.1(2)(d) or (f) applies, the amount to be included in the judgment for the claimant's legal representative's charges is the total of—

(i) the fixed commencement costs; and

(ii) the sum of £57.25.

(2) Where an order for possession is made in a claim to which rule 45.1(2)(e) applies, the amount allowed for the claimant's legal representative's charges for preparing and filing—

(a) the claim form;

(b) the documents that accompany the claim form; and

(c) the request for possession,

is £79.50.

Miscellaneous fixed costs

45.7. Table 4 shows the amount to be allowed in respect of legal representative's charges in the circumstances mentioned.

TABLE 4 Miscellaneous Fixed Costs

For service by a party of any document other than the claim form required to be served personally including preparing and copying a certificate of service for each individual served	£15.00
Where service by an alternative method or at an alternative place is permitted by an order under rule 6.15 for each individual served	£53.25
Where a document is served out of the jurisdiction—	
(a) in Scotland, Northern Ireland, the Isle of Man or the Channel Islands;	£68.25
(b) in any other place	£77.00

Fixed enforcement costs

45.8. Table 5 shows the amount to be allowed in respect of legal representatives' costs in the circumstances mentioned. The amounts shown in Table 4 are to be allowed in addition, if applicable.

TABLE 5 Fixed Enforcement Costs

For an application under rule 70.5(4) that an award may be enforced as if payable under a court order, where the amount outstanding under the award:	
exceeds £25 but does not exceed £250	£30.75
exceeds £250 but does not exceed £600	£41.00
exceeds £600 but does not exceed £2,000	£69.50
exceeds £2,000	£75.50

(Continued)

TABLE 5 (*Continued*)

On attendance to question a judgment debtor (or officer of a company or other corporation) who has been ordered to attend court under rule 71.2 where the questioning takes place before a court officer, including attendance by a responsible representative of the legal representative	for each half hour or part, £15.00
On the making of a final third party debt order under rule 72.8(6)(a) or an order for the payment to the judgment creditor of money in court under rule 72.10(1)(b):	
if the amount recovered is less than £150	one-half of the amount recovered
otherwise	£98.50
On the making of a final charging order under rule 73.8(2)(a):	£110.00
	The court may also allow reasonable disbursements in respect of search fees and the registration of the order.
Where a certificate is issued and registered under Schedule 6 to the Civil Jurisdiction and Judgments Act 1982, the costs of registration	£39.00
Where permission is given under RSC Order 45, rule 3 to enforce a judgment or order giving possession of land and costs are allowed on the judgment or order, the amount to be added to the judgment or order for costs—	
(a) basic costs	£42.50
(b) where notice of the proceedings is to be to more than one person, for each additional person	£2.75
Where a writ of execution as defined in the RSC Order 46, rule 1, is issued against any party	£51.75
Where a request is filed for the issue of a warrant of execution under CCR Order 26, rule 1, for a sum exceeding £25	£2.25
Where an application for an attachment of earnings order is made and costs are allowed under CCR Order 27, rule 9 or CCR Order 28, rule 10, for each attendance on the hearing of the application	£8.50

SECTION II

Road Traffic Accidents—Fixed Recoverable Costs

Scope and interpretation

45.9.—(1) Subject to paragraph (3), this Section sets out the costs which are to be allowed in—

(a) proceedings to which rule 46.14(1) applies (costs-only proceedings); or

(b) proceedings for approval of a settlement or compromise under rule 21.10(2),

in cases to which this Section applies.

(2) This Section applies where—
　(a) the dispute arises from a road traffic accident occurring on or after 6 October 2003;
　(b) the agreed damages include damages in respect of personal injury, damage to property, or both;
　(c) the total value of the agreed damages does not exceed £10,000; and
　(d) if a claim had been issued for the amount of the agreed damages, the small claims track would not have been the normal track for that claim.

(3) This Section does not apply where—
　(a) the claimant is a litigant in person; or
　(b) Section III of this Part applies.

(4) In this Section—
　'road traffic accident' means an accident resulting in bodily injury to any person or damage to property caused by, or arising out of, the use of a motor vehicle on a road or other public place in England and Wales;
　'motor vehicle' means a mechanically propelled vehicle intended for use on roads; and
　'road' means any highway and any other road to which the public has access and includes bridges over which a road passes.

Application of fixed recoverable costs

45.10. Subject to rule 45.13, the only costs which are to be allowed are—
　(a) fixed recoverable costs calculated in accordance with rule 45.11; and
　(b) disbursements allowed in accordance with rule 45.12.
　(Rule 45.13 provides for where a party issues a claim for more than the fixed recoverable costs.)

Amount of fixed recoverable costs

45.11.—(1) Subject to paragraphs (2) and (3), the amount of fixed recoverable costs is the total of—
　(a) £800;
　(b) 20% of the damages agreed up to £5,000; and
　(c) 15% of the damages agreed between £5,000 and £10,000.

(2) Where the claimant—
　(a) lives or works in an area set out in Practice Direction 45; and
　(b) instructs a legal representative who practises in that area,
　the fixed recoverable costs will include, in addition to the costs specified in paragraph (1), an amount equal to 12.5% of the costs allowable under that paragraph.

(3) Where appropriate, VAT may be recovered in addition to the amount of fixed recoverable costs and any reference in this Section to fixed recoverable costs is a reference to those costs net of any such VAT.

Disbursements

45.12.—(1) The court—
　(a) may allow a claim for a disbursement of a type mentioned in paragraph (2); but
　(b) will not allow a claim for any other type of disbursement.

(2) The disbursements referred to in paragraph (1) are—
    (a) the cost of obtaining—
        (i)   medical records;
        (ii) a medical report;
        (iii) a police report;
        (iv) an engineer's report; or
        (v)   a search of the records of the Driver Vehicle Licensing Authority;[2]
    (b) where they are necessarily incurred by reason of one or more of the claimants being a child or protected party as defined in Part 21—
        (i)   fees payable for instructing counsel; or
        (ii) court fees payable on an application to the court; or
    (c) any other disbursement that has arisen due to a particular feature of the dispute.

Claims for an amount of costs exceeding fixed recoverable costs

45.13.—(1) The court will entertain a claim for an amount of costs (excluding any success fee or disbursements) greater than the fixed recoverable costs but only if it considers that there are exceptional circumstances making it appropriate to do so.

(2) If the court considers such a claim appropriate, it may—
    (a) summarily assess the costs; or
    (b) make an order for the costs to be subject to detailed assessment.

(3) If the court does not consider the claim appropriate, it will make an order for fixed recoverable costs (and any permitted disbursements) only.

Failure to achieve costs greater than fixed recoverable costs

45.14.—(1) This rule applies where—
    (a) costs are assessed in accordance with rule 45.13(2); and
    (b) the court assesses the costs (excluding any VAT) as being an amount which is less than 20% greater than the amount of the fixed recoverable costs.

(2) The court must order the defendant to pay to the claimant the lesser of—
    (a) the fixed recoverable costs; and
    (b) the assessed costs.

Costs of the costs-only proceedings or the detailed assessment

45.15. Where—
    (a) the court makes an order for fixed recoverable costs in accordance with rule 45.13(3); or
    (b) rule 45.14 applies, the court may—
        (i)   decide not to make an award of the payment of the claimant's costs in bringing the proceedings under rule 46.14; and
        (ii) make orders in relation to costs that may include an order that the claimant pay the defendant's costs of defending those proceedings.

---

[2] *Sic.* The correct title is the Driver and Vehicle Licensing Agency.

SECTION III

Pre-Action Protocol for Low Value Personal Injury
Claims in Road Traffic Accidents

Scope and interpretation

45.16.—(1) This Section applies to claims that have been or should have been started under Part 8 in accordance with Practice Direction 8B ('the Stage 3 Procedure').

(2) Where a party has not complied with the RTA Protocol rule 45.24 will apply.

'RTA Protocol' means the Pre-Action Protocol for Low Value Personal Injury Claims in Road Traffic Accidents.

(3) A reference to 'Claim Notification Form' is a reference to the form used in the RTA Protocol.

Application of fixed costs, and disbursements

45.17. The only costs allowed are—

(a) fixed costs in rule 45.18; and

(b) disbursements in accordance with rule 45.19.

Amount of fixed costs

45.18.—(1) Subject to paragraph (4), the amount of fixed costs is set out in Table 6.

(2) In Table 6—

'Type A fixed costs' means the legal representative's costs;

'Type B fixed costs' means the advocate's costs; and

'Type C fixed costs' means the costs for the advice on the amount of damages where the claimant is a child.

(3) 'Advocate' has the same meaning as in rule 45.37(2)(a).

(4) Subject to rule 45.24(2) the court will not award more or less than the amounts shown in Table 1.[3]

(5) Where the claimant—

(a) lives or works in an area set out in Practice Direction 45; and

(b) instructs a legal representative who practices in that area,

the fixed costs will include, in addition to the costs set out in Table 6, an amount equal to 12.5% of the Stage 1 and 2 and Stage 3 Type A fixed costs.

(6) Where appropriate, value added tax (VAT) may be recovered in addition to the amount of fixed costs and any reference in this Section to fixed costs is a reference to those costs net of any such VAT.

---

[3] *Sic.* The reference should be to Table 6.

TABLE 6 Fixed costs in relation to the RTA Protocol

Stage 1 fixed costs		£400
Stage 2 fixed costs		£800
Stage 3—	Type A fixed costs	£250
	Type B fixed costs	£250
	Type C fixed costs	£150

Disbursements

45.19.—(1) The court—

    (a) may allow a claim for a disbursement of a type mentioned in paragraph (2); but

    (b) will not allow a claim for any other type of disbursement.

  (2) The disbursements referred to in paragraph (1) are—

    (a) the cost of obtaining—

      (i)   medical records;

      (ii) a medical report or reports as provided for in the RTA Protocol;

      (iii) an engineer's report;

      (iv) a search of the records of the—

        (aa) Driver Vehicle Licensing Authority;[4]

        (bb) Motor Insurance Database;

    (b) court fees as a result of Part 21 being applicable;

    (c) court fees payable where proceedings are started as a result of a limitation period that is about to expire;

    (d) court fees in respect of the Stage 3 Procedure;

    (e) any other disbursement that has arisen due to a particular feature of the dispute.

Where the claimant obtains judgment for an amount more than the defendant's RTA Protocol offer

45.20. Where rule 36.21(1)(b) or (c) applies, the court will order the defendant to pay—

    (a) where not already paid by the defendant, the Stage 1 and 2 fixed costs;

    (b) where the claim is determined—

      (i)   on the papers, Stage 3 Type A fixed costs;

      (ii) at a Stage 3 hearing, Stage 3 Type A and B fixed costs; or

      (iii) at a Stage 3 hearing and the claimant is a child, Type A, B and C fixed costs; and

    (c) disbursements allowed in accordance with rule 45.19.

Settlement at Stage 2 where the claimant is a child

45.21.—(1) This rule applies where—

    (a) the claimant is a child;

    (b) there is a settlement at Stage 2 of the RTA Protocol; and

    (c) an application is made to the court to approve the settlement.

---

[4] *Sic.* The correct title is the Driver and Vehicle Licensing Agency.

(2) Where the court approves the settlement at a settlement hearing it will order the defendant to pay—
    (a) the Stage 1 and 2 fixed costs;
    (b) the Stage 3 Type A, B and C fixed costs; and
    (c) disbursements allowed in accordance with rule 45.19.
(3) Where the court does not approve the settlement at a settlement hearing it will order the defendant to pay the Stage 1 and 2 fixed costs.
(4) Paragraphs (5) and (6) apply where the court does not approve the settlement at the first settlement hearing but does approve the settlement at a second settlement hearing.
(5) At the second settlement hearing the court will order the defendant to pay—
    (a) the Stage 3 Type A and C fixed costs for the first settlement hearing;
    (b) disbursements allowed in accordance with rule 45.19; and
    (c) the Stage 3 Type B fixed costs for one of the hearings.
(6) The court in its discretion may also order—
    (a) the defendant to pay an additional amount of either or both the Stage 3—
        (i) Type A fixed costs;
        (ii) Type B fixed costs; or
    (b) he[5] claimant to pay an amount equivalent to either or both the Stage 3—
        (i) Type A fixed costs;
        (ii) Type B fixed costs.

Settlement at Stage 3 where the claimant is a child

45.22.—(1) This rule applies where—
    (a) the claimant is a child;
    (b) there is a settlement after proceedings are started under the Stage 3 Procedure;
    (c) the settlement is more than the defendant's RTA Protocol offer; and
    (d) an application is made to the court to approve the settlement.
(2) Where the court approves the settlement at the settlement hearing it will order the defendant to pay—
    (a) the Stage 1 and 2 fixed costs;
    (b) the Stage 3 Type A, B and C fixed costs; and
    (c) disbursements allowed in accordance with rule 45.19.
(3) Where the court does not approve the settlement at the settlement hearing it will order the defendant to pay the Stage 1 and 2 fixed costs.
(4) Paragraphs (5) and (6) apply where the court does not approve the settlement at the first settlement hearing but does approve the settlement at the Stage 3 hearing.
(5) At the Stage 3 hearing the court will order the defendant to pay—
    (a) the Stage 3 Type A and C fixed costs for the settlement hearing;
    (b) disbursements allowed in accordance with rule 45.19; and
    (c) the Stage 3 Type B fixed costs for one of the hearings.

---

[5] *Sic.* 'he' should be 'the'.

(6) The court in its discretion may also order—
    (a) he[6] defendant to pay an additional amount of either or both the Stage 3—
        (i) Type A fixed costs;
        (ii) Type B fixed costs; or
    (b) the claimant to pay an amount equivalent to either or both of the Stage 3—
        (i) Type A fixed costs;
        (ii) Type B fixed costs.

(7) Where the settlement is not approved at the Stage 3 hearing the court will order the defendant to pay the Stage 3 Type A fixed costs.

Where the court orders that the claim is not suitable to be determined under the Stage 3 Procedure and the claimant is a child

45.23. Where—
    (a) the claimant is a child; and
    (b) at a settlement hearing or the Stage 3 hearing the court orders that the claim is not suitable to be determined under the Stage 3 Procedure, the court will order the defendant to pay—
        (i) the Stage 1 and 2 fixed costs; and
        (ii) the Stage 3 Type A, B and C fixed costs.

Failure to comply or electing not to continue with the RTA Protocol—costs consequences

45.24.—(1) This rule applies where the claimant—
    (a) does not comply with the process set out in the RTA Protocol; or
    (b) elects not to continue with that process,
and starts proceedings under Part 7.

(2) Where a judgment is given in favour of the claimant but—
    (a) the court determines that the defendant did not proceed with the process set out in the RTA Protocol because the claimant provided insufficient information on the Claim Notification Form;
    (b) the court considers that the claimant acted unreasonably—
        (i) by discontinuing the process set out in the RTA Protocol and starting proceedings under Part 7;
        (ii) by valuing the claim at more than £10,000, so that the claimant did not need to comply with the RTA Protocol; or
        (iii) except for paragraph (2)(a), in any other way that caused the process in the RTA Protocol to be discontinued; or
    (c) the claimant did not comply with the RTA Protocol at all despite the claim falling within the scope of the RTA Protocol,

---

[6] *Sic.* 'he' should be 'the'.

the court may order the defendant to pay no more than the fixed costs in rule 45.18 together with the disbursements allowed in accordance with rule 45.19.

(3) Where the claimant starts proceedings under paragraph 7.22 of the RTA Protocol and the court orders the defendant to make an interim payment of no more than the interim payment made under paragraph 7.14(2) or (3) of that Protocol the court will, on the final determination of the proceedings, order the defendant to pay no more than—

(a) the Stage 1 and 2 fixed costs; and

(b) the disbursements allowed in accordance with rule 45.19.

Where the parties have settled after proceedings have started

45.25.—(1) This rule applies where an application is made under rule 45.29 (costs-only application after a claim is started under Part 8 in accordance with Practice Direction 8B).

(2) Where the settlement is more than the defendant's RTA Protocol offer the court will order the defendant to pay—

(a) the Stage 1 and 2 fixed costs where not already paid by the defendant;

(b) the Stage 3 Type A fixed costs; and

(c) disbursements allowed in accordance with rule 45.19.

(3) Where the settlement is less than or equal to the defendant's RTA Protocol offer the court will order the defendant to pay—

(a) the Stage 1 and 2 fixed costs where not already paid by the defendant; and

(b) disbursements allowed in accordance with rule 45.19.

(4) The court may, in its discretion, order either party to pay the costs of the application.

Where the claimant obtains judgment for an amount equal to or less than the defendant's RTA Protocol offer

45.26. Where rule 36.21(1)(a) applies, the court will order the claimant to pay—

(a) where the claim is determined—

(i)   on the papers, Stage 3 Type A fixed costs; or

(ii) at a hearing, Stage 3 Type A and B fixed costs;

(b) any Stage 3 disbursements allowed in accordance with rule 45.19.

Adjournment

45.27. Where the court adjourns a settlement hearing or a Stage 3 hearing it may, in its discretion, order a party to pay—

(a) an additional amount of the Stage 3 Type B fixed costs; and

(b) any court fee for that adjournment.

Account of payment of Stage 1 fixed costs

45.28. Where a claim no longer continues under the RTA Protocol the court will, when making any order as to costs including an order for fixed recoverable costs under Section II of this Part, take into account the Stage 1 fixed costs that have been paid by the defendant.

Costs-only application after a claim is started under Part 8 in accordance with Practice Direction 8B

45.29.—(1) This rule sets out the procedure where—

(a) the parties to a dispute have reached an agreement on all issues (including which party is to pay the costs) which is made or confirmed in writing; but

(b) they have failed to agree the amount of those costs; and

(c) proceedings have been started under Part 8 in accordance with Practice Direction 8B.

(2) Either party may make an application for the court to determine the costs.

(3) Where an application is made under this rule the court will assess the costs in accordance with rule 45.22 or rule 45.25.

(4) Rule 44.5 (amount of costs where costs are payable pursuant to a contract) does not apply to an application under this rule.

SECTION IV

Scale Costs for Claims in a Patents County Court

Scope and interpretation

45.30.—(1) Subject to paragraph (2), this Section applies to proceedings in a patents county court.

(2) This Section does not apply where—

(a) the court considers that a party has behaved in a manner which amounts to an abuse of the court's process; or

(b) the claim concerns the infringement or revocation of a patent or registered design the validity of which has been certified by a court in earlier proceedings.

(3) The court will make a summary assessment of the costs of the party in whose favour any order for costs is made. Rules 44.2(8), 44.7(b) and Part 47 do not apply to this Section.

(4) 'Scale costs' means the costs set out in Table A and Table B of the Practice Direction supplementing this Part.

Amount of scale costs

45.31.—(1) Subject to rule 45.32, the court will not order a party to pay total costs of more than—

(a) £50,000 on the final determination of a claim in relation to liability; and

(b) £25,000 on an inquiry as to damages or account of profits.

(2) The amounts in paragraph (1) apply after the court has applied the provision on set off in accordance with rule 44.12(a).

(3) The maximum amount of scale costs that the court will award for each stage of the claim is set out in Practice Direction 45.

(4) The amount of the scale costs awarded by the court in accordance with paragraph (3) will depend on the nature and complexity of the claim.

(5) Where appropriate, value added tax (VAT) may be recovered in addition to the amount of the scale costs and any reference in this Section to scale costs is a reference to those costs net of any such VAT.

Summary assessment of the costs of an application where a party has behaved unreasonably

45.32. Costs awarded to a party under rule 63.26(2) are in addition to the total costs that may be awarded to that party under rule 45.31.

SECTION V

Fixed Costs: HM Revenue and Customs

Scope, interpretation and application

45.33.—(1) This Section sets out the amounts which, unless the court orders otherwise, are to be allowed in respect of HM Revenue and Customs charges in the cases to which this Section applies.

(2) For the purpose of this Section—

(a) 'HMRC Officer' means a person appointed by the Commissioners under section 2 of the Commissioners for Revenue and Customs Act 2005 and authorised to conduct county court proceedings for recovery of debt under section 25(1A) of that Act;

(b) 'Commissioners' means commissioners for HMRC appointed under section 1 of the Commissioners for Revenue and Customs Act 2005;

(c) 'debt' means any sum payable to the Commissioners under or by virtue of an enactment or under a contract settlement; and

(d) 'HMRC charges' means the fixed costs set out in Tables 7 and 8 in this Section.

(3) HMRC charges must, for the purpose of this Section, be claimed as 'legal representative's costs' on relevant court forms.

(4) This Section applies where the only claim is a claim conducted by an HMRC Officer in the county court for recovery of a debt and the Commissioners obtain judgment on the claim.

(5) Any appropriate court fee will be allowed in addition to the costs set out in this Section.

(6) The claim form may include a claim for fixed commencement costs.

Amount of fixed commencement costs in a county court claim for the recovery of money

45.34. The amount of fixed commencement costs in a claim to which rule 45.33 applies—

(a) will be calculated by reference to Table 7; and

(b) the amount claimed in the claim form is to be used for determining which claim band in Table 7 applies.

TABLE 7 Fixed costs on commencement of a County Court claim conducted by an HMRC Officer

Where the value of the claim does not exceed £25	Nil
Where the value of the claim exceeds £25 but does not exceed £500	£33
Where the value of the claim exceeds £500 but does not exceed £1,000	£47
Where the value of the claim exceeds £1,000 but does not exceed £5,000	£53
Where the value of the claim exceeds £5,000 but does not exceed £15,000	£67
Where the value of the claim exceeds £15,000 but does not exceed £50,000	£90
Where the value of the claim exceeds £50,000 but does not exceed £100,000	£113
Where the value of the claim exceeds £100,000 but does not exceed £150,000	£127
Where the value of the claim exceeds £150,000 but does not exceed £200,000	£140
Where the value of the claim exceeds £200,000 but does not exceed £250,000	£153
Where the value of the claim exceeds £250,000 but does not exceed £300,000	£167
Where the value of the claim exceeds £300,000	£180

Costs on entry of judgment in a county court claim for recovery of money

45.35. Where—

    (a) an HMRC Officer has claimed fixed commencement costs under Rule 45.34; and

    (b) judgment is entered in a claim to which rule 45.33 applies, the amount to be included in the judgment for HMRC charges is the total of—

        (i)   the fixed commencement costs; and

        (ii)   the amount in Table 8 relevant to the value of the claim.

TABLE 8 Fixed costs on entry of judgment in a County Court claim conducted by an HMRC Officer

Where the value of the claim does not exceed £5,000	£15
Where the value of the claim exceeds £5,000	£20

When the defendant is only liable for fixed commencement costs

45.36. Where—

    (a) the only claim is for a specified sum of money; and

    (b) the defendant pays the money claimed within 14 days after service of the particulars of claim, together with the fixed commencement costs stated in the claim form, the defendant is not liable for any further costs unless the court orders otherwise.

SECTION VI

Fast Track Trial Costs

Scope of this Section

45.37.—(1) This Section deals with the amount of costs which the court may award as the costs of an advocate for preparing for and appearing at the trial of a claim in the fast track (referred to in this rule as 'fast track trial costs').

(2) For the purposes of this Section—

'advocate' means a person exercising a right of audience as a representative of, or on behalf of, a party;

'fast track trial costs' means the costs of a party's advocate for preparing for and appearing at the trial, but does not include—

(i) any other disbursements; or

(ii) any value added tax payable on the fees of a party's advocate; and

'trial' includes a hearing where the court decides an amount of money or the value of goods following a judgment under Part 12 (default judgment) or Part 14 (admissions) but does not include—

(i) the hearing of an application for summary judgment under Part 24; or

(ii) the court's approval of a settlement or other compromise under rule 21.10.

Amount of fast track trial costs

45.38.—(1) Table 9 shows the amount of fast track trial costs which the court may award (whether by summary or detailed assessment).

TABLE 9

Value of the claim	Amount of fast track trial costs which the court may award
No more than £3,000	£485
More than £3,000 but not more than £10,000	£690
More than £10,000 but not more than £15,000	£1,035
For proceedings issued on or after 6th April 2009, more than £15,000	£1,650

(2) The court may not award more or less than the amount shown in the table except where—

(a) it decides not to award any fast track trial costs; or

(b) rule 45.39 applies,

but the court may apportion the amount awarded between the parties to reflect their respective degrees of success on the issues at trial.

(3) Where the only claim is for the payment of money—

(a) for the purpose of quantifying fast track trial costs awarded to a claimant, the value of the claim is the total amount of the judgment excluding—

(i) interest and costs; and

(ii) any reduction made for contributory negligence.

273

(b) for the purpose of quantifying fast track trial costs awarded to a defendant, the value of the claim is—

    (i) the amount specified in the claim form (excluding interest and costs);

    (ii) if no amount is specified, the maximum amount which the claimant reasonably expected to recover according to the statement of value included in the claim form under rule 16.3; or

    (iii) more than £15,000, if the claim form states that the claimant cannot reasonably say how much is likely to be recovered.

(4) Where the claim is only for a remedy other than the payment of money, the value of the claim is deemed to be more than £3,000 but not more than £10,000, unless the court orders otherwise.

(5) Where the claim includes both a claim for the payment of money and for a remedy other than the payment of money, the value of the claim is deemed to be the higher of—

    (a) the value of the money claim decided in accordance with paragraph (3); or

    (b) the deemed value of the other remedy decided in accordance with paragraph (4),

unless the court orders otherwise.

(6) Where—

    (a) a defendant has made a counterclaim against the claimant;

    (b) the counterclaim has a higher value than the claim; and

    (c) the claimant succeeds at trial both on the claim and the counterclaim,

for the purpose of quantifying fast track trial costs awarded to the claimant, the value of the claim is the value of the defendant's counterclaim calculated in accordance with this rule.

Power to award more or less than the amount of fast track trial costs

45.39.—(1) This rule sets out when a court may award—

    (a) an additional amount to the amount of fast track trial costs shown in Table 9 in rule 45.38(1); or

    (b) less than those amounts.

(2) If—

    (a) in addition to the advocate, a party's legal representative attends the trial;

    (b) the court considers that it was necessary for a legal representative to attend to assist the advocate; and

    (c) the court awards fast track trial costs to that party,

the court may award an additional £345 in respect of the legal representative's attendance at the trial.

(3) If the court considers that it is necessary to direct a separate trial of an issue then the court may award an additional amount in respect of the separate trial but that amount is limited in accordance with paragraph (4) of this rule.

(4) The additional amount the court may award under paragraph (3) will not exceed two-thirds of the amount payable for that claim, subject to a minimum award of £485.

(5) Where the party to whom fast track trial costs are to be awarded is a litigant in person, the court will award—

(a) if the litigant in person can prove financial loss, two-thirds of the amount that would otherwise be awarded; or

(b) if the litigant in person fails to prove financial loss, an amount in respect of the time spent reasonably doing the work at the rate specified in Practice Direction 46.

(6) Where a defendant has made a counterclaim against the claimant, and—

(a) the claimant has succeeded on his claim; and

(b) the defendant has succeeded on his counterclaim,

the court will quantify the amount of the award of fast track trial costs to which—

(i) but for the counterclaim, the claimant would be entitled for succeeding on his claim; and

(ii) but for the claim, the defendant would be entitled for succeeding on his counterclaim,

and make one award of the difference, if any, to the party entitled to the higher award of costs.

(7) Where the court considers that the party to whom fast track trial costs are to be awarded has behaved unreasonably or improperly during the trial, it may award that party an amount less than would otherwise be payable for that claim, as it considers appropriate.

(8) Where the court considers that the party who is to pay the fast track trial costs has behaved improperly during the trial the court may award such additional amount to the other party as it considers appropriate.

Fast track trial costs where there is more than one claimant or defendant

45.40.—(1) Where the same advocate is acting for more than one party—

(a) the court may make only one award in respect of fast track trial costs payable to that advocate; and

(b) the parties for whom the advocate is acting are jointly entitled to any fast track trial costs awarded by the court.

(2) Where—

(a) the same advocate is acting for more than one claimant; and

(b) each claimant has a separate claim against the defendant,

the value of the claim, for the purpose of quantifying the award in respect of fast track trial costs is to be ascertained in accordance with paragraph (3).

(3) The value of the claim in the circumstances mentioned in paragraph (2) or (5) is—

(a) where the only claim of each claimant is for the payment of money—

(i) if the award of fast track trial costs is in favour of the claimants, the total amount of the judgment made in favour of all the claimants jointly represented; or

(ii) if the award is in favour of the defendant, the total amount claimed by the claimants,

and in either case, quantified in accordance with rule 45.38(3);

    (b) where the only claim of each claimant is for a remedy other than the payment of money, deemed to be more than £3,000 but not more than £10,000; and

    (c) where claims of the claimants include both a claim for the payment of money and for a remedy other than the payment of money, deemed to be—

        (i) more than £3,000 but not more than £10,000; or

        (ii) if greater, the value of the money claims calculated in accordance with subparagraph (a) above.

(4) Where—

    (a) there is more than one defendant; and

    (b) any or all of the defendants are separately represented,

the court may award fast track trial costs to each party who is separately represented.

(5) Where—

    (a) there is more than one claimant; and

    (b) a single defendant,

the court may make only one award to the defendant of fast track trial costs, for which the claimants are jointly and severally liable.

(6) For the purpose of quantifying the fast track trial costs awarded to the single defendant under paragraph (5), the value of the claim is to be calculated in accordance with paragraph (3) of this rule.

SECTION VII

Costs Limits in Aarhus Convention Claims

Scope and interpretation

45.41.—(1) This Section provides for the costs which are to be recoverable between the parties in Aarhus Convention claims.

    (2) In this Section, 'Aarhus Convention claim' means a claim for judicial review of a decision, act or omission all or part of which is subject to the provisions of the UNECE Convention on Access to Information, Public Participation in Decision-Making and Access to Justice in Environmental Matters done at Aarhus, Denmark on 25 June 1998, including a claim which proceeds on the basis that the decision, act or omission, or part of it, is so subject.

    (Rule 52.9A makes provision in relation to costs of an appeal.)

Opting out

45.42. Rules 45.43 to 45.44 do not apply where the claimant—

    (a) has not stated in the claim form that the claim is an Aarhus Convention claim; or

    (b) has stated in the claim form that—

        (i) the claim is not an Aarhus Convention claim, or

        (ii) although the claim is an Aarhus Convention claim, the claimant does not wish those rules to apply.

Limit on costs recoverable from a party in an Aarhus Convention claim

45.43.—(1) Subject to rule 45.44, a party to an Aarhus Convention claim may not be ordered to pay costs exceeding the amount prescribed in Practice Direction 45.

(2) Practice Direction 45 may prescribe a different amount for the purpose of paragraph (1) according to the nature of the claimant.

Challenging whether the claim is an Aarhus Convention claim

45.44.—(1) If the claimant has stated in the claim form that the claim is an Aarhus Convention claim, rule 45.43 will apply unless—

(a) the defendant has in the acknowledgment of service filed in accordance with rule 54.8—

(i)   denied that the claim is an Aarhus Convention claim; and

(ii) set out the defendant's grounds for such denial; and

(b) the court has determined that the claim is not an Aarhus Convention claim.

(2) Where the defendant argues that the claim is not an Aarhus Convention claim, the court will determine that issue at the earliest opportunity.

(3) In any proceedings to determine whether the claim is an Aarhus Convention claim—

(a) if the court holds that the claim is not an Aarhus Convention claim, it will normally make no order for costs in relation to those proceedings;

(b) if the court holds that the claim is an Aarhus Convention claim, it will normally order the defendant to pay the claimant's costs of those proceedings on the indemnity basis, and that order may be enforced notwithstanding that this would increase the costs payable by the defendant beyond the amount prescribed in Practice Direction 45.

PART 46

COSTS—SPECIAL CASES

Contents of this Part

SECTION I

Costs Payable by or to Particular Persons

Pre-commencement disclosure and orders for disclosure against a person who is not a party

46.1.—(1) This paragraph applies where a person applies—
  (a) for an order under—
      (i)   section 33 of the Senior Courts Act 1981; or
      (ii) section 52 of the County Courts Act 1984,
      (which give the court powers exercisable before commencement of proceedings); or
  (b) for an order under—
      (i)   section 34 of the Senior Courts Act 1981; or
      (ii) section 53 of the County Courts Act 1984,
      (which give the court power to make an order against a non-party for disclosure of documents, inspection of property etc.).
(2) The general rule is that the court will award the person against whom the order is sought that person's costs—
  (a) of the application; and
  (b) of complying with any order made on the application.
(3) The court may however make a different order, having regard to all the circumstances, including—
  (a) the extent to which it was reasonable for the person against whom the order was sought to oppose the application; and
  (b) whether the parties to the application have complied with any relevant pre-action protocol.

Costs orders in favour of or against non-parties

46.2.—(1) Where the court is considering whether to exercise its power under section 51 of the Senior Courts Act 1981 (costs are in the discretion of the court) to make a costs order in favour of or against a person who is not a party to proceedings, that person must—

   (a) be added as a party to the proceedings for the purposes of costs only; and

   (b) be given a reasonable opportunity to attend a hearing at which the court will consider the matter further.

(2) This rule does not apply—

   (a) where the court is considering whether to—

      (i) make an order against the Lord Chancellor in proceedings in which the Lord Chancellor has provided legal aid to a party to the proceedings;

      (ii) make a wasted costs order (as defined in rule 46.8); and

   (b) in proceedings to which rule 46.1 applies (pre-commencement disclosure and orders for disclosure against a person who is not a party).

Limitations on court's power to award costs in favour of trustee or personal representative

46.3.—(1) This rule applies where—

   (a) a person is or has been a party to any proceedings in the capacity of trustee or personal representative; and

   (b) rule 44.5 does not apply.

(2) The general rule is that that person is entitled to be paid the costs of those proceedings, insofar as they are not recovered from or paid by any other person, out of the relevant trust fund or estate.

(3) Where that person is entitled to be paid any of those costs out of the fund or estate, those costs will be assessed on the indemnity basis.

Costs where money is payable by or to a child or protected party

46.4.—(1) This rule applies to any proceedings where a party is a child or protected party and—

   (a) money is ordered or agreed to be paid to, or for the benefit of, that party; or

   (b) money is ordered to be paid by that party or on that party's behalf.

('Child' and 'protected party' have the same meaning as in rule 21.1(2).)

(2) The general rule is that—

   (a) the court must order a detailed assessment of the costs payable by, or out of money belonging to, any party who is a child or protected party; and

   (b) on an assessment under paragraph (a), the court must also assess any costs payable to that party in the proceedings, unless—

      (i) the court has issued a default costs certificate in relation to those costs under rule 47.11; or

      (ii) the costs are payable in proceedings to which Section II or Section III of Part 45 applies.

(3) The court need not order detailed assessment of costs in the circumstances set out in Practice Direction 46.

(4) Where—
    (a) a claimant is a child or protected party; and
    (b) a detailed assessment has taken place under paragraph (2)(a),
the only amount payable by the child or protected party is the amount which the court certifies as payable.
(This rule applies to a counterclaim by or on behalf of a child or protected party by virtue of rule 20.3.)

Litigants in person

46.5.—(1) This rule applies where the court orders (whether by summary assessment or detailed assessment) that the costs of a litigant in person are to be paid by any other person.

(2) The costs allowed under this rule will not exceed, except in the case of a disbursement, two-thirds of the amount which would have been allowed if the litigant in person had been represented by a legal representative.

(3) The litigant in person shall be allowed—
    (a) costs for the same categories of—
        (i)   work; and
        (ii) disbursements,
    which would have been allowed if the work had been done or the disbursements had been made by a legal representative on the litigant in person's behalf;
    (b) the payments reasonably made by the litigant in person for legal services relating to the conduct of the proceedings; and
    (c) the costs of obtaining expert assistance in assessing the costs claim.

(4) The amount of costs to be allowed to the litigant in person for any item of work claimed will be—
    (a) where the litigant can prove financial loss, the amount that the litigant can prove to have been lost for time reasonably spent on doing the work; or
    (b) where the litigant cannot prove financial loss, an amount for the time reasonably spent on doing the work at the rate set out in Practice Direction 46.

(5) A litigant who is allowed costs for attending at court to conduct the case is not entitled to a witness allowance in respect of such attendance in addition to those costs.

(6) For the purposes of this rule, a litigant in person includes—
    (a) a company or other corporation which is acting without a legal representative; and
    (b) any of the following who acts in person (except where any such person is represented by a firm in which that person is a partner)—
        (i)   a barrister;
        (ii)   a solicitor;
        (iii) a solicitor's employee;
        (iv) a manager of a body recognised under section 9 of the Administration of Justice Act 1985; or

(v) a person who, for the purposes of the 2007 Act, is an authorised person in relation to an activity which constitutes the conduct of litigation (within the meaning of that Act).

Costs where the court has made a group litigation order

46.6.—(1) This rule applies where the court has made a Group Litigation Order ('GLO').

(2) In this rule—

'individual costs' means costs incurred in relation to an individual claim on the group register;

'common costs' means—

(i)   costs incurred in relation to the GLO issues;

(ii) individual costs incurred in a claim while it is proceeding as a test claim, and

(iii) costs incurred by the lead legal representative in administering the group litigation; and

'group litigant' means a claimant or defendant, as the case may be, whose claim is entered on the group register.

(3) Unless the court orders otherwise, any order for common costs against group litigants imposes on each group litigant several liability for an equal proportion of those common costs.

(4) The general rule is that where a group litigant is the paying party, he will, in addition to any costs he is liable to pay to the receiving party, be liable for—

(a) the individual costs of his claim; and

(b) an equal proportion, together with all the other group litigants, of the common costs.

(5) Where the court makes an order about costs in relation to any application or hearing which involved—

(a) one or more GLO issues; and

(b) issues relevant only to individual claims,

the court will direct the proportion of the costs that is to relate to common costs and the proportion that is to relate to individual costs.

(6) Where common costs have been incurred before a claim is entered on the group register, the court may order the group litigant to be liable for a proportion of those costs.

(7) Where a claim is removed from the group register, the court may make an order for costs in that claim which includes a proportion of the common costs incurred up to the date on which the claim is removed from the group register.

(Part 19 sets out rules about group litigation.)

Orders in respect of pro bono representation

46.7.—(1) Where the court makes an order under section 194(3) of the 2007 Act—

(a) he[7] court may order the payment to the prescribed charity of a sum no greater than the costs specified in Part 45 to which the party with pro

---

[7] *Sic.* 'he' should be 'the'.

bono representation would have been entitled in accordance with that Part and in respect of that representation had it not been provided free of charge; or

    (b) where Part 45 does not apply, the court may determine the amount of the payment (other than a sum equivalent to fixed costs) to be made by the paying party to the prescribed charity by—

        (i) making a summary assessment; or

        (ii) making an order for detailed assessment,

of a sum equivalent to all or part of the costs the paying party would have been ordered to pay to the party with pro bono representation in respect of that representation had it not been provided free of charge.

(2) Where the court makes an order under section 194(3) of the 2007 Act, the order must direct that the payment by the paying party be made to the prescribed charity.

(3) The receiving party must send a copy of the order to the prescribed charity within 7 days of receipt of the order.

(4) Where the court considers making or makes an order under section 194(3) of the 2007 Act, Parts 44 to 47 apply, where appropriate, with the following modifications—

    (a) references to 'costs orders', 'orders about costs' or 'orders for the payment of costs' are to be read, unless otherwise stated, as if they refer to an order under section 194(3);

    (b) references to 'costs' are to be read as if they referred to a sum equivalent to the costs that would have been claimed by, incurred by or awarded to the party with pro bono representation in respect of that representation had it not been provided free of charge; and

    (c) references to 'receiving party' are to be read, as meaning a party who has pro bono representation and who would have been entitled to be paid costs in respect of that representation had it not been provided free of charge.

SECTION II

Costs relating to Legal Representatives

Personal liability of legal representative for costs—wasted costs orders

46.8.—(1) This rule applies where the court is considering whether to make an order under section 51(6) of the Senior Courts Act 1981 (court's power to disallow or (as the case may be) order a legal representative to meet, 'wasted costs').

(2) The court will give the legal representative a reasonable opportunity to make written submissions or, if the legal representative prefers, to attend a hearing before it makes such an order.

(3) When the court makes a wasted costs order, it will—

    (a) specify the amount to be disallowed or paid; or

    (b) direct a costs judge or a district judge to decide the amount of costs to be disallowed or paid.

(4) The court may direct that notice must be given to the legal representative's client, in such manner as the court may direct—
(a) of any proceedings under this rule; or
(b) of any order made under it against his legal representative.

Basis of detailed assessment of solicitor and client costs

46.9.—(1) This rule applies to every assessment of a solicitor's bill to a client except a bill which is to be paid out of the Community Legal Service Fund under the Legal Aid Act 1988 or the Access to Justice Act 1999.

(2) Section 74(3) of the Solicitors Act 1974 applies unless the solicitor and client have entered into a written agreement which expressly permits payment to the solicitor of an amount of costs greater than that which the client could have recovered from another party to the proceedings.

(3) Subject to paragraph (2), costs are to be assessed on the indemnity basis but are to be presumed—
(a) to have been reasonably incurred if they were incurred with the express or implied approval of the client;
(b) to be reasonable in amount if their amount was expressly or impliedly approved by the client;
(c) to have been unreasonably incurred if—
  (i) they are of an unusual nature or amount; and
  (ii) the solicitor did not tell the client that as a result the costs might not be recovered from the other party.

(4) Where the court is considering a percentage increase on the application of the client, the court will have regard to all the relevant factors as they reasonably appeared to the solicitor or counsel when the conditional fee agreement was entered into or varied.

Assessment procedure

46.10.—(1) This rule sets out the procedure to be followed where the court has made an order under Part III of the Solicitors Act 1974 for the assessment of costs payable to a solicitor by the solicitor's client.

(2) The solicitor must serve a breakdown of costs within 28 days of the order for costs to be assessed.

(3) The client must serve points of dispute within 14 days after service on the client of the breakdown of costs.

(4) The solicitor must serve any reply within 14 days of service on the solicitor of the points of dispute.

(5) Either party may file a request for a hearing date—
(a) after points of dispute have been served; but
(b) no later than 3 months after the date of the order for the costs to be assessed.

(6) This procedure applies subject to any contrary order made by the court.

SECTION III

Costs on Allocation and Re-allocation

Costs on the small claims track and fast track

46.11.—(1) Part 27 (small claims) and Part 45 Section VI (fast track trial costs) contain special rules about—

(a) liability for costs;

(b) the amount of costs which the court may award; and

(c) the procedure for assessing costs.

(2) Once a claim is allocated to a particular track, those special rules shall apply to the period before, as well as after, allocation except where the court or a practice direction provides otherwise.

Limitation on amount court may allow where a claim allocated to the fast track settles before trial

46.12.—(1) Where the court—

(a) assesses costs in relation to a claim which—

(i)   has been allocated to the fast track; and

(ii) settles before the start of the trial; and

(b) is considering the amount of costs to be allowed in respect of a party's advocate for preparing for the trial,

it may not allow, in respect of those advocate's costs, an amount that exceeds the amount of fast track trial costs which would have been payable in relation to the claim had the trial taken place.

(2) When deciding the amount to be allowed in respect of the advocate's costs, the court will have regard to—

(a) when the claim was settled; and

(b) when the court was notified that the claim had settled.

(3) In this rule, 'advocate' and 'fast track trial costs' have the meanings given to them by Part 45 Section VI.

Costs following allocation, re-allocation and non-allocation

46.13.—(1) Any costs orders made before a claim is allocated will not be affected by allocation.

(2) Where—

(a) claim is allocated to a track; and

(b) the court subsequently re-allocates that claim to a different track,

then unless the court orders otherwise, any special rules about costs applying—

(i)   to the first track, will apply to the claim up to the date of re-allocation; and

(ii) to the second track, will apply from the date of re-allocation.

(3) Where the court is assessing costs on the standard basis of a claim which concluded without being allocated to a track, it may restrict those costs to costs that would have been allowed on the track to which the claim would have been allocated if allocation had taken place.

SECTION IV

Costs-only Proceedings

Costs-only proceedings

46.14.—(1) This rule applies where—

(a) the parties to a dispute have reached an agreement on all issues (including which party is to pay the costs) which is made or confirmed in writing; but

(b) they have failed to agree the amount of those costs; and

(c) no proceedings have been started.

(2) Where this rule applies, the procedure set out in this rule must be followed.

(3) Proceedings under this rule are commenced by issuing a claim form in accordance with Part 8.

(4) The claim form must contain or be accompanied by the agreement or confirmation.

(5) In proceedings to which this rule applies the court may make an order for the payment of costs the amount of which is to be determined by assessment and/or, where appropriate, for the payment of fixed costs.

(6) Where this rule applies but the procedure set out in this rule has not been followed by a party—

(a) that party will not be allowed costs greater than those that would have been allowed to that party had the procedure been followed; and

(b) the court may award the other party the costs of the proceedings up to the point where an order for the payment of costs is made.

(7) Rule 44.5 (amount of costs where costs are payable pursuant to a contract) does not apply to claims started under the procedure in this rule.

PART 47

PROCEDURE FOR DETAILED ASSESSMENT OF COSTS
AND DEFAULT PROVISIONS

Contents of this Part

SECTION I

General Rules about Detailed Assessment

Time when detailed assessment may be carried out

47.1. The general rule is that the costs of any proceedings or any part of the proceedings are not to be assessed by the detailed procedure until the conclusion of the proceedings, but the court may order them to be assessed immediately.

(Practice Direction 47 gives further guidance about when proceedings are concluded for the purpose of this rule.)

No stay of detailed assessment where there is an appeal

47.2. Detailed assessment is not stayed pending an appeal unless the court so orders.

Powers of an authorised court officer

47.3.—(1) An authorised court officer has all the powers of the court when making a detailed assessment, except—

    (a) power to make a wasted costs order as defined in rule 46.8;

    (b) power to make an order under—

        (i)   rule 44.11 (powers in relation to misconduct);

        (ii) rule 47.8 (sanction for delay in commencing detailed assessment proceedings);

        (iii) paragraph (2) (objection to detailed assessment by authorised court officer); and

    (c) power to make a detailed assessment of costs payable to a solicitor by that solicitor's client, unless the costs are being assessed under rule 46.4 (costs where money is payable to a child or protected party).

  (2) Where a party objects to the detailed assessment of costs being made by an authorised court officer, the court may order it to be made by a costs judge or a district judge.

(Practice Direction 47 sets out the relevant procedure.)

Venue for detailed assessment proceedings

47.4.—(1) All applications and requests in detailed assessment proceedings must be made to or filed at the appropriate office.

(Practice Direction 47 sets out the meaning of 'appropriate office' in any particular case.)

  (2) The court may direct that the appropriate office is to be the Costs Office.

  (3) A county court may direct that another county court is to be the appropriate office.

  (4) A direction under paragraph (3) may be made without proceedings being transferred to that court.

(Rule 30.2 makes provision for any county court to transfer the proceedings to another county court for detailed assessment of costs.)

SECTION II

Costs Payable by one Party to another—Commencement of Detailed Assessment
Proceedings

Application of this Section

47.5. This Section of Part 47 applies where a cost officer is to make a detailed assessment of—

    (a) costs which are payable by one party to another; or

(b) the sum which is payable by one party to the prescribed charity pursuant to an order under section 194(3) of the 2007 Act.

Commencement of detailed assessment proceedings

47.6.—(1) Detailed assessment proceedings are commenced by the receiving party serving on the paying party—

(a) notice of commencement in the relevant practice form; and

(b) a copy of the bill of costs.

(Rule 47.7 sets out the period for commencing detailed assessment proceedings.)

(2) The receiving party must also serve a copy of the notice of commencement and the bill on any other relevant persons specified in Practice Direction 47.

(3) A person on whom a copy of the notice of commencement is served under paragraph (2) is a party to the detailed assessment proceedings (in addition to the paying party and the receiving party).

(Practice Direction 47 deals with—

other documents which the party must file when requesting detailed assessment;

the court's powers where it considers that a hearing may be necessary;

the form of a bill; and

the length of notice which will be given if a hearing date is fixed.)

Period for commencing detailed assessment proceedings

47.7. The following table shows the period for commencing detailed assessment proceedings.

Source of right to detailed assessment	Time by which detailed assessment proceedings must be commenced
Judgment, direction, order, award or other determination	3 months after the date of the judgment etc. Where detailed assessment is stayed pending an appeal, 3 months after the date of the order lifting the stay
Discontinuance under Part 38	3 months after the date of service of notice of discontinuance under rule 38.3; or 3 months after the date of the dismissal of application to set the notice of discontinuance aside under rule 38.4
Acceptance of an offer to settle under Part 36	3 months after the date when the right to costs arose

Sanction for delay in commencing detailed assessment proceedings

47.8.—(1) Where the receiving party fails to commence detailed assessment proceedings within the period specified—

(a) in rule 47.7; or

(b) by any direction of the court,

the paying party may apply for an order requiring the receiving party to commence detailed assessment proceedings within such time as the court may specify.

(2) On an application under paragraph (1), the court may direct that, unless the receiving party commences detailed assessment proceedings within the time specified by the court, all or part of the costs to which the receiving party would otherwise be entitled will be disallowed.

(3) If—

    (a) the paying party has not made an application in accordance with paragraph (1); and

    (b) the receiving party commences the proceedings later than the period specified in rule 47.7,

the court may disallow all or part of the interest otherwise payable to the receiving party under—

    (i) section 17 of the Judgments Act 1838; or

    (ii) section 74 of the County Courts Act 1984,

but will not impose any other sanction except in accordance with rule 44.11 (powers in relation to misconduct).

(4) Where the costs to be assessed in a detailed assessment are payable out of the Community Legal Service Fund, this rule applies as if the receiving party were the solicitor to whom the costs are payable and the paying party were the Legal Services Commission.

Points of dispute and consequence of not serving

47.9.—(1) The paying party and any other party to the detailed assessment proceedings may dispute any item in the bill of costs by serving points of dispute on—

    (a) the receiving party; and

    (b) every other party to the detailed assessment proceedings.

(2) The period for serving points of dispute is 21 days after the date of service of the notice of commencement.

(3) If a party serves points of dispute after the period set out in paragraph (2), that party may not be heard further in the detailed assessment proceedings unless the court gives permission.

(Practice Direction 47 sets out requirements about the form of points of dispute.)

(4) The receiving party may file a request for a default costs certificate if—

    (a) the period set out in paragraph (2) for serving points of dispute has expired; and

    (b) the receiving party has not been served with any points of dispute.

(5) If any party (including the paying party) serves points of dispute before the issue of a default costs certificate the court may not issue the default costs certificate.

(Section IV of this Part sets out the procedure to be followed after points of dispute have been served.)

Procedure where costs are agreed

47.10.—(1) If the paying party and the receiving party agree the amount of costs, either party may apply for a costs certificate (either interim or final) in the amount agreed.

(Rule 47.16 and rule 47.17 contain further provisions about interim and final costs certificates respectively.)

(2) An application for a certificate under paragraph (1) must be made to the court which would be the venue for detailed assessment proceedings under rule 47.4.

SECTION III

Costs Payable by one Party to another—Default Provisions

Default costs certificate

47.11.—(1) Where the receiving party is permitted by rule 47.9 to obtain a default costs certificate, that party does so by filing a request in the relevant practice form.
(Practice Direction 47 deals with the procedure by which the receiving party may obtain a default costs certificate.)
(2) A default costs certificate will include an order to pay the costs to which it relates.
(3) Where a receiving party obtains a default costs certificate, the costs payable to that party for the commencement of detailed assessment proceedings will be the sum set out in Practice Direction 47.
(4) A receiving party who obtains a default costs certificate in detailed assessment proceedings pursuant to an order under section 194(3) of the 2007 Act must send a copy of the default costs certificate to the prescribed charity.

Setting aside a default costs certificate

47.12.—(1) The court will set aside a default costs certificate if the receiving party was not entitled to it.
(2) In any other case, the court may set aside or vary a default costs certificate if it appears to the court that there is some good reason why the detailed assessment proceedings should continue.
(Practice Direction 47 contains further details about the procedure for setting aside a default costs certificate and the matters which the court must take into account.)
(3) Where the court sets aside or varies a default costs certificate in detailed assessment proceedings pursuant to an order under section 194(3) of the Legal Services Act 2007, the receiving party must send a copy of the order setting aside or varying the default costs certificate to the prescribed charity.

SECTION IV

Costs Payable by one Party to another—Procedure where Points of Dispute are Served

Optional Reply

47.13.—(1) Where any party to the detailed assessment proceedings serves points of dispute, the receiving party may serve a reply on the other parties to the assessment proceedings.

(2) The receiving party may do so within 21 days after being served with the points of dispute to which the reply relates.
(Practice Direction 47 sets out the meaning of 'reply'.)

Detailed assessment hearing

47.14.—(1) Where points of dispute are served in accordance with this Part, the receiving party must file a request for a detailed assessment hearing within 3 months of the expiry of the period for commencing detailed assessment proceedings as specified—

(a) in rule 47.7; or
(b) by any direction of the court.

(2) Where the receiving party fails to file a request in accordance with paragraph (1), the paying party may apply for an order requiring the receiving party to file the request within such time as the court may specify.

(3) On an application under paragraph (2), the court may direct that, unless the receiving party requests a detailed assessment hearing within the time specified by the court, all or part of the costs to which the receiving party would otherwise be entitled will be disallowed.

(4) If—

(a) the paying party has not made an application in accordance with paragraph (2); and
(b) the receiving party files a request for a detailed assessment hearing later than the period specified in paragraph (1),

the court may disallow all or part of the interest otherwise payable to the receiving party under—

(i) section 17 of the Judgments Act 1838; or
(ii) section 74 of the County Courts Act 1984,

but will not impose any other sanction except in accordance with rule 44.11 (powers in relation to misconduct).

(5) No party other than—

(a) the receiving party;
(b) the paying party; and
(c) any party who has served points of dispute under rule 47.9,

may be heard at the detailed assessment hearing unless the court gives permission.

(6) Only items specified in the points of dispute may be raised at the hearing, unless the court gives permission.

(7) If an assessment is carried out at more than one hearing, then for the purposes of rule 52.4 time for appealing shall not start to run until the conclusion of the final hearing, unless the court orders otherwise.
(Practice Direction 47 specifies other documents which must be filed with the request for hearing and the length of notice which the court will give when it fixes a hearing date.)

Provisional Assessment

47.15.—(1) This rule applies to any detailed assessment proceedings commenced in the High Court or a county court on or after 1 April 2013 in which the costs claimed are the amount set out in paragraph 14.1 of the practice direction supplementing this Part, or less.

(2) In proceedings to which this rule applies, the parties must comply with the procedure set out in Part 47 as modified by paragraph 14 Practice Direction 47.

(3) The court will undertake a provisional assessment of the receiving party's costs on receipt of Form N258 and the relevant supporting documents specified in Practice Direction 47.

(4) The provisional assessment will be based on the information contained in the bill and supporting papers and the contentions set out in Precedent G (the points of dispute and any reply).

(5) The court will not award more than £1,500 to any party in respect of the costs of the provisional assessment.

(6) The court may at any time decide that the matter is unsuitable for a provisional assessment and may give directions for the matter to be listed for hearing. The matter will then proceed under rule 47.14 without modification.

(7) When a provisional assessment has been carried out, the court will send a copy of the bill, as provisionally assessed, to each party with a notice stating that any party who wishes to challenge any aspect of the provisional assessment must, within 21 days of the receipt of the notice, file and serve on all other parties a written request for an oral hearing. If no such request is filed and served within that period, the provisional assessment shall be binding upon the parties, save in exceptional circumstances.

(8) The written request referred to in paragraph (7) must—
    (a) identify the item or items in the court's provisional assessment which are sought to be reviewed at the hearing; and
    (b) provide a time estimate for the hearing.

(9) The court then will fix a date for the hearing and give at least 14 days' notice of the time and place of the hearing to all parties.

(10) Any party which has requested an oral hearing, will pay the costs of and incidental to that hearing unless—
    (a) it achieves an adjustment in its own favour by 20% or more of the sum provisionally assessed; or
    (b) the court otherwise orders.

SECTION V

Interim Costs Certificate and Final Costs Certificate

Power to issue an interim certificate

47.16.—(1) The court may at any time after the receiving party has filed a request for a detailed assessment hearing—
    (a) issue an interim costs certificate for such sum as it considers appropriate; or
    (b) amend or cancel an interim certificate.

(2) An interim certificate will include an order to pay the costs to which it relates, unless the court orders otherwise.

(3) The court may order the costs certified in an interim certificate to be paid into court.

(4) Where the court—

(a) issues an interim costs certificate; or

(b) amends or cancels an interim certificate,

in detailed assessment proceedings pursuant to an order under section 194(3) of the 2007 Act, the receiving party must send a copy of the interim costs certificate or the order amending or cancelling the interim costs certificate to the prescribed charity.

Final costs certificate

47.17.—(1) In this rule a 'completed bill' means a bill calculated to show the amount due following the detailed assessment of the costs.

(2) The period for filing the completed bill is 14 days after the end of the detailed assessment hearing.

(3) When a completed bill is filed the court will issue a final costs certificate and serve it on the parties to the detailed assessment proceedings.

(4) Paragraph (3) is subject to any order made by the court that a certificate is not to be issued until other costs have been paid.

(5) A final costs certificate will include an order to pay the costs to which it relates, unless the court orders otherwise.

(Practice Direction 47 deals with the form of a final costs certificate.)

(6) Where the court issues a final costs certificate in detailed assessment proceedings pursuant to an order under section 194(3) of the 2007 Act, the receiving party must send a copy of the final costs certificate to the prescribed charity.

SECTION VI

Detailed Assessment Procedure for Costs of a LSC Funded Client or an Assisted Person where Costs are Payable out of the Community Legal Service Fund

Detailed assessment procedure where costs are payable out of the Community Legal Services Fund

47.18.—(1) Where the court is to assess costs of a LSC funded client or an assisted person which are payable out of the Community Legal Services Fund, that person's solicitor may commence detailed assessment proceedings by filing a request in the relevant practice form.

(2) A request under paragraph (1) must be filed within 3 months after the date when the right to detailed assessment arose.

(3) The solicitor must also serve a copy of the request for detailed assessment on the LSC funded client or the assisted person, if notice of that person's interest has been given to the court in accordance with community legal service or legal aid regulations.

(4) Where the solicitor has certified that the LSC funded client or that person wishes to attend an assessment hearing, the court will, on receipt of the request for assessment, fix a date for the assessment hearing.

(5) Where paragraph (3) does not apply, the court will, on receipt of the request for assessment provisionally assess the costs without the attendance of the solicitor, unless it considers that a hearing is necessary.

(6) After the court has provisionally assessed the bill, it will return the bill to the solicitor.

(7) The court will fix a date for an assessment hearing if the solicitor informs the court, within 14 days after receiving the provisionally assessed bill, that the solicitor wants the court to hold such a hearing.

Detailed assessment procedure where costs are payable out of a fund other than the community legal service fund

47.19.—(1) Where the court is to assess costs which are payable out of a fund other than the Community Legal Service Fund, the receiving party may commence detailed assessment proceedings by filing a request in the relevant practice form.

(2) A request under paragraph (1) must be filed within 3 months after the date when the right to detailed assessment arose.

(3) The court may direct that the party seeking assessment serve a copy of the request on any person who has a financial interest in the outcome of the assessment.

(4) The court will, on receipt of the request for assessment, provisionally assess the costs without the attendance of the receiving party, unless the court considers that a hearing is necessary.

(5) After the court has provisionally assessed the bill, it will return the bill to the receiving party.

(6) The court will fix a date for an assessment hearing if the receiving party informs the court, within 14 days after receiving the provisionally assessed bill, that the receiving party wants the court to hold such a hearing.

SECTION VII

Costs of Detailed Assessment Proceedings

Liability for costs of detailed assessment proceedings

47.20.—(1) The receiving party is entitled to the costs of the detailed assessment proceedings except where—

(a) the provisions of any Act, any of these Rules or any relevant practice direction provide otherwise; or

(b) the court makes some other order in relation to all or part of the costs of the detailed assessment proceedings.

(2) Paragraph (1) does not apply where the receiving party has pro bono representation in the detailed assessment proceedings but that party may apply for

an order in respect of that representation under section 194(3) of the 2007 Act.

(3) In deciding whether to make some other order, the court must have regard to all the circumstances, including—

    (a) the conduct of all the parties;

    (b) the amount, if any, by which the bill of costs has been reduced; and

    (c) whether it was reasonable for a party to claim the costs of a particular item or to dispute that item.

(4) The provisions of Part 36 apply to the costs of detailed assessment proceedings with the following modifications—

    (a) 'claimant' refers to 'receiving party' and 'defendant' refers to 'paying party';

    (b) 'trial' refers to 'detailed assessment hearing';

    (c) in rule 36.9(5), at the end insert 'or, where the Part 36 offer is made in respect of the detailed assessment proceedings, after the commencement of the detailed assessment hearing.';

    (d) for rule 36.11(7) substitute 'If the accepted sum is not paid within 14 days or such other period as has been agreed the offeree may apply for a final costs certificate for the unpaid sum.';

    (e) a reference to 'judgment being entered' is to the completion of the detailed assessment, and references to a 'judgment' being advantageous or otherwise are to the outcome of the detailed assessment.

(5) The court will usually summarily assess the costs of detailed assessment proceedings at the conclusion of those proceedings.

(6) Unless the court otherwise orders, interest on the costs of detailed assessment proceedings will run from the date of default, interim or final costs certificate, as the case may be.

(7) For the purposes of rule 36.14, detailed assessment proceedings are to be regarded as an independent claim.

SECTION VIII

Appeals from Authorised Court Officers in Detailed Assessment Proceedings

Right to appeal

47.21. Any party to detailed assessment proceedings may appeal against a decision of an authorised court officer in those proceedings.

Court to hear appeal

47.22. An appeal against a decision of an authorised court officer lies to a costs judge or a district judge of the High Court.

Appeal procedure

47.23.—(1) The appellant must file an appeal notice within 21 days after the date of the decision against which it is sought to appeal.

(2) On receipt of the appeal notice, the court will—

(a) serve a copy of the notice on the parties to the detailed assessment proceedings; and

(b) give notice of the appeal hearing to those parties.

Powers of the court on appeal

47.24. On an appeal from an authorised court officer the court will—

(a) re-hear the proceedings which gave rise to the decision appealed against; and

(b) make any order and give any directions as it considers appropriate.

PART 48

PART 2 OF THE LEGAL AID, SENTENCING AND PUNISHMENT OF OFFENDERS ACT 2012 RELATING TO CIVIL LITIGATION FUNDING AND COSTS: TRANSITIONAL PROVISION IN RELATION TO PRE-COMMENCEMENT FUNDING ARRANGEMENTS

48.1.—(1) The provisions of CPR Parts 43 to 48 relating to funding arrangements, and the attendant provisions of the Costs Practice Direction, will apply in relation to a pre-commencement funding arrangement as they were in force immediately before 1 April 2013, with such modifications (if any) as may be made by a practice direction on or after that date.

(2) A reference in rule 48.2 to a rule is to that rule as it was in force immediately before 1 April 2013.

48.2.—(1) A pre-commencement funding arrangement is—

(a) in relation to proceedings other than insolvency-related proceedings, publication and privacy proceedings or a mesothelioma claim—

(i) a funding arrangement as defined by rule 43.2(1)(k)(i) where—

(aa) the agreement was entered into before 1 April 2013 specifically for the purposes of the provision to the person by whom the success fee is payable of advocacy or litigation services in relation to the matter that is the subject of the proceedings in which the costs order is to be made; or

(bb) the agreement was entered into before 1 April 2013 and advocacy or litigation services were provided to that person under the agreement in connection with that matter before 1 April 2013;

(ii) a funding arrangement as defined by rule 43.2(1)(k)(ii) where the party seeking to recover the insurance premium took out the insurance policy in relation to the proceedings before 1 April 2013;

(iii) a funding arrangement as defined by rule 43.2(1)(k)(iii) where the agreement with the membership organisation to meet the costs was made before 1 April 2013 specifically in respect of the costs of other parties to proceedings relating to the matter which is the subject of the proceedings in which the costs order is to be made;

(b) in relation to insolvency-related proceedings, publication and privacy proceedings or a mesothelioma claim—

    (i)   a funding arrangement as defined by rule 43.2(1)(k)(i) where—

        (aa) the agreement was entered into before the relevant date specifically for the purposes of the provision to the person by whom the success fee is payable of advocacy or litigation services in relation to the matter that is the subject of the proceedings in which the costs order is to be made; or

        (bb) the agreement was entered into before the relevant date and advocacy or litigation services were provided to that person under the agreement in connection with that matter before the relevant date;

    (ii) a funding arrangement as defined by rule 43.2(1)(k)(ii) where the party seeking to recover the insurance premium took out the insurance policy in relation to the proceedings before the relevant date.

(2) In paragraph (1)—

  (a) 'insolvency-related proceedings' means any proceedings—

    (i)   in England and Wales brought by a person acting in the capacity of—

        (aa) a liquidator of a company which is being wound up in England and Wales or Scotland under Parts IV or V of the Insolvency Act 1986; or

        (bb) a trustee of a bankrupt's estate under Part IX of the Insolvency Act 1986;

    (ii) brought by a person acting in the capacity of an administrator appointed pursuant to the provisions of Part II of the Insolvency Act 1986;

    (iii) in England and Wales brought by a company which is being wound up in England and Wales or Scotland under Parts IV or V of the Insolvency Act 1986; or

    (iv) brought by a company which has entered administration under Part II of the Insolvency Act 1986;

  (b) 'news publisher' means a person who publishes a newspaper, magazine or website containing news or information about or comment on current affairs;

  (c) 'publication and privacy proceedings' means proceedings for—

    (i)   defamation;

    (ii) malicious falsehood;

    (iii) breach of confidence involving publication to the general public;

    (iv) misuse of private information; or

    (v) harassment, where the defendant is a news publisher.

  (d) 'a mesothelioma claim' is a claim for damages in respect of diffuse mesothelioma (within the meaning of the Pneumoconiosis etc. (Workers' Compensation) Act 1979; and

  (e) 'the relevant date' is the date on which sections 44 and 46 of the Legal Aid, Sentencing and Punishment of Offenders Act 2012 came into force in relation to proceedings of the sort in question.'

EXPLANATORY NOTE

(This note is not part of the Order)

These Rules make the following amendments to the Civil Procedure Rules 1998 (CPR)—

A series of amendments to implement recommendations made in the Review of Civil Litigation Costs: Final Report, 21 December 2009 (the Costs Review), in particular— Amendments in relation to costs management, as follows—

— CPR rule 1.1(1) and (2) are amended to change the overriding objective to include the objective to deal with cases at proportionate cost (rule 4 of these Rules);
— the division of Part 3 of the CPR into Sections, the first containing current rules on case management (CPR rules 3.1 to 3.11) the second containing new rules on costs management (CPR rules 3.12 to 3.18) and the third containing rules on costs capping (CPR rules 3.19 to 3.21) (rule 5(a) to (c) and (h) of these Rules);
— an insertion into the Glossary of the definition of 'budget' (rule 21(a) of these Rules);

A new rule 3.1(8) is added, relating to monitoring parties' compliance with directions (rule 5(d) of these Rules);

Amendments to replace allocation questionnaires with directions questionnaires (rules 5(e), 8(a) to (e) and (h) of these Rules);

A new rule 3.9(1) is substituted for the existing provision, and a consequential amendment is made to rule 3.8 relating to sanctions (rules 5(f) and (g) of these Rules);

An amendment to rule 29.1 in relation to standard directions in the multi-track, to add a provision that the parties and the court should take standard and model directions as a starting point for directions (rule 10(a) of these Rules);

Amendments to rules 29.2, 29.4 and 29.8 in relation to timetabling and the steps following allocation to the multi-track (rule 10(b), (c) and (d) of these Rules);

The replacement of rule 31.5 in relation to disclosure in multi-track cases (rule 11 of these Rules);

The insertion of a new paragraph into rule 32.2 in relation to court directions about factual witness statements (rule 12 of these Rules);

Amendments to rule 35.4 in relation to the costs of expert evidence (rule 13 of these Rules);

Amendments to rule 36.14 in relation to Part 36 offers (rule 14 of these Rules);

The revocation of Part 43 and the replacement of Parts 44 to 48 with the following new Parts on costs:

— Part 44—General rules about costs;
— Part 45—Fixed costs;
— Part 46—Costs—special cases;
— Part 47—Procedure for detailed assessment of costs and default provisions; and
— Part 48—Part 2 of the Legal Aid, Sentencing and Punishment of Offenders Act 2012 relating to civil litigation funding and costs: transition provision in relation to pre-commencement funding arrangements (rules 15 and 16 of and the Schedule to these Rules);

Various consequential amendments resulting from the introduction of new Parts 44 to 48 (in particular rule 7 of these Rules);

The introduction of a new rule 52.9A in relation to appeal costs (rule 17 of these Rules); and

An addition of the definition of 'damages-based agreement' to the Glossary (rule 21(b) of these Rules); and

—the following amendments which are other than in relation to the Costs Review—

Amendments to increase the small claims track limit from £5,000 to £10,000 (rules 6, 8(f) and (g), 9(a) and (c) and 18 of these Rules);

Amendment to rule 27.5 to correct a cross-reference (rule 9(b) of these Rules);

Amendment to rule 54.6 in relation to Aarhus Convention claims (rule 18 of these Rules); and

The omission of CCR Order 27 rule 7A(3) as a consequence of the introduction of Part 81 of the Civil Procedure Rules (Applications and proceedings in relation to contempt of court) (rule 20 of these Rules).

AMENDMENT TO CPR RULE 3.12(1)

At its meeting on 8 February 2013, the Civil Procedure Rule Committee approved the following amended r 3.12(1):

(1) This Section and Practice Direction 3E apply to all multi-track cases commenced on or after 1st April 2013, except—

  (a) cases in the Admiralty and Commercial Courts;

  (b) such cases in the Chancery Division as the Chancellor of the High Court may direct; and

  (c) such cases in the Technology and Construction Court and the Mercantile Courts as the President of the Queen's Bench Division may direct,

  unless the proceedings are the subject of fixed costs or scale costs or the court otherwise orders. This Section and the Practice Direction 3E will apply to any other proceedings (including applications) where the court so orders.

On 8 February 2013, the President of the Queen's Bench Division and the Chancellor of the High Court announced that a direction will be made under the amended r 3.12(1) in these terms:

Pursuant to CPR, r 3.12(1)(b) and (c), the Chancellor of the High Court directs that in the Chancery Division and the President of the Queen's Bench Division directs that in the Technology and Construction Court and Mercantile Courts, Section II of CPR, Part 3, and PD 3E shall not apply to cases where at the date of the first case management conference the sums in dispute in the proceedings exceed £2,000,000, excluding interest and costs, except where the court so orders.

The announcement went on to say that the Master of the Rolls has been consulted on and agrees with this direction. Parity of approach in relation to costs management between these courts is considered to be important to avoid any inappropriate forum shopping as parties get used to the new rules. The revised rule is an interim measure, as it is thought that the case for any exception should be revisited, given that under the rules there is a discretion which might be exercised in particular cases not to make a costs management order, which could deal with any remaining concerns as to the appropriateness of costs management in high-value cases. Also, after that review of the position, it will be desirable for the principle finally decided on to be incorporated in r 3.12(1) itself rather than in a direction.

Subject to the limited exceptions which will be dealt with in the direction, it is envisaged that costs management orders would be made in all cases except where there is good reason not to do so. Even when the exceptions in the rule and the direction apply, the use of costs management should always be considered.

Other Statutory Instruments

Recovery of Costs Insurance Premiums in Clinical Negligence Proceedings Regulations 2013 (SI 2013/92)
Offers to Settle in Civil Proceedings Order 2013 (SI 2013/93)
Conditional Fee Agreements Order 2013
Damages-Based Agreements Regulations 2013

RECOVERY OF COSTS INSURANCE PREMIUMS IN CLINICAL NEGLIGENCE PROCEEDINGS REGULATIONS 2013 (SI 2013/92)

The Lord Chancellor, in exercise of the powers conferred on him by section 58C(2) to (4) of the Courts and Legal Services Act 1990 makes the following Regulations:

Citation and commencement

1. These Regulations may be cited as the Recovery of Costs Insurance Premiums in Clinical Negligence Proceedings Regulations 2013 and shall come into force on 1st April 2013.

Costs order may require payment of an amount of the relevant part of the premium

2.—(1) Subject to paragraph (2), a costs order made in favour of a party to clinical negligence proceedings may include provision requiring the payment of an amount in respect of the relevant part of the premium of a costs insurance policy taken out by that party which insures against the risk of incurring liability to pay for one or more expert reports in connection with the proceedings (or against that risk and other risks).

(2) A costs order may not require the payment of an amount in respect of the relevant part of the premium which relates to the liability to pay for any expert report if—

(a) the report was not in the event obtained;

(b) the report did not relate to liability or causation; or

(c) the cost of the report is not allowed under the costs order.

OFFERS TO SETTLE IN CIVIL PROCEEDINGS
ORDER 2013 (SI 2013/93)

The Lord Chancellor, in exercise of the powers conferred by section 55 of the Legal Aid, Sentencing and Punishment of Offenders Act 2012, makes the following Order:

Citation and commencement

1. This Order may be cited as the Offers to Settle in Civil Proceedings Order 2013 and shall come into force on 12th February 2013.

Additional amount to be paid where a claim is only for an amount of money

2. Where rules of court make provision for a court to order a defendant in civil proceedings to pay an additional amount to a claimant in those proceedings and the claim is for (and only for) an amount of money then, for the purposes of section 55(3) of the Legal Aid, Sentencing and Punishment of Offenders Act 2012, the prescribed percentage shall be—

Amount awarded by the court	Prescribed percentage
Up to £500,000	10% of the amount awarded.
Above £500,000, up to £1,000,000	10% of the first £500,000 and 5% of the amount awarded above that figure.
Above £1,000,000	7.5% of the first £1,000,000 and 0.001% of the amount awarded above that figure.

Amount to be paid where a claim is or includes a non-monetary claim

3.—(1) Rules of court may make provision for a court to order a defendant in civil proceedings to pay an amount to a claimant ('the amount to be paid') in those proceedings where—
   (a) the claim is or includes a non-monetary claim;
   (b) judgment is given in favour of the claimant; and
   (c) the judgment in respect of the claim is at least as advantageous as an offer to settle the claim which the claimant made in accordance with rules of court and has not withdrawn in accordance with those rules.
(2) The amount to be paid shall be calculated as prescribed in paragraph (4).
(3) Rules made under paragraph (1) may—
   (a) include provision as to the assessment of whether a judgment is at least as advantageous as an offer to settle; and
   (b) make provision as to the calculation of the value of a non-monetary benefit awarded to a claimant.

(4) Subject to subparagraph (5), the amount to be paid shall be—

    (a) if a claim includes both a claim for an amount of money and a non-monetary claim, the following percentages of the amount awarded to the claimant by the court (excluding any amount awarded in respect of the claimant's costs)—

Amount awarded by the court	*Amount to be paid by the defendant*
Up to £500,000	10% of the amount awarded.
Above £500,000, up to £1,000,000	10% of the first £500,000 and 5% of the amount awarded above that figure; and

    (b) in a non-monetary claim only, the following percentages of any costs ordered by the court to be paid to the claimant by the defendant—

Costs ordered to be paid to the claimant	*Amount to be paid by the defendant*
Up to £500,000	10% of the costs ordered to be paid.
Above £500,000, up to £1,000,000	10% of the first £500,000 and 5% of any costs ordered to be paid above that figure.

(5) The amount to be paid shall not exceed £75,000.

CONDITIONAL FEE AGREEMENTS ORDER 2013

The Lord Chancellor in exercise of the powers conferred on him by sections 58(4)(a) and (c), 58(4A)(b), (4B)(c) and (d) and 120(3) of the Courts and Legal Services Act 1990, having consulted in accordance with section 58A(5) of that Act, makes the following Order, a draft of which has been laid and approved by each House of Parliament in accordance with section 120(4) of that Act.

Citation, commencement, interpretation and application

1.—(1) This Order may be cited as the Conditional Fee Agreements Order 2013 and will come into force on 1st April 2013.

(2) In this Order—

'the 1986 Act' means the Insolvency Act 1986;

'the 1990 Act' means the Courts and Legal Services Act 1990;

'claim for personal injuries' has the same meaning as in Rule 2.3 of the Civil Procedure Rules 1998;

'company' means a company within the meaning of section 1 of the Companies Act 2006 or a company which may be wound up under Part V of the 1986 Act;

'diffuse mesothelioma' has the same meaning as in section 48(2) of the Legal Aid, Sentencing and Punishment of Offenders Act 2012;

'news publisher' means a person who publishes a newspaper, magazine or website containing news or information about or comment on current affairs;

'publication and privacy proceedings' means proceedings for—

(a) defamation;

(b) malicious falsehood;

(c) breach of confidence involving publication to the general public;

(d) misuse of private information; or

(e) harassment, where the defendant is a news publisher.

'representative' means the person or persons providing the advocacy services or litigation services to which the conditional fee agreement relates.

Agreements providing for a success fee

2. All proceedings which, under section 58 of the Act, can be the subject of an enforceable conditional fee agreement, except proceedings under section 82 of the Environmental Protection Act 1990, are proceedings specified for the purpose of section 58(4)(a) of the Act.

Amount of success fee

3. In relation to all proceedings specified in article 2, the percentage specified for the purposes of section 58(4)(c) of the Act is 100%.

Specified proceedings

4. A claim for personal injuries shall be proceedings specified for the purpose of section 58(4A)(b) of the Act.

Amount of success fee in specified proceedings

5.—(1) In relation to the proceedings specified in article 4, the percentage prescribed for the purposes of section 58(4B)(c) of the Act is—

(a) in proceedings at first instance, 25%; and

(b) in all other proceedings, 100%.

(2) The descriptions of damages specified for the purposes of section 58(4B)(d) of the Act are—

(a) general damages for pain, suffering, and loss of amenity; and

(b) damages for pecuniary loss, other than future pecuniary loss,

net of any sums recoverable by the Compensation Recovery Unit of the Department for Work and Pensions.

Transitional and saving provisions

6.—(1) Articles 4 and 5 do not apply to a conditional fee agreement which is entered into before the date upon which this Order comes into force if—

(a) the agreement was entered into specifically for the purposes of the provision to a person ('P') of advocacy or litigation services in connection with the matter which is the subject of the proceedings; or

(b) advocacy or litigation services were provided to P under the agreement in connection with those proceedings before that date.

(2) Articles 4 and 5 do not apply to any conditional fee agreement entered into in relation to—

(a) proceedings relating to a claim for damages in respect of diffuse mesothelioma;

(b) publication and privacy proceedings;

(c) proceedings in England and Wales brought by a person acting in the capacity of—

(i) a liquidator of a company which is being wound up in England and Wales or Scotland under Parts IV or V of the 1986 Act; or

(ii) a trustee of a bankrupt's estate under Part IX of the 1986 Act;

(d) proceedings brought by a person acting in the capacity of an administrator appointed pursuant to the provisions of Part II of the 1986 Act;

(e) proceedings in England and Wales brought by a company which is being wound up in England and Wales or Scotland under Parts IV or V of the 1986 Act; or

(f) proceedings brought by a company which has entered administration under Part II of the 1986 Act.

Revocation of 2000 Order

7. The Conditional Fee Agreements Order 2000 is revoked.

DAMAGES-BASED AGREEMENTS REGULATIONS 2013

The Lord Chancellor in exercise of the powers conferred by sections 58AA(4) and (5) and 120(3) of the Courts and Legal Services Act 1990, having consulted in accordance with section 58AA(6) of that Act, makes the following Regulations, a draft of which has been laid before and approved by resolution of each House of Parliament in accordance with section 120(4) of that Act.

Citation, commencement, interpretation and application

1.—(1) These Regulations may be cited as the Damages-Based Agreements Regulations 2013 and come into force on 1st April 2013.

(2) In these Regulations—

'the Act' means the Courts and Legal Services Act 1990;

'claim for personal injuries' has the same meaning as in Rule 2.3 of the Civil Procedure Rules 1998;

'client' means the person who has instructed the representative to provide advocacy services, litigation services (within section 119 of the Act) or claims management services (within the meaning of section 4(2)(b) of the Compensation Act 2006) and is liable to make a payment for those services;

'costs' means the total of the representative's time reasonably spent, in respect of the claim or proceedings, multiplied by the reasonable hourly rate of remuneration of the representative;

'employment matter' means a matter that is, or could become, the subject of proceedings before an employment tribunal;

'expenses' means disbursements incurred by the representative, including the expense of obtaining an expert's report and, in an employment matter only, counsel's fees;

'payment' means that part of the sum recovered in respect of the claim or damages awarded that the client agrees to pay the representative, and excludes expenses but includes, in respect of any claim or proceedings to which these regulations apply other than an employment matter, any disbursements incurred by the representative in respect of counsel's fees;

'representative' means the person providing the advocacy services, litigation services or claims management services to which the damages-based agreement relates.

(3) Subject to paragraphs (4), (5) and (6), these Regulations shall apply to all damages-based agreements entered into on or after the date on which these Regulations come into force.

(4) Subject to paragraph (6), these Regulations shall not apply to any damages-based agreement to which section 57 of the Solicitors Act 1974 (non-contentious business agreements between solicitor and client) applies.

(5) In these Regulations—

(a) regulation 4 does not apply; and

(b) regulations 5, 6, 7 and 8 only apply,

to any damages-based agreement in respect of an employment matter.

(6) Where these Regulations relate to an employment matter, they apply to all damages-based agreements signed on or after the date on which these Regulations come into force.

Revocation of 2010 Regulations and transitional provision

2.—(1) Subject to paragraph (2), the Damages-Based Agreements Regulations 2010 ('the 2010 Regulations') are revoked.

(2) The 2010 Regulations shall continue to have effect in respect of any damages-based agreement to which those Regulations applied and which was signed before the date on which these Regulations come into force.

Requirements of an agreement in respect of all damages-based agreements

3. The requirements prescribed for the purposes of section 58AA(4)(c) of the Act are that the terms and conditions of a damages-based agreement must specify—

(a) the claim or proceedings or parts of them to which the agreement relates;

(b) the circumstances in which the representative's payment, expenses and costs, or part of them, are payable; and

(c) the reason for setting the amount of the payment at the level agreed, which, in an employment matter, shall include having regard to, where appropriate, whether the claim or proceedings is one of several similar claims or proceedings.

Payment in respect of claims or proceedings other than an employment matter

4.—(1) In respect of any claim or proceedings, other than an employment matter, to which these Regulations apply, a damages-based agreement must not require an amount to be paid by the client other than—

(a) the payment, net of—

(i) any costs (including fixed costs under Part 45 of the Civil Procedure Rules 1998); and

(ii) where relevant, any sum in respect of disbursements incurred by the representative in respect of counsel's fees,

that have been paid or are payable by another party to the proceedings by agreement or order; and

(b) any expenses incurred by the representative, net of any amount which has been paid or is payable by another party to the proceedings by agreement or order.

(2) In a claim for personal injuries—

(a) the only sums recovered by the client from which the payment shall be met are—

(i) general damages for pain, suffering and loss of amenity; and

(ii) damages for pecuniary loss other than future pecuniary loss,

net of any sums recoverable by the Compensation Recovery Unit of the Department for Work and Pensions; and

(b) subject to paragraph (4), a damages-based agreement must not provide for a payment above an amount which, including VAT, is equal to 25% of the combined sums in paragraph (2)(a)(i) and (ii) which are ultimately recovered by the client.

(3) Subject to paragraph (4), in any other claim or proceedings to which this regulation applies, a damages-based agreement must not provide for a payment above

an amount which, including VAT, is equal to 50% of the sums ultimately recovered by the client.

(4) The amounts prescribed in paragraphs (2)(b) and (3) shall only apply to claims or proceedings at first instance.

Information required to be given before an agreement is made in an employment matter

5.—(1) In an employment matter, the requirements prescribed for the purposes of section 58AA(4)(d) of the Act are to provide—

(a) information to the client in writing about the matters in paragraph (2); and

(b) such further explanation, advice or other information about any of those matters as the client may request.

(2) Those matters are—

(a) the circumstances in which the client may seek a review of costs and expenses of the representative and the procedure for doing so;

(b) the dispute resolution service provided by the Advisory, Conciliation and Arbitration Service (ACAS) in regard to actual and potential claims;

(c) whether other methods of pursuing the claim or financing the proceedings, including—

(i) advice under the Community Legal Service,

(ii) legal expenses insurance,

(iii) pro bono representation, or

(iv) trade union representation,

are available, and, if so, how they apply to the client and the claim or proceedings in question; and

(d) the point at which expenses become payable; and

(e) a reasonable estimate of the amount that is likely to be spent upon expenses, inclusive of VAT.

Additional causes of action in an employment matter

6. In an employment matter, any amendment to a damages-based agreement to cover additional causes of action must be in writing and signed by the client and the representative.

Payment in an employment matter

7. In an employment matter, a damages-based agreement must not provide for a payment above an amount which, including VAT, is equal to 35% of the sums ultimately recovered by the client in the claim or proceedings.

Terms and conditions of termination in an employment matter

8.—(1) In an employment matter, the additional requirements prescribed for the purposes of section 58AA(4)(c) of the Act are that the terms and conditions of a damages-based agreement must be in accordance with paragraphs (2), (3) and (4).

(2) If the agreement is terminated, the representatives may not charge the client more than the representative's costs and expenses for the work undertaken in respect of the client's claim or proceedings.

(3) The client may not terminate the agreement—
   (a) after settlement has been agreed; or
   (b) within seven days before the start of the tribunal hearing.

(4) The representative may not terminate the agreement and charge costs unless the client has behaved or is behaving unreasonably.

(5) Paragraphs (3) and (4) are without prejudice to any right of either party under general law of contract to terminate the agreement.

Index